2005 SUPPLEMENT

CIVIL RIGHTS ACTIONS:
ENFORCING THE CONSTITUTION

by

JOHN C. JEFFRIES, JR.
Emerson Spies Professor of Law
Arnold H. Leon Professor and Dean of the Law School
University of Virginia

PAMELA S. KARLAN
Kenneth and Harle Montgomery Professor of Public Interest Law
Stanford University

PETER W. LOW
Hardy Cross Dillard Professor of Law
University of Virginia

GEORGE A. RUTHERGLEN
John Barbee Minor Distinguished Professor of Law
University of Virginia

FOUNDATION PRESS
NEW YORK, NEW YORK
2005

Foundation Press, of Thomson/West, has created this publication to provide you with accurate and authoritative information concerning the subject matter covered. However, this publication was not necessarily prepared by persons licensed to practice law in a particular jurisdiction. Foundation Press is not engaged in rendering legal or other professional advice, and this publication is not a substitute for the advice of an attorney. If you require legal or other expert advice, you should seek the services of a competent attorney or other professional.

© 2000–2004 FOUNDATION PRESS
© 2005 By FOUNDATION PRESS
       395 Hudson Street
       New York, NY 10014
       Phone Toll Free 1–877–888–1330
       Fax (212) 367–6799
       fdpress.com
Printed in the United States of America

ISBN 1–58778–858–6

PREFACE

Five years have now elapsed since the publication of *Civil Rights Actions: Enforcing the Constitution*. A new edition is scheduled for next year. In the meantime, this Supplement brings the casebook up-to-date through the 2004-2005 term of the Supreme Court.

The 2005 Supplement adds one new main case. *Brosseau v. Haugen* (2004) is the Court's most recent pronouncement on qualified immunity. On that issue, the Court divided eight-one in favor of the defendant, with only Justice Stevens dissenting. Interestingly, however, Justice Breyer, joined by Justices Scalia and Ginsburg, concurred to ask for reconsideration of the rule requiring adjudication of the merits before reaching questions of qualified immunity. Partly for that reason, *Brosseau* has been substituted for the much longer opinions in *Hope v. Pelzer* (2002), which now appears as a note case following *Brosseau*.

The other main cases are carried over from the 2004 Supplement. They include:

Brentwood Academy v. Tennessee Secondary School Athletic Association (2001), which held that a non-governmental statewide association created to regulate athletic competition among secondary schools in Tennessee acted "under color of" state law under § 1983;

Buckhannon Board and Care Home v. West Virginia Department of Health and Human Resources (2001), which rejected outright the "catalyst theory" for awarding attorney's fees;

Hibbs v. Winn (2004), which held that the Tax Injunction Act, 28 U.S.C. § 1341, does not bar § 1983 suits challenging state tax-credits as violations of the Establishment Clause; and

Miller v. French (2000), which was the Supreme Court's first response to the provisions of the Prison Litigation Reform Act that seek to curtail structural reform litigation.

Many more cases are covered in Notes, some of which are quite extensive. Additionally, the Supplement updates references to secondary literature.

PERMISSION TO DUPLICATE

There are many intersections between **Civil Rights Actions: Enforcing the Constitution** (4th ed. 2000) and Low and Jeffries, **Federal**

Courts and the Law of Federal-State Relations (5th ed. 2004). Occasionally, a teacher using one book may wish to use material from the other book or its supplement. To facilitate such borrowings, we authorize teachers who have adopted either book to duplicate limited portions of the other or its annual supplement for distribution to their students. We are grateful to Foundation Press for agreeing to make this option available.

JCJJr

PSK

PWL

GAR

Charlottesville and Palo Alto
July 2005

TABLE OF CONTENTS

	Supplement Page
PREFACE	iii
TABLE OF CASES	ix
TABLE OF SECONDARY AUTHORITIES	xv

INTRODUCTION: STATE SOVEREIGN IMMUNITY AND THE ELEVENTH AMENDMENT

Casebook Page		
21	Additional Citation	1
23	Additional Citations	1
24	Additional Citations	1
25	Add Note on Section 5 of 14th Amendment	2

CHAPTER I: 42 U.S.C. § 1983

Section 1: "Under Color of" Law

40	Additional Citations	6

Section 2: The Eleventh Amendment and § 1983

49	Additional Citation	6

Section 3: Official Immunity

90	Additional Citations	6
92	Additional Citation	7
112	***Saucier v. Katz, Groh v. Ramirez***	7
113	Additional Citations	13
114	Additional Citations	13
114	Additional Citations	13
115	Add new main case and Notes:	
	BROSSEAU v. HAUGEN	13
	Notes on Clearly Established Law	18
	1. Required Similarity Between Challenged Conduct and Prior Precedent: ***Hope v. Pelzer***	18
	2. Unintended Effect of the *Saucier* Sequencing Requirement: ***Bunting v. Mellen***	22
	3. The Sources of Clearly Established Law	25
129	Additional Citation	26

Section 4: Governmental Liability

Casebook Page		Supplement Page
147	*Inyo County v. Paiute-Shoshone Indians*	27
175	**Correctional Services Corp. v. Malesko**	27
205	Additional Citations	28
216	Add New Section 4A	28

Section 4A: State Action and § 1983

	BRENTWOOD ACADEMY v. TENNESSEE SECONDARY SCHOOL ATHLETIC ASSOCIATION	28
	Notes on the State Action Doctrine	35
	1. Introduction	35
	2. Private Actors as Public Actors	35
	3. Public Actors as Private Actors	37
	4. Why It Matters	38

Section 5: For What Wrongs?

235	Additional Citation	39
248	*Chavez v. Martinez*	39
295	*Alexander v. Sandoval*	40
	Gonzaga University v. Doe	40
	City of Rancho Palos Verdes v. Abrams	44

CHAPTER II: ATTORNEY'S FEES

Section 1: Determining Fee Awards

361	**BUCHANNON BOARD AND CARE HOME v. WEST VIRGINIA DEPARTMENT OF HEALTH AND HUMAN RESOURCES**	45

Section 2: Risk Enhancement

373	Additional Citation	59

Section 3: Attorney's Fees and Settlement Negotiations

403	Add Note on Taxation of Attorney's Fees	59

CHAPTER III: ADMINISTRATION OF THE CIVIL RIGHTS ACTS: INTERSECTIONS OF STATE AND FEDERAL LAW

418	Additional Citation	61
419	*Booth v. Churner; Porter v. Nussle*	61
437	*Nelson v. Campbell*	61
524	**HIBBS v. WINN**	66

CHAPTER IV: ADDITIONAL RECONSTRUCTION LEGISLATION

Section 1: 42 U.S.C. § 1982

540	Additional Citation	84

Section 2: 42 U.S.C. § 1981

571	*Jones v. R.R. Donnelley & Sons, Co.*	84

Casebook Page		Supplement Page
591	Additional Citations	84
612	Additional Citations	85

CHAPTER V: MODERN CIVIL RIGHTS LEGISLATION: LAWS AGAINST SEX DISCRIMINATION

Section 1: Title VII of the Civil Rights Act of 1964

654	Additional Citations	86
655	*Pollard v. E.I. du Pont de Nemours Co.*	87
681	*Clark County School District v. Breeden*	87
683	Additional Citations	87
688	**Pennsylvania State Police v. Suders**	89
689	Additional Citations	90
691	Additional Citations	90
692	Additional Citations	90
697	Additional Citations	91

Section 2: Title IX of the Education Amendments of 1972

701	*Alexander v. Sandoval*	92
	Barnes v. Gorman	93
715	**Jackson v. Birmingham Board of Education**	93
734	Additional Citations	94
734	**United States v. Morrison**	94
	Nevada Department of Human Resources v. Hibbs	100
735	Additional Citations	101

CHAPTER VI: STRUCTURAL REFORM LITIGATION

Section 1: School Desegregation

768	Add Note on Unitariness Litigation	103
792	Add Note on Subsequent Developments in *Jenkins*	104

Section 3: Prisons

852	Delete Note on Prison Litigation Reform Act	105
856	Additional Citation	105
856	Add new material:	
	Introductory Note on the Prison Litigation Reform Act	105
	MILLER v. FRENCH	108
	Add Note on Retroactive Application of the PLRA	120

*

TABLE OF CASES

Principal cases are in bold type. Non-principal cases are in roman type. References are to Pages.

ACLU Foundation of Louisiana v. Bridges, 334 F.3d 416 (5th Cir.2003), 75
Adickes v. S.H. Kress & Co., 398 U.S. 144, 90 S.Ct. 1598, 26 L.Ed.2d 142 (1970), 6, 35
African Trade & Information Center, Inc. v. Abromaitis, 294 F.3d 355 (2nd Cir.2002), 25
Alden v. Maine, 527 U.S. 706, 119 S.Ct. 2240, 144 L.Ed.2d 636 (1999), 2
Alexander v. Sandoval, 532 U.S. 275, 121 S.Ct. 1511, 149 L.Ed.2d 517 (2001), 40, 41, 42, 92, 93
Alyeska Pipeline Service Co. v. Wilderness Society, 421 U.S. 240, 95 S.Ct. 1612, 44 L.Ed.2d 141 (1975), 46, 49
American Mfrs. Mut. Ins. Co. v. Sullivan, 526 U.S. 40, 119 S.Ct. 977, 143 L.Ed.2d 130 (1999), 34
Anderson v. Creighton, 483 U.S. 635, 107 S.Ct. 3034, 97 L.Ed.2d 523 (1987), 8, 9, 10, 11, 16, 17
Arkansas v. Farm Credit Services of Cent. Arkansas, 520 U.S. 821, 117 S.Ct. 1776, 138 L.Ed.2d 34 (1997), 72

Barnes v. Gorman, 536 U.S. 181, 122 S.Ct. 2097, 153 L.Ed.2d 230 (2002), 93
Belk v. Charlotte–Mecklenburg Bd. of Educ., 211 F.3d 853 (4th Cir.2000), 103
Bivens v. Six Unknown Named Agents of Federal Bureau of Narcotics, 403 U.S. 388, 91 S.Ct. 1999, 29 L.Ed.2d 619 (1971), 6, 12, 27
Blessing v. Freestone, 520 U.S. 329, 117 S.Ct. 1353, 137 L.Ed.2d 569 (1997), 42, 43, 44
Blum v. Yaretsky, 457 U.S. 991, 102 S.Ct. 2777, 73 L.Ed.2d 534 (1982), 30, 31
Board of Educ. of Oklahoma City Public Schools, Independent School Dist. No. 89, Oklahoma County, Okl. v. Dowell, 498 U.S. 237, 111 S.Ct. 630, 112 L.Ed.2d 715 (1991), 103
Board of Trustees v. Garrett, 531 U.S. 356, 121 S.Ct. 955, 148 L.Ed.2d 866 (2001), 3, 4
Bob Jones University v. Simon, 416 U.S. 725, 94 S.Ct. 2038, 40 L.Ed.2d 496 (1974), 70

Boerne, City of v. Flores, 521 U.S. 507, 117 S.Ct. 2157, 138 L.Ed.2d 624 (1997), 2, 3, 4
Bonitz v. Fair, 804 F.2d 164 (1st Cir.1986), 86
Booth v. Churner, 532 U.S. 731, 121 S.Ct. 1819, 149 L.Ed.2d 958 (2001), 61
Boyd v. Benton County, 374 F.3d 773 (9th Cir.2004), 26
Brentwood Academy v. Tennessee Secondary School Athletic Ass'n, 531 U.S. 288, 121 S.Ct. 924, 148 L.Ed.2d 807 (2001), 28, 35, 36, 37
Brosseau v. Haugen, 543 U.S. ___, 125 S.Ct. 596, 160 L.Ed.2d 583 (2004), 13, 18, 22
Brown v. Board of Education, 347 U.S. 483, 74 S.Ct. 686, 98 L.Ed. 873 (1954), 66, 75
Buckhannon Bd. and Care Home, Inc. v. West Virginia Dept. of Health and Human Resources, 532 U.S. 598, 121 S.Ct. 1835, 149 L.Ed.2d 855 (2001), 45
Buckley v. Rogerson, 133 F.3d 1125 (8th Cir. 1998), 26
Bunting v. Mellen, 541 U.S. 1019, 124 S.Ct. 1750, 158 L.Ed.2d 636 (2004), 17, 22, 23
Burgess v. Lowery, 201 F.3d 942 (7th Cir. 2000), 26
Burlington v. Dague, 505 U.S. 557, 112 S.Ct. 2638, 120 L.Ed.2d 449 (1992), 49
Burlington Industries, Inc. v. Ellerth, 524 U.S. 742, 118 S.Ct. 2257, 141 L.Ed.2d 633 (1998), 89, 90
Butts v. Volusia County, 222 F.3d 891 (11th Cir.2000), 85

Califano v. Yamasaki, 442 U.S. 682, 99 S.Ct. 2545, 61 L.Ed.2d 176 (1979), 112
California v. Grace Brethren Church, 457 U.S. 393, 102 S.Ct. 2498, 73 L.Ed.2d 93 (1982), 71, 72, 73, 80, 81
California v. Rooney, 483 U.S. 307, 107 S.Ct. 2852, 97 L.Ed.2d 258 (1987), 23
California v. Sierra Club, 451 U.S. 287, 101 S.Ct. 1775, 68 L.Ed.2d 101 (1981), 43
Cannon v. University of Chicago, 441 U.S. 677, 99 S.Ct. 1946, 60 L.Ed.2d 560 (1979), 40, 42, 93

Table of Cases

Capacchione v. Charlotte–Mecklenburg Schools, 57 F.Supp.2d 228 (W.D.N.C. 1999), 103

Carlson v. Green, 446 U.S. 14, 100 S.Ct. 1468, 64 L.Ed.2d 15 (1980), 27

Case of (see name of party)

Chapman v. Higbee Co., 319 F.3d 825 (6th Cir.2003), 85

Chavez v. Martinez, 538 U.S. 760, 123 S.Ct. 1994, 155 L.Ed.2d 984 (2003), 12, 39, 40

Christiansburg Garment Co. v. Equal Employment Opportunity Commission, 434 U.S. 412, 98 S.Ct. 694, 54 L.Ed.2d 648 (1978), 57

Commissioner v. Banks, 541 U.S. 958, 124 S.Ct. 1712, 158 L.Ed.2d 398 (2004), 60

City of (see name of city)

Civil Rights Cases, 109 U.S. 3, 3 S.Ct. 18, 27 L.Ed. 835 (1883), 98

Clark County School Dist. v. Breeden, 532 U.S. 268, 121 S.Ct. 1508, 149 L.Ed.2d 509 (2001), 88

Clarks, Estate of v. United States, 202 F.3d 854 (6th Cir.2000), 60

Cleveland–Perdue v. Brutsche, 881 F.2d 427 (7th Cir.1989), 25

Cole v. Bone, 993 F.2d 1328 (8th Cir.1993), 16

Committee For Public Ed. & Religious Liberty v. Nyquist, 413 U.S. 756, 93 S.Ct. 2955, 37 L.Ed.2d 948 (1973), 75

Commonwealth of (see name of Commonwealth)

Correctional Services Corp. v. Malesko, 534 U.S. 61, 122 S.Ct. 515, 151 L.Ed.2d 456 (2001), 27

County of (see name of county)

Crawford–El v. Britton, 523 U.S. 574, 118 S.Ct. 1584, 140 L.Ed.2d 759 (1998), 26

Davis v. Passman, 442 U.S. 228, 99 S.Ct. 2264, 60 L.Ed.2d 846 (1979), 27

Dothard v. Rawlinson, 433 U.S. 321, 97 S.Ct. 2720, 53 L.Ed.2d 786 (1977), 86

Dunn v. Carey, 808 F.2d 555 (7th Cir.1986), 73

Edward J. DeBartolo Corp. v. Florida Gulf Coast Bldg. & Const. Trades Council, 485 U.S. 568, 108 S.Ct. 1392, 99 L.Ed.2d 645 (1988), 112

Edwards v. Balisok, 520 U.S. 641, 117 S.Ct. 1584, 137 L.Ed.2d 906 (1997), 64

Employment Division v. Smith, 494 U.S. 872, 110 S.Ct. 1595, 108 L.Ed.2d 876 (1990), 2

Estate of (see name of party)

Estelle v. Gamble, 429 U.S. 97, 97 S.Ct. 285, 50 L.Ed.2d 251 (1976), 63

Evans v. Jeff D., 475 U.S. 717, 106 S.Ct. 1531, 89 L.Ed.2d 747 (1986), 47, 49, 59

Evans v. Newton, 382 U.S. 296, 86 S.Ct. 486, 15 L.Ed.2d 373 (1966), 31

Exeter–West Greenwich Regional School Dist. v. Pontarelli, 788 F.2d 47 (1st Cir. 1986), 56

Fair Assessment in Real Estate Ass'n, Inc. v. McNary, 454 U.S. 100, 102 S.Ct. 177, 70 L.Ed.2d 271 (1981), 72, 81

Faragher v. City of Boca Raton, 524 U.S. 775, 118 S.Ct. 2275, 141 L.Ed.2d 662 (1998), 89, 90

Farrar v. Hobby, 506 U.S. 103, 113 S.Ct. 566, 121 L.Ed.2d 494 (1992), 46, 47, 48, 53, 58, 59

F.D.I.C. v. Meyer, 510 U.S. 471, 114 S.Ct. 996, 127 L.Ed.2d 308 (1994), 27

Federal Election Com'n v. NRA Political Victory Fund, 513 U.S. 88, 115 S.Ct. 537, 130 L.Ed.2d 439 (1994), 82

Federation of African American Contractors v. City of Oakland, 96 F.3d 1204 (9th Cir.1996), 85

Feliciano v. Barcelo, 497 F.Supp. 14 (D.Puerto Rico 1979), 116

Fesel v. Masonic Home of Delaware, Inc., 447 F.Supp. 1346 (D.Del.1978), 86

Fitzpatrick v. Bitzer, 427 U.S. 445, 96 S.Ct. 2666, 49 L.Ed.2d 614 (1976), 2

Florida Prepaid Postsecondary Educ. Expense Bd. v. College Sav. Bank, 527 U.S. 627, 119 S.Ct. 2199, 144 L.Ed.2d 575 (1999), 3, 98

Forts v. Ward, 621 F.2d 1210 (2nd Cir.1980), 86

Franklin v. Gwinnett County Public Schools, 503 U.S. 60, 112 S.Ct. 1028, 117 L.Ed.2d 208 (1992), 93

Friends of the Earth, Inc. v. Laidlaw Environmental Services (TOC), Inc., 528 U.S. 167, 120 S.Ct. 693, 145 L.Ed.2d 610 (2000), 49, 53, 56

Galletti, United States v., 541 U.S. 114, 124 S.Ct. 1548, 158 L.Ed.2d 279 (2004), 69, 77

Gates v. Collier, 501 F.2d 1291 (5th Cir. 1974), 20

Gebser v. Lago Vista Independent School Dist., 524 U.S. 274, 118 S.Ct. 1989, 141 L.Ed.2d 277 (1998), 93, 99

General Dynamics Land Systems, Inc. v. Cline, 540 U.S. 581, 124 S.Ct. 1236, 157 L.Ed.2d 1094 (2004), 69

Gibson v. City of Chicago, 910 F.2d 1510 (7th Cir.1990), 38

Gillis, In re, 836 F.2d 1001 (6th Cir.1988), 75

Gomez v. United States Dist. Court for Northern Dist. of California, 503 U.S. 653, 112 S.Ct. 1652, 118 L.Ed.2d 293 (1992), 64, 65

Gonzaga University v. Doe, 536 U.S. 273, 122 S.Ct. 2268, 153 L.Ed.2d 309 (2002), 41, 42, 44

Gonzalez v. Ingersoll Mill. Mach. Co., 133 F.3d 1025 (7th Cir.1998), 85

Graham v. Connor, 490 U.S. 386, 109 S.Ct. 1865, 104 L.Ed.2d 443 (1989), 7, 8, 9, 11, 15, 16, 40

Great Lakes Dredge & Dock Co. v. Huffman, 319 U.S. 293, 63 S.Ct. 1070, 87 L.Ed. 1407 (1943), 72

Green v. County School Board, 391 U.S. 430, 88 S.Ct. 1689, 20 L.Ed.2d 716 (1968), 105

Gregory, United States v., 818 F.2d 1114 (4th Cir.1987), 86

Griffin v. County School Bd. of Prince Edward County, 377 U.S. 218, 84 S.Ct. 1226, 12 L.Ed.2d 256 (1964), 74, 75

Groh v. Ramirez, 540 U.S. 551, 124 S.Ct. 1284, 157 L.Ed.2d 1068 (2004), 12

Hagans v. Lavine, 415 U.S. 528, 94 S.Ct. 1372, 39 L.Ed.2d 577 (1974), 83

Hanrahan v. Hampton, 446 U.S. 754, 100 S.Ct. 1987, 64 L.Ed.2d 670 (1980), 46, 47, 48, 58

Harlow v. Fitzgerald, 457 U.S. 800, 102 S.Ct. 2727, 73 L.Ed.2d 396 (1982), 11, 17, 21

Harris, United States v., 106 U.S. 629, 16 Otto 629, 1 S.Ct. 601, 27 L.Ed. 290 (1883), 97, 98

Harrison v. Eddy Potash, 248 F.3d 1014 (10th Cir.2001), 90

Hayburn, Case of, 2 U.S. 408, 2 Dall. 409, 1 L.Ed. 436 (1792), 112, 113, 115

Heart of Atlanta Motel, Inc. v. United States, 379 U.S. 241, 85 S.Ct. 348, 13 L.Ed.2d 258 (1964), 96

Heck v. Humphrey, 512 U.S. 477, 114 S.Ct. 2364, 129 L.Ed.2d 383 (1994), 64

Hennigan v. Ouachita Parish School Bd., 749 F.2d 1148 (5th Cir.1985), 55

Hensley v. Eckerhart, 461 U.S. 424, 103 S.Ct. 1933, 76 L.Ed.2d 40 (1983), 46, 49, 59

Hewitt v. Helms, 482 U.S. 755, 107 S.Ct. 2672, 96 L.Ed.2d 654 (1987), 46, 47, 55, 58, 59

Hibbs v. Winn, 542 U.S. 88, 124 S.Ct. 2276, 159 L.Ed.2d 172 (2004), **66**

Higgins v. New Balance Athletic Shoe, Inc., 194 F.3d 252 (1st Cir.1999), 91

Ho v. San Francisco Unified School Dist., 147 F.3d 854 (9th Cir.1998), 104

Hodel v. Virginia Surface Min. & Reclamation Ass'n, Inc., 452 U.S. 264, 101 S.Ct. 2352, 69 L.Ed.2d 1 (1981), 96, 99

Holman v. Indiana, 211 F.3d 399 (7th Cir. 2000), 91

Hope v. Pelzer, 536 U.S. 730, 122 S.Ct. 2508, 153 L.Ed.2d 666 (2002), 17, 18

Horne v. Coughlin, 191 F.3d 244 (2nd Cir. 1999), 24

Hunter v. Bryant, 502 U.S. 224, 112 S.Ct. 534, 116 L.Ed.2d 589 (1991), 7

Indest v. Freeman Decorating, Inc., 168 F.3d 795 (5th Cir.1999), 90

Indest v. Freeman Decorating, Inc., 164 F.3d 258 (5th Cir.1999), 90

In re (see name of party)

Inyo County v. Paiute–Shoshone Indians of the Bishop Community of the Bishop Colony, 538 U.S. 701, 123 S.Ct. 1887, 155 L.Ed.2d 933 (2003), 26

Jackson v. Birmingham Bd. of Educ., 544 U.S. ___, 125 S.Ct. 1497, 161 L.Ed.2d 361 (2005), 93

Jackson v. Metropolitan Edison Co., 419 U.S. 345, 95 S.Ct. 449, 42 L.Ed.2d 477 (1974), 30, 31

Jefferson County v. Acker, 527 U.S. 423, 119 S.Ct. 2069, 144 L.Ed.2d 408 (1999), 70

Jenkins v. Missouri, 205 F.3d 361 (8th Cir. 2000), 104

Jenkins v. Missouri, 959 F.Supp. 1151 (W.D.Mo.1997), 104

Jennings v. New York State Office of Mental Health, 786 F.Supp. 376 (S.D.N.Y.1992), 86

Jett v. Dallas Independent School Dist., 491 U.S. 701, 109 S.Ct. 2702, 105 L.Ed.2d 598 (1989), 85

Johnson v. Railway Exp. Agency, Inc., 421 U.S. 454, 95 S.Ct. 1716, 44 L.Ed.2d 295 (1975), 84

Jones v. Alfred H. Mayer Co., 392 U.S. 409, 88 S.Ct. 2186, 20 L.Ed.2d 1189 (1968), 84

Jones v. Clinton, 993 F.Supp. 1217 (E.D.Ark. 1998), 90

Jones v. R.R. Donnelley & Sons Co., 541 U.S. 369, 124 S.Ct. 1836, 158 L.Ed.2d 645 (2004), 84

Kalka v. Hawk, 215 F.3d 90 (D.C.Cir.2000), 24

Kenseth v. Commissioner 114 T.C. 399 (U.S.Tax Ct.2000), 60

Key Tronic Corp. v. United States, 511 U.S. 809, 114 S.Ct. 1960, 128 L.Ed.2d 797 (1994), 46

Kimel v. Florida Bd. of Regents, 528 U.S. 62, 120 S.Ct. 631, 145 L.Ed.2d 522 (2000), 3, 4

Kissimmee River Valley Sportsman Ass'n v. City of Lakeland, 250 F.3d 1324 (11th Cir.2001), 41

Klein, United States v., 80 U.S. 128, 20 L.Ed. 519 (1871), 115

Laing v. United States, 423 U.S. 161, 96 S.Ct. 473, 46 L.Ed.2d 416 (1976), 69, 76

Table of Cases

Lanier, United States v., 520 U.S. 259, 117 S.Ct. 1219, 137 L.Ed.2d 432 (1997), 17, 19

L.A. Tucker Truck Lines, Inc., United States v., 344 U.S. 33, 73 S.Ct. 67, 97 L.Ed. 54 (1952), 82

Lawrence v. Texas, 539 U.S. 558, 123 S.Ct. 2472, 156 L.Ed.2d 508 (2003), 92

Lebron v. National R.R. Passenger Corp., 513 U.S. 374, 115 S.Ct. 961, 130 L.Ed.2d 902 (1995), 31

Liddell v. Missouri, 731 F.2d 1294 (8th Cir. 1984), 74

Lopez, United States v., 514 U.S. 549, 115 S.Ct. 1624, 131 L.Ed.2d 626 (1995), 95, 96, 98

Lorillard v. Pons, 434 U.S. 575, 98 S.Ct. 866, 55 L.Ed.2d 40 (1978), 76

Lugar v. Edmondson Oil Co., 457 U.S. 922, 102 S.Ct. 2744, 73 L.Ed.2d 482 (1982), 27, 30, 31, 32, 34

Maher v. Gagne, 448 U.S. 122, 100 S.Ct. 2570, 65 L.Ed.2d 653 (1980), 47, 48, 52, 54, 57, 58

Malley v. Briggs, 475 U.S. 335, 106 S.Ct. 1092, 89 L.Ed.2d 271 (1986), 22

Martin v. Hadix, 527 U.S. 343, 119 S.Ct. 1998, 144 L.Ed.2d 347 (1999), 121

McClendon v. City of Columbia, 305 F.3d 314 (5th Cir.2002), 25

McDaniel v. Barresi, 402 U.S. 39, 91 S.Ct. 1287, 28 L.Ed.2d 582 (1971), 104

McGlotten v. Connally, 338 F.Supp. 448 (D.D.C.1972), 70, 71, 79

Merchants' Ins. Co. v. Ritchie, 72 U.S. 541, 18 L.Ed. 540 (1866), 82

Miller v. French, 530 U.S. 327, 120 S.Ct. 2246, 147 L.Ed.2d 326 (2000), **108**, 120

Miranda v. Arizona, 384 U.S. 436, 86 S.Ct. 1602, 16 L.Ed.2d 694 (1966), 39

Missouri v. Jenkins, 495 U.S. 33, 110 S.Ct. 1651, 109 L.Ed.2d 31 (1990), 74

Mitchell v. Forsyth, 472 U.S. 511, 105 S.Ct. 2806, 86 L.Ed.2d 411 (1985), 7

Monell v. Department of Social Services of City of New York, 436 U.S. 658, 98 S.Ct. 2018, 56 L.Ed.2d 611 (1978), 38

Moore v. Vega, 371 F.3d 110 (2nd Cir.2004), 25

Moorer v. Grumman Aerospace Corp., 964 F.Supp. 665 (E.D.N.Y.1997), 85

Morales Feliciano v. Rossello Gonzalez, 13 F.Supp.2d 151 (D.Puerto Rico 1998), 117

Morrison, United States v., 529 U.S. 598, 120 S.Ct. 1740, 146 L.Ed.2d 658 (2000), 95, 96, 97, 99, 100, 101

Mueller v. Allen, 463 U.S. 388, 103 S.Ct. 3062, 77 L.Ed.2d 721 (1983), 75

Nadeau v. Helgemoe, 581 F.2d 275 (1st Cir. 1978), 58

National Collegiate Athletic Ass'n v. Tarkanian, 488 U.S. 179, 109 S.Ct. 454, 102 L.Ed.2d 469 (1988), 30, 34

National Private Truck Council, Inc. v. Oklahoma Tax Com'n, 515 U.S. 582, 115 S.Ct. 2351, 132 L.Ed.2d 509 (1995), 72, 81

Nelson v. Campbell, 541 U.S. 637, 124 S.Ct. 2117, 158 L.Ed.2d 924 (2004), 61

Nevada Dept. of Human Resources v. Hibbs, 538 U.S. 721, 123 S.Ct. 1972, 155 L.Ed.2d 953 (2003), 4, 100, 101

Olsen v. Marriott Intern., Inc., 75 F.Supp.2d 1052 (D.Ariz.1999), 86

Oncale v. Sundowner Offshore Services, Inc., 523 U.S. 75, 118 S.Ct. 998, 140 L.Ed.2d 201 (1998), 91, 92

Ort v. White, 813 F.2d 318 (11th Cir.1987), 20, 21

Owens v. Lott, 372 F.3d 267 (4th Cir.2004), 25

Padelford, United States v., 76 U.S. 531, 19 L.Ed. 788 (1869), 115

Parham v. Southwestern Bell Telephone Co., 433 F.2d 421 (8th Cir.1970), 48, 56

Parrilla–Burgos v. Hernandez–Rivera, 108 F.3d 445 (1st Cir.1997), 37

Paul v. Davis, 424 U.S. 693, 96 S.Ct. 1155, 47 L.Ed.2d 405 (1976), 39

Pennhurst State School and Hospital v. Halderman, 451 U.S. 1, 101 S.Ct. 1531, 67 L.Ed.2d 694 (1981), 41

Pennsylvania v. Board of Directors of City Trusts of City of Philadelphia, 353 U.S. 230, 77 S.Ct. 806, 1 L.Ed.2d 792 (1957), 31

Pennsylvania v. Union Gas Co., 491 U.S. 1, 109 S.Ct. 2273, 105 L.Ed.2d 1 (1989), 1

Pennsylvania State Police v. Suders, 542 U.S. 129, 124 S.Ct. 2342, 159 L.Ed.2d 204 (2004), 89

Perry v. Woodward, 199 F.3d 1126 (10th Cir. 1999), 85

Peters v. Jenney, 327 F.3d 307 (4th Cir. 2003), 41

Peterson v. Jensen, 371 F.3d 1199 (10th Cir. 2004), 26

Pitchell v. Callan, 13 F.3d 545 (2nd Cir.1994), 38

Plaut v. Spendthrift Farm, Inc., 514 U.S. 211, 115 S.Ct. 1447, 131 L.Ed.2d 328 (1995), 112, 113, 115

Polk County v. Dodson, 454 U.S. 312, 102 S.Ct. 445, 70 L.Ed.2d 509 (1981), 33, 34, 37, 38

Pollard v. E.I. du Pont de Nemours & Co., 532 U.S. 843, 121 S.Ct. 1946, 150 L.Ed.2d 62 (2001), 87

Porter v. Nussle, 534 U.S. 516, 122 S.Ct. 983, 152 L.Ed.2d 12 (2002), 61

Table of Cases

Porter v. Warner Holding Co., 328 U.S. 395, 66 S.Ct. 1086, 90 L.Ed. 1332 (1946), 112

Powell v. City of Pittsfield, 143 F.Supp.2d 94 (D.Mass.2001), 85

Quinn v. Green Tree Credit Corp., 159 F.3d 759 (2nd Cir.1998), 90

Rancho Palos Verdes, City of v. Abrams, 544 U.S. ___, 125 S.Ct. 1453, 161 L.Ed.2d 316 (2005), 44

Rendell–Baker v. Kohn, 457 U.S. 830, 102 S.Ct. 2764, 73 L.Ed.2d 418 (1982), 32, 33, 36

Rhodes v. Stewart, 488 U.S. 1, 109 S.Ct. 202, 102 L.Ed.2d 1 (1988), 57, 106

Richardson v. McKnight, 521 U.S. 399, 117 S.Ct. 2100, 138 L.Ed.2d 540 (1997), 36

Rosewell v. LaSalle Nat. Bank, 450 U.S. 503, 101 S.Ct. 1221, 67 L.Ed.2d 464 (1981), 72, 73, 81

Roy v. Inhabitants of City of Lewiston, 42 F.3d 691 (1st Cir.1994), 11

Rufo v. Inmates of Suffolk County Jail, 502 U.S. 367, 112 S.Ct. 748, 116 L.Ed.2d 867 (1992), 114

Sacramento, County of v. Lewis, 523 U.S. 833, 118 S.Ct. 1708, 140 L.Ed.2d 1043 (1998), 24

Saucier v. Katz, 533 U.S. 194, 121 S.Ct. 2151, 150 L.Ed.2d 272 (2001), 7, 12, 14, 15, 16, 17, 22, 23

Save Our Valley v. Sound Transit, 335 F.3d 932 (9th Cir.2003), 41

Seminole Tribe of Florida v. Florida, 517 U.S. 44, 116 S.Ct. 1114, 134 L.Ed.2d 252 (1996), 1, 2

Shelley v. Kraemer, 334 U.S. 1, 68 S.Ct. 836, 92 L.Ed. 1161 (1948), 97

Siegert v. Gilley, 500 U.S. 226, 111 S.Ct. 1789, 114 L.Ed.2d 277 (1991), 7

Simonton v. Runyon, 232 F.3d 33 (2nd Cir.2000), 91

Smith v. Freland, 954 F.2d 343 (6th Cir.1992), 16

South Camden Citizens in Action v. New Jersey Department of Environmental Protection, 274 F.3d 771 (3rd Cir.2001), 41

South Carolina v. Regan, 465 U.S. 367, 104 S.Ct. 1107, 79 L.Ed.2d 372 (1984), 80, 83

Starks, Estate of v. Enyart, 5 F.3d 230 (7th Cir.1993), 16

Street v. Parham, 929 F.2d 537 (10th Cir.1991), 11

Suter v. Artist M., 503 U.S. 347, 112 S.Ct. 1360, 118 L.Ed.2d 1 (1992), 42

Swann v. Charlotte–Mecklenburg Bd. of Ed., 402 U.S. 1, 91 S.Ct. 1267, 28 L.Ed.2d 554 (1971), 103

Tarpley, United States v., 945 F.2d 806 (5th Cir.1991), 37

Tax Analysts and Advocates v. Shultz, 376 F.Supp. 889 (D.D.C.1974), 70, 71, 79

Tennessee v. Garner, 471 U.S. 1, 105 S.Ct. 1694, 85 L.Ed.2d 1 (1985), 15, 16, 18

Tennessee v. Lane, 541 U.S. 509, 124 S.Ct. 1978, 158 L.Ed.2d 820 (2004), 4

Texas State Teachers Ass'n v. Garland Independent School Dist., 489 U.S. 782, 109 S.Ct. 1486, 103 L.Ed.2d 866 (1989), 47, 48, 49, 58

Thomas ex rel. Thomas v. Roberts, 323 F.3d 950 (11th Cir.2003), 25

Torres v. Wisconsin Dept. of Health & Social Services, 859 F.2d 1523 (7th Cir.1988), 86

Touche Ross & Co. v. Redington, 442 U.S. 560, 99 S.Ct. 2479, 61 L.Ed.2d 82 (1979), 42

Tuttle v. Arlington Cty. School Bd., 195 F.3d 698 (4th Cir.1999), 104

Tyler v. Corner Const. Corp., 167 F.3d 1202 (8th Cir.1999), 57

United States v. _____ (see opposing party)

Vermont Low Income Advocacy Council v. Usery, 546 F.2d 509 (2nd Cir.1976), 55

Virginia v. Rives, 100 U.S. 313, 10 Otto 313, 25 L.Ed. 667 (1879), 98

Walton v. City of Southfield, 995 F.2d 1331 (6th Cir.1993), 25

Wardlaw v. Pickett, 1 F.3d 1297 (D.C.Cir.1993), 11

West v. Atkins, 487 U.S. 42, 108 S.Ct. 2250, 101 L.Ed.2d 40 (1988), 38

Whitley v. Albers, 475 U.S. 312, 106 S.Ct. 1078, 89 L.Ed.2d 251 (1986), 19

Wickard v. Filburn, 317 U.S. 111, 63 S.Ct. 82, 87 L.Ed. 122 (1942), 99

Wilder v. Virginia Hosp. Ass'n, 496 U.S. 498, 110 S.Ct. 2510, 110 L.Ed.2d 455 (1990), 42, 43, 44

Will v. Michigan Dept. of State Police, 491 U.S. 58, 109 S.Ct. 2304, 105 L.Ed.2d 45 (1989), 25, 26, 83

Wilson v. Layne, 526 U.S. 603, 119 S.Ct. 1692, 143 L.Ed.2d 818 (1999), 8, 24, 35

Wilson v. Spain, 209 F.3d 713 (8th Cir.2000), 11

Winn v. Killian, 321 F.3d 911 (9th Cir.2003), 77

Wright v. City of Roanoke Redevelopment and Housing Authority, 479 U.S. 418, 107 S.Ct. 766, 93 L.Ed.2d 781 (1987), 42, 43

TABLE OF SECONDARY AUTHORITIES

Achampong, The Evolution of Same-Sex Hostile-Environment Sexual Harassment Law: A Critical Examination of the Latest Developments in Workplace Sexual Harassment Litigation, 73 John's L. Rev. 701 (1999)--p. 92

Aden, "Harm in Asking": A Reply to Eugene Scalia and an Analysis of the Paradigm Shift in the Supreme Court's Title VII Sexual Harassment Jurisprudence, 8 Temp. Pol. & Civ. Rts. L. Rev. 477 (1999)--p. 90

Anderson, The Legacy of the Prompt Complaint Requirement, Corroboration Requirement, and Cautionary Instructions on Campus Sexual Assault, 84 B.U. L.Rev. 945 (2004)--p. 94

Anderson, "Thinking Within the Box": How Proof Models Are Used to Limit the Scope of Sexual Harassment Law, 19 Hofstra Lab. & Emp. L.J. 125 (2001)--p. 88

Armacost, Race and Reputation: The Real Legacy of *Paul v. Davis*, 85 Va. L. Rev. 569 (1999)--p. 39

Avery, Paying for Silence: The Liability of Police Officers under Section 1983 for Suppressing Exculpatory Evidence, 13 Temple Pol. & C.R. L. Rev. 1 (2003)--p. 13

Baker, *Seminole* Speaks to Sovereign Immunity and *Ex Parte Young*, 71 St. John's L. Rev. 739 (1997)--p. 1

Bandes, Introduction: The Emperor's New Clothes, 48 DePaul L. Rev. 619 (1999)--p. 28

Beermann, Municipal Responsibility for Constitutional Torts, 48 DePaul L. Rev. 627 (1999)--p. 28

Beiner, Gender Myths v. Working Realities: Using Social Science to Reformulate Sexual Harassment Law (NYU Press 2005)--p. 89

Beiner, Let the Jury Decide: The Gap Between What Judges and Reasonable People Believe Is Sexually Harassing, 75 S. Cal. L. Rev. 791 (2002)--p. 88

Bernstein, Defending the First Amendment From Antidiscrimination Laws, 2 N.C. L. Rev. 223 (2003)--p. 89

Bland and Knox, EEOC's Guidance on Vicarious Liability for Supervisory Harassment: Are the Courts Following the EEOC's Lead? 30 U. Mem. L. Rev. 793 (2000)--p. 91

Block, Whitehead, and Hardin, Gender Equity in Athletics: Should We Adopt a Non-Discriminatory Model?, 30 Toledo L. Rev. 223 (1999)--p. 102

Blum, Municipal Liability: Derivative or Direct? Statutory or Constitutional? Distinguishing the *Canton* Case from the *Collins* Case, 48 DePaul L. Rev. 687 (2000)--p. 28

Bodensteiner, Peer Harassment—Interference with an Equal Educational Opportunity in Elementary and Secondary Schools, 79 Neb. L. Rev. 1 (2000)--p. 94

Bohannan, Beyond Abrogation of Sovereign Immunity: State Waivers, Private Contracts, and Federal Incentives, 77 N.Y.U.L. Rev. 273 (2002)--p. 1

Brake, The Struggle for Sex Equality in Sport and the Theory Behind Title IX, 34 U. Mich. J.L. Ref. 12 (2000–01)--p. 102

Brown, Deterring Bully Government: A Sovereign Dilemma, 76 Tul. L. Rev. 149 (2001)--p. 7

Browne, Zero Tolerance for the First Amendment: Title VII's Regulation of Employee Speech, 27 Ohio N.U.L. Rev. 563 (2001)--p. 89

Bullman, Abuse of Female Sweatshop Laborers: Another Form of Sexual Harassment That Does Not Fit Neatly Into the Judiciary's Current Understanding of Discrimination Because of Sex, 78 Ind. L.J. 1019 (2003)--p. 87

Burke, Workplace Harassment: A Proposal for a Bright Line Test Consistent with the First Amendment, 21 Hofstra Lab. & Emp. L.J. 591 (2004)--p. 89

Caminker, "Appropriate" Means–Ends Constraints on Section 5 Powers, 53 Stan. L. Rev. 1127 (2001)--p. 5

Chamallas, Title VII's Midlife Crisis: The Case of Constructive Discharge, 77 S. Cal. L. Rev. 307 (2004)--p. 90

Chambers, (Un)welcome Conduct and the Sexually Hostile Environment, 53 Ala. L. Rev. 733 (2002)--p. 89

Chase and Chase, *Monell*: The Story Behind the Landmark, 31 Urb. Law. 491 (1999)--p. 28

Chaudhry & Greenberger, Seasons of Change: *Communities for Equity v. Michigan High School Athletic Association*, 13 UCLA Women's L.J. 1 (2003)--p. 102

Colker and Brudney, Dissing Congress, 100 Mich. L. Rev. 80 (2001)--p. 5

Collins Woodford and Rissetto, Tangible Employment Action: What Did the Supreme Court Really Mean in *Faragher* and *Ellerth*?, 19 Lab. Law. 63 (2003)--p. 91

Connell & Euben, Evolving Law in Same-Sex Sexual Harassment and Sexual Orientation Discrimination, 31 J. Coll. & U.L. 193 (2004)--p. 92

Coombs, Title VII and Homosexual Harassment After Oncale: Was It a Victory? 6 Duke J. Gender L. & Pol'y 113 (1999)--p. 92

Craswell, Deterrence and Damages: The Multiplier Principle and Its Alternatives, 97 Mich. L. Rev. 2185 (1999)--p. 59

Cunningham, Preserving Normal Heterosexual Male Fantasy: The "Severe or Pervasive" Missed–Interpretation of Sexual Harassment in the Absence of a Tangible Job Consequence, 1999 U. Chi. Legal F. 199 (1999)--p. 88

Dalley, All in a Day's Work: Employers' Vicarious Liability for Sexual Harassment, 104 W. Va. L. Rev. 517 (2002)--p. 91

Dauenhauer & Wells, Corrective Justice and Constitutional Torts, 35 Ga. L. Rev. 903 (2001)--p. 6

Davies, Assessing Institutional Responsibility for Sexual Harassment in Education, 77 Tul. L. Rev. 387 (2002)--p. 94

Deese, Case Note: Civil Rights–42 U.S.C. section 1981–Scope of the Equal Benefit Clause, 71 Tenn. L. Rev. 199 (2003)--p. 85

Del Po, The Thin Line Between Love and Hate: Same-Sex Sexual Harassment, 40 Santa Clara L. Rev. 1 (1999)--p. 92

Doran & Mason, Disproportionate Incongruity: State Sovereign Immunity and the Future of Federal Employment Discrimination Law, 2003 L. Rev. Mich. St. U. Det. C.L. 1 (2003)--p. 100

Dosanjh, Calling on Oncale: Federal Courts' Post-Oncale Approach to the "Evidentiary Routes" to Discriminatory Intent in Title VII Same-Sex Harassment Claims, 33 Urb. Law. 547 (2001)--p. 92

Drobac, Sex and the Workplace: Consenting Adolescents and a Conflict of Laws, 79 Wash. L. Rev. 471 (2004)--p. 87

Epstein, Foreword–"Just do It!": Title IX as a Threat to University Autonomy, 101 Mich. L. Rev. 1365 (2003)--p. 94

Farber, Pledging a New Allegiance: An Essay on Sovereignty and the New Federalism, 75 Notre Dame L. Rev. 1133 (2000)--p. 2

Feeley and Rubin, Judicial Policy Making and the Modern State: How the Courts Reformed America's Prisons (1998, paperback ed. 2000)--p. 105

Findlay, The Case for Requiring a Proportionality Test to Assess Compliance with Title IX in High School Athletics, 23 N. Ill. U. L. Rev. 29 (2002)--p. 101

Fleming, Title IX from The Red Rose Crew to Grutter: The Law and Literature of Sports, 14 Fordham Intell. Prop. Media & Ent. L.J. 793 (2004)--p. 102

Fletcher, The Eleventh Amendment: Unfinished Business, 75 Notre Dame L. Rev. 843 (2000)--p. 1

Fremling and Posner, Status Signaling and the Law, with Particular Application to Sexual Harassment, 147 U. Pa. L. Rev. 1069 (1999)--p. 88

Galle, Can Federal Agencies Authorize Private Suits Under Section 1983?: A Theoretical Approach, 69 Brooklyn L. Rev. 163 (2003)--p. 41

Gavora, Tilting the Playing Field: Schools, Sports, Sex and Title IX (2002)--p. 102

Gelfand, Introduction, Reconsidering *Monell*'s Limitation on Municipal Liability for Civil Rights Violations, 31 Urb. Law. 395 (1999)--p. 28

George, Fifty/Fifty: Ending Sex Segregation in School Sports, 63 Ohio St. L.J. 1107 (2002)--p. 101

George, If You're Not Part of the Solution, You're Part of the Problem: Employer Liability for Sexual Harassment, 13 Yale J.L. & Feminism 133 (2001)--p. 91

George, Title IX and the Scholarship Dilemma, 9 Marq. Sports L.J. 273 (1999)--p. 102

Gerhardt, Institutional Analysis of Municipal Liability Under Section 1983, 48 DePaul L. Rev. 669 (2000)--p. 28

Gilles, Breaking the Code of Silence: Rediscovering "Custom" in Section 1983 Municipal Liability, 80 B.U. L. Rev. 17 (2000)--p. 28

Gilles, In Defense of Making Government Pay: The Deterrent Effect of Constitutional Tort Remedies, 35 Ga. L. Rev. 845 (2001)--p. 6

Grossman, Making a Federal Case Out of It: Section 1981 and At-Will Employment, 67 Brook. L. Rev. 329 (2001)--p. 85

Grossman, The Culture of Compliance: The Final Triumph of Form Over Substance in Sexual Harassment Law, 26 Harv. Women's L.J. 3 (2003)--p. 91

Grover, After *Ellerth*: The Tangible Employment Action in Sexual Harassment Analysis, 35 U. Mich. J.L. Reform 809 (2002)--p. 91

Hamilton, The Importance and Overuse of Policy and Custom Claims: A View from One Trench, 48 DePaul L. Rev. 723 (2000)--p. 28

Harris, Shopping While Black: Applying 42 U.S.C. Section 1981 to Cases of Consumer Racial Profiling, 23 B.C. Third World L.J. 1 (2003)--p. 85

Healy, The Rise of Unnecessary Constitutional Rulings, 83 N.C.L. Rev. 847 (2005)--p. 13

Hebert, The Disparate Impact of Sexual Harassment: Does Motive Matter?, 53 U. Kan. L. Rev. 341 (2005)--p. 89

Heckman, Is Notice Required in a Title IX Athletic Action Not Involving Sexual Harassment?, 14 Marq. Sports L. Rev. 175 (2003)--p. 94

Heckman, The Glass Sneaker: Thirty Years of Victories and Defeats Involving Title IX and Sex Discrimination in Athletics, 13 Fordham Intell. Prop. Media & Ent. L.J. 551 (2003)--p. 101

Herbert, Sexual Harassment as Discrimination "Because of Sex": Have We Come Full Circle?, 27 Ohio N.U.L. Rev. 439 (2001)--p. 88

Hill, The Feminist Misspeak of Sexual Harassment, 57 Fla. L. Rev. 133 (2005)--p. 89

Hoffmann, Selective Sexual Harassment Differential Treatment of Similar Groups of Women Workers, 28 Law & Hum. Behav. 29 (2004)--p. 87

Hogshead–Makar & Steinbach, Intercollegiate Athletics' Unique Environment for Sexual Harassment Claims: Balancing the Realities of Athletics with Preventing Potential Claims, 13 Marq. Sports L. Rev. 173 (2003)--p. 94

Hutchens, The Legal Effect of College and University Policies Prohibiting Romantic Relationships Between Students and Professors, 32 J.L. & Educ. 411 (2003)--p. 94

Hutchinson, The Collision of Employment-at-Will, Section 1981 & *Gonzalez*: Discharge, Consent and Contract Sufficiency, 3 U. Pa. J. Lab. & Empl. L. 207 (2001)--p. 85

Jackson, Principle and Compromise in Constitutional Adjudication: The Eleventh Amendment and State Sovereign Immunity, 75 Notre Dame L. Rev. 953 (2000)--p. 1

Jeffries, Disaggregating Constitutional Torts, 110 Yale L.J. 259 (2000)--p. 13

Johnson, License to Harass Women: Requiring Hostile Environment Sexual Harassment to Be "Severe or Pervasive" Discriminates Among "Terms and Conditions" of Employment, 62 Md. L. Rev. 85 (2003)--p. 89

Juliano & Schwab, The Sweep of Sexual Harassment Cases, 86 Cornell L. Rev. 548 (2001)--p. 88

Kabat, How (Not) to Litigate a Sexual Harassment Class Action, 9 Lab. Law. 129 (2003)--p. 87

Kaczorowski, Reflections on *Monell*'s Analysis of the Legislative History of Section 1983, 31 Urb. L. Law. 407 (1999)--p. 28

Kaczorowski, The Supreme Court and Congress's Power to Enforce Constitutional Rights: An Overlooked Moral Anomaly, 73 Fordham L. Rev. 153 (2004)--p. 101

Kamin, Harmless Error and the Rights/Remedies Split, 88 Va.L.Rev. (2002)--p. 13

Karlan, Disarming the Private Attorney General, 2003 U. Ill. L. Rev. 183 (2003)--pp. 5, 41

Katz, Re–Considering Attraction in Sexual Harassment, 79 Ind. L.J. 101 (2004)--p. 88

Kean, Municipal Liability for Off–Duty Police Misconduct Under Section 1983: The "Under Color of Law Requirement," 79 B.U.L. Rev. 195 (1999)--p. 37

King, Sexual Harassment Claims in the New Millenium: A Litigator's Point of View, 27 Ohio N.U.L. Rev. 539 (2001)--p. 88

Kinports, Habeas Corpus, Qualified Immunity, and Crystal Balls: Predicting the Course of Constitutional Law, 33 Ariz. L. Rev. 115 (1991)--p. 26

Kinports, Implied Waiver After *Seminole Tribe*, 82 Minn. L. Rev. 793 (1998)--p. 1

Kirshenbaum, Hostile Environment Sexual Harassment Law and the First Amendment: Can the Two Peacefully Coexist?, 12 Tex. J. Women & L. 67 (2002)--p. 89

Korb and Bales, A Permanent Stop Sign: Why Courts Should Yield to the Temptation to Impose Heightened Pleading Standards in § 1983 Cases, 41 Brandeis L.J. 267 (2002)--p. 26

Kritchevsky, Reexamining *Monell*: Basing Section 1983 Municipal Liability Doctrine on the Statutory Language, 31 Urb. Law. 437 (1999)--p. 28

TABLE OF SECONDARY AUTHORITIES

Lawton, Tipping the Scales of Justice in Sexual Harassment Law, 27 Ohio N.U.L. Rev. 517 (2001)--p. 88

Lehman, The Equal Protection Problem in Sexual Harassment Doctrine, 10 Colum. J. Gender & L. 125 (2000)--p. 88

Lehman, Why Title VII Should Prohibit All Workplace Sexual Harassment, 12 Yale J.L. & Feminism 225 (2000)--p. 92

Levinson, Making Government Pay: Markets, Politics, and the Allocation of Constitutional Costs, 67 U. Chi. L. Rev. 345 (2000)--p. 6

Levinson, Parsing the Meaning of "Adverse Employment Action" in Title VII Disparate Treatment, Sexual Harassment, and Retaliation Claims: What Should Be Actionable Wrongdoing? 56 Okla. L. Rev. 623 (2003)--p. 88

Lombardi, Media in the Spotlight: Private Parties Liable For Violating the Fourth Amendment, 6 Roger Williams U.L. Rev. 393 (2000)--p. 35

Lyon and Phillips, Faragher v. City of Boca Raton and Burlington Industries, Inc. v. Ellerth: Sexual Harassment Under Title VII Reaches Adolescence, 29 U. Mem. L. Rev. 601 (1999)--p. 91

MacKinnon, The Logic of Experience: Reflections on the Development of Sexual Harassment Law, 90 Geo. L.J. 813 (2002)--p. 88

MacKinnon and Siegel, Directions in Sexual Harassment Law (2004)--p. 87

Macready, Statutory Construction as a Means of Judicial Restraint on Government: A case Study in Bisexual Harassment Under Title VII, 27 Ohio N.U.L. Rev. 659 (2001)--p. 92

Mank, Are Anti-Retaliation Regulations in Title VI or Title IX Enforceable in a Private Right of Action: Does Sandoval or Sullivan Control this Question?, 35 Seton Hall L. Rev. 47 (2004)--p. 94

Mank, Suing Under Section 1983: The Future After *Gonzaga University v. Doe,* 39 Hous. L. Rev. 1417 (2003)--pp. 41, 44

Manley, Effective But Messy, *Monell* Should Endure, 31 Urb. Law. 481 (1999)--p. 28

Mansfield & Gabel, An Analysis of the *Burlington* and *Faragher* Affirmative Defense: When Are Employers Liable?, 19 Lab. Law. 107 (2003)--p. 91

Marks, Smoke, Mirrors, and the Disappearance of "Vicarious" Liability: The Emergence of a Dubious Summary-Judgment Safe Harbor for Employers Whose Supervisory Personnel Commit Hostile Environment Workplace Harassment, 38 Hous. L. Rev. 1401 (2002)--p. 91

Marshall, Injustice Frames, Legality, and the Everyday Construction of Sexual Harassment, 28 Law & Soc. Inquiry 659 (2003)--p. 88

Mawdsley, A Section 1983 Cause of Action Under IDEA? Measuring the Effect of *Gonzaga University v. Doe,* 170 Ed. L. Rep. 425 (2002)--p. 44

McGough, Same-Sex Harassment: Do Either Price Waterhouse or Oncale Support the Ninth Circuit's Holding in Nichols v. Azteca Restaurant Enterprises, Inc. that Same-Sex Harassment Based on Failure to Conform to Gender Stereotypes is Actionable?, 22 Hofstra Lab. & Emp. L.J. 206 (2004)--p. 92

McGowan, The Bona Fide Body: Title VII's Last Bastion of Intentional Sex Discrimination, 12 Colum. J. Gender & L. 77 (2003)--p. 86

Meltzer, State Sovereign Immunity: Five Authors in Search of a Theory, 75 Notre Dame L. Rev. 1011 (2000)--p. 1

Michaelis, Title IX and Same-Gender Sexual Harassment: School District Liability for Damages, 2000 B.Y.U. Educ. & L.J. 47 (2000)--p. 94

Montz, Shifting Paramets: An Examination of Recent Changes in the Baseline of Actionable Conduct for Hostile Working Environment Sexual Harassment, 3 Geo. J. Gender & L. 809 (2002)--p. 89

Morris, The Impact of Constitutional Liability on the Privatization Movement After *Richardson v. McKnight,* 52 Vand. L. Rev. 489 (1999)--p. 36

Nahmod, From the Courtroom to the Street: Court Orders and Section 1983, 29 Hat. Const'l L.Q. 613 (2002)--p. 13

Noonan, Narrowing the Nation's Power: The Supreme Court Sides with the States (2002)--p. 5

Nowak, The Gang of Five & the Second Coming of an Anti-Reconstruction Supreme Court, 75 Notre Dame L. Rev. 1091 (2000)--p. 2

Olmstead, In Defense of the Indefensible: Title VII Hostile Environment Claims Unconstitutionally Restrict Free Speech, 27 Ohio N.U.L. Rev. 691 (2001)--p. 89

Oppenheimer, Investigating Workplace Harassment and Discrimination, 29 Employee Rel. L.J. 56 (2004)--p. 88

Oren, If *Monell* Were Reconsidered: Sexual Abuse and the Scope-of-Employment Doctrine in the Common Law, 31 Urb. Law. 527 (1999)--p. 28

Orth, History and the Eleventh Amendment, 75 Notre Dame L. Rev. 1147 (2000)--p. 2

Paetzold, Same-Sex Sexual Harassment, Revisited: The Aftermath of Oncale v. Sundowner Offshore Services, Inc., 3 Employee Rts. & Employ. Pol'y J. 251 (1999)--p. 92

Palmer, Baer, Jasperson, and DeLaat, Low-Life-Sleazy-Big-Haired Trailer-Park Girl v. The President: The Paula Jones Case and the Law of Sexual Harassment, 9 Am. U. Gender Soc. Pol'y & L. 283 (2001)--p. 90

Park, The Constitutional Tort Action as Individual Remedy, 38 Harv. C.R.-C.L.L. Rev. 393 (2003)--p. 7

Parker, The Decline of Judicial Decisionmaking: School Desegregation and District Court Judges, 81 N.C.L. Rev. 1623 (2003)--p. 104

Perry, Kulik & Bourhis, The Reasonable Woman Standard Effects on Sexual Harassment Court Decisions, 28 Law & Hum. Behav. 9 (2004)--p. 88

Pfander, Once More Unto the Breach: Eleventh Amendment Scholarship and the Court, 75 Notre Dame L. Rev. 817 (2000)--p. 1

Pieronek, Title IX Beyond Thirty: A Review of Recent Developments, 30 J. Coll. & Univ. L. 75 (2003)--p. 94

Pillard, Taking Fiction Seriously: The Strange Results of Public Officials' Individual Liability Under *Bivens*, 88 Geo. L.J. 65 (1999)--pp. 6, 13

Pope, Everything You Wanted to Know About Sexual Harassment But Were Too Politically Correct to Ask (or, the Use and Abuse of "But For" Analysis in Sexual Harassment Law Under Title VII, 30 Sw. U.L. Rev. 253 (2001)--p. 88

Posner, Employment Discrimination: Age Discrimination and Sexual Harassment, 19 Int'l Rev. L. & Econ. 421 (1999)--p. 88

Post, Fashioning the Legal Constitution: Culture, Courts, and Law, 117 Harv. L. Rev. 4 (2003)--p. 5

Post and Siegel, Equal Protection by Law: Federal Antidiscrimination Legislation After *Morrison* and *Kimel*, 110 Yale L.J. 441 (2000)--p. 100

Post & Siegel, Legislative Constitutionalism and Section Five Power: Policentric Interpretation of the Family and Medical Leave Act, 112 Yale L.J. 1943 (2003)--p. 101

Quereshi and Vaupel, Should Sexual Harassment Based Upon Sexual Orientation be Covered by Title VII or Prohibited?, 27 Ohio N.U.L. Rev. 679 (2001)--p. 92

Quinn, The Paradox of Complaining: Law, Humor, and Harassment in the Everyday Work World, 25 Law & Soc. Inquiry 1151 (2000)--p. 88

Reardon, Integrating Neighborhoods, Segregating Schools: The Retreat from School Desegregation in the South, 81 N.C.L. Rev. 1563 (2003)--p. 104

Reich, All the [Athletes] Are Equal, But Some Are More Equal Than Others: An Objective Evaluation of Title IX's Past, Present, and Recommendations for Its Future, 108 Penn St. L. Rev. 525 (2003)--p. 102

Rich–Chappell, Child's Play or Sex Discrimination?: School Liability for Peer Sexual Harassment Under Title IX, 3 J. Gender Race & Just. 311 (1999)--p. 94

Roberts, Evaluating Gender Equity Within the Framework of Intercollegiate Athletics' Conflicting Value Systems, 77 Tul. L. Rev. 997 (2003)--p. 102

Romano Davis v. Monroe County Board of Education: Title IX Recipients' "Head in the Sand" Approach to Peer Sexual Harassment May Incur Liability, 30 J.L. & Educ. 63 (2001)--p. 94

Roosevelt, Exhaustion under the Prison Litigation Reform Act: The Consequences of Procedural Error, 52 Emory L.J. 1771 (2003)--p. 61

Rotunda, The Eleventh Amendment, *Garrett*, and Protection for Civil Rights, 53 Ala. L. Rev. 1183 (2002)--pp. 5, 100

Rubin, Square Pegs and Round Holes: Substantive Due Process, Procedural Due Process, and the Bill of Rights, 103 Colum. L. Rev. 833 (2003)--p. 40

Ruescher, Saving Title VII: Using Intent to Distinguish Harassment from Expression, 23 Rev. Litig. 349 (2004)--p. 89

Rutherglen, Custom and Usage as Action Under Color of State Law: An Essay on the Forgotten Terms of Section 1983, 89 Va. L. Rev. 925 (2003)--p. 6

Rutherglen, The Improbable History of Section 1981: Clio Still Bemused and Confused, 2003 Sup. Ct. Rev. 303 (2003)--pp. 84, 85

Sangree, Title IX and the Contact Sports Exemption: Gender Stereotypes in a Civil Rights Statute, 32 Conn. L. Rev. 381 (2000)--p. 101

Schlanger, Inmate Litigation, 116 Harv. L. Rev. 1555 (2003)--p. 105

Schlanger, Prison Litigation, 116 Harv. L. Rev. 1555 (2003)--p. 108

Schnapper, Some of Them Still Don't Get It: Hostile Work Environment Litigation in the Lower Courts, 1999 U. Chi. Legal F. 277 (1999)--p. 88

Schultz, Talking About Harassment, 9 J. L. & Policy 417 (2001)--p. 88

Schultz, The Sanitized Workplace, 112 Yale L.J. 2061 (2003)--p. 88

Schwartz, Should Juries Be Informed that Municipality Will Indemnify Officer's § 1983 Liability for Constitutional Wrongdoing?, 86 Iowa L. Rev. 1209 (2001)--p. 6

Schwartz, When is Sex Because of Sex? The Causation Problem in Sexual Harassment Law, 150 U. Pa. L. Rev. 1697 (2002)--p. 88

Seinfeld, Waiver-in-Litigation: Eleventh Amendment Immunity and the Voluntariness Question, 63 Ohio St. L.J. 871 (2002)--p. 1

Serr, Turning Section 1983's Protection of Civil Rights Into an Attractive Nuisance: Extra-Textual Barriers in Municipal Liability Under *Monell*, 35 Ga. L. Rev. 881 (2001)--p. 6

Sherry, States Are People Too, 75 Notre Dame L. Rev. 1121 (2000)--p. 2

Singer, Statutes and Statutory Construction § 46.06, pp. 181–86 (rev. 6th ed. 2000)--p. 69

Sklansky, The Private Police, 46 U.C.L.A. L. Rev. 1165 (1999)--p. 36

Stein, Bullying or Sexual Harassment? The Missing Discourse of Rights in an Era of Zero Tolerance, 45 Ariz. L. Rev. 783 (2003)---p. 88

Stockdale, Bisom-Rapp, O'Connor & Gutek, Coming to Terms with Zero Tolerance Sexual Harassment Policies, 4 J. Forensic Psych. Prac. 65 (2004)--p. 91

Symposium, Title IX at Thirty, 14 Marq. Sports L. Rev. 1 (2003)--p. 94

Symposium, Title IX Women, Athletics and the Law, 3 Margins L.J. 209 (2003)--p. 94

Taylor, A Litigator's View of Discovery and Proof in Police Misconduct Policy and Practice Cases, 48 DePaul L. Rev. 723 (2000)--p. 28

Taylor, Let's Talk About Sex: A Clarification of Employer Liability for Supervisor Sexual Harassment Under Title VII, 27 Ohio N.U.L. Rev. 607 (2001)--p. 91

Tidmarsh, A Dialogic Defense of *Alden*, 75 Notre Dame L. Rev. 1161 (2000)--p. 2

Timmons, Sexual Harassment and Disparate Impact: Should Non-Targeted Workplace Sexual Conduct Be Actionable Under Title VII, 81 Neb. L. Rev. 1152 (2003)--p. 88

Turner, Employer Liability for Supervisory Hostile Environment Sexual Harassment: Comparing Title VII's and Section 1983's Regulatory Regimes, 31 Urb. Law. 503 (1999)--pp. 28, 91

Turner, The Unenvisaged Case, Interpretive Progression, and the Justiciability of Title VII Same-Sex Sexual Harassment Claims, 7 Duke J. Gender L. & Pol'y 57 (2000)--p. 92

Turner, Title VII and the Inequality–Enhancing Effects of the Bisexual and Equal Opportunity Harasser Defenses, 7 U. Pa. J. Lab. & Emp. L. 341 (2005)--p. 92

Vaughn, The Customer Is Always Right . . . Not! Employer Liability for Third Party Sexual Harassment, 9 Mich. J. Gender & L. 1 (2002)--p. 91

Vázquez, Eleventh Amendment Schizophrenia, 75 Notre Dame L. Rev. 859 (2000)--p. 1

Volokh, Speech as Conduct: Generally Applicable Laws, Illegal Courses of Conduct, Situation-Altering Utterances, and the Uncharted Zones, 90 Cornell L. Rev. ___ (2005)--p. 89

Wagman Roisman, The Impact of the Civil Rights Act of 1866 on Racially Discriminatory Donative Transfers, 53 Ala. L. Rev. 463 (2002)--p. 85

Wells, Identifying State Actors in Constitutional Litigation: Reviving the Role of Substantive Context, 26 Cardozo L. Rev. 99 (2004)--p. 35

West, Preventing Sexual Harassment: The Federal Courts' Wake-Up Call for Women, 68 Brook L. Rec. 457 (2002)--p. 89

White, Rule of Law and the Limits of Sovereignty: The Private Prison in Jurisprudential Perspective, 38 Am. Crim. L. Rev. 111 (2001)--p. 36

White, The Making of the President 1960, pp. 293–94 (1961)--p. 54

Woolhandler, Old Property, New Property, and Sovereign Immunity, 75 Notre Dame L. Rev. 919 (2000)--p. 1

Yuracko, One for You and One for Me: Is Title IX's Sex-Based Proportionality Requirement for College Varsity Athletic Positions Defensible?, 97 Nw. U. L. Rev. 731 (2003)--p. 101

Yuracko, Private Nurses and Playboy Bunnies: Explaining Permissible Sex Discrimination, 92 Cal. L. Rev. 147 (2004)--p. 86

2005 SUPPLEMENT

CIVIL RIGHTS ACTIONS: ENFORCING THE CONSTITUTION

*

INTRODUCTION

STATE SOVEREIGN IMMUNITY AND THE ELEVENTH AMENDMENT

Page 21, add a footnote at the end of Note 2:

a. For commentary on 11th Amendment waiver, see Christina Bohannan, Beyond Abrogation of Sovereign Immunity: State Waivers, Private Contracts, and Federal Incentives, 77 N.Y.U.L. Rev. 273 (2002), and Gil Seinfeld, Waiver-in-Litigation: Eleventh Amendment Immunity and the Voluntariness Question, 63 Ohio St. L.J. 871 (2002).

Page 23, add at the end of footnote b:

Additional commentary appears in William A. Fletcher, The Eleventh Amendment: Unfinished Business, 75 Notre Dame L. Rev. 843 (2000) (arguing for *Union Gas* and against *Seminole Tribe* on the ground that state sovereign immunity from private suit is less justified when a state engages in commercial activity than when it exercises sovereign functions); Kit Kinports, Implied Waiver After *Seminole Tribe*, 82 Minn. L. Rev. 793 (1998) (pointing out that while Congress exercising Article I power may not unilaterally abrogate Eleventh Amendment immunity, it can use the conditional grant of federal funds to solicit state waivers); Wayne L. Baker, *Seminole* Speaks to Sovereign Immunity and *Ex Parte Young*, 71 St. John's L. Rev. 739 (1997) (concluding that Congress could easily evade *Seminole Tribe* by creating a private right of action against state officials).

Page 24, add at the end of footnote c:

Alden has provoked a substantial literature. For a sample, see James E. Pfander, Once More Unto the Breach: Eleventh Amendment Scholarship and the Court, 75 Notre Dame L. Rev. 817 (2000) (introducing a symposium on state sovereign immunity and exploring the implications of *Alden* for Eleventh Amendment scholarship); Carlos Manuel Vázquez, Eleventh Amendment Schizophrenia, 75 Notre Dame L. Rev. 859 (2000) (exploring the "schizophrenia" of saying on the one hand that state sovereign immunity from private suits is constitutionally fundamental and beyond Congressional control and allowing on the other hand unlimited federal enforcement actions against states, as well as private suits against state officers); Ann Woolhandler, Old Property, New Property, and Sovereign Immunity, 75 Notre Dame L. Rev. 919 (2000) (arguing that while all "property" might be entitled to some due process protection, only traditional property interests trigger a constitutional right to compensation); Vicki C. Jackson, Principle and Compromise in Constitutional Adjudication: The Eleventh Amendment and State Sovereign Immunity, 75 Notre Dame L. Rev. 953 (2000) (arguing that state sovereign immunity should be de-emphasized, in part because it conflicts with the rule of law and with federal supremacy); Daniel J. Meltzer, State Sovereign Immunity: Five Authors in Search of a Theory, 75 Notre Dame L. Rev. 1011 (2000) (criticizing the Court's efforts to promote federalism by limiting the enforcement of valid federal laws against states rather than by restricting the reach of federal legislative authority as "fail[ing] to promote any coherent conception of states' rights or state autonomy while harming legitimate national objectives"); John E. Nowak, The Gang of Five & the Second Coming of an Anti–Reconstruction Supreme Court, 75 Notre Dame L. Rev. 1091 (2000) (comparing recent decisions to those that dismantled or curtailed Reconstruction-era legislation); Suzanna Sherry, States Are People Too, 75 Notre Dame L. Rev. 1121 (2000) (criticizing analogies between state sovereign immunity and individuals rights); Daniel A. Farber, Pledging a New Allegiance: An Essay on Sovereignty and the New Federalism, 75 Notre Dame L. Rev. 1133 (2000) (examining *Alden* as reflecting a "new federalism" credo of state sovereignty); John V. Orth, History and the Eleventh Amendment, 75 Notre Dame L. Rev. 1147 (2000) (examining the use of history to justify various positions on state sovereign immunity); Jay Tidmarsh, A Dialogic Defense of *Alden*, 75 Notre Dame L. Rev. 1161 (2000) (defending the result in *Alden* as "within the range of permissible constitutional choice").

Page 25, add a new Note:

4a. Congressional Enforcement Power under the 14th Amendment. The decisions in *Seminole Tribe* and *Alden* on the one hand and *Fitzpatrick* on the other, place pressure on the question of which source of congressional authority undergirds a statute. While Congress can create quite similar rights and duties under both the Commerce Clause and the 14th Amendment, the mechanisms available to enforce those obligations differ significantly. Only in cases where Congress is using its authority under the 14th Amendment (or one of the other Reconstruction Amendments) can Congress provide individuals with the right to bring suit against a state.

In a series of cases beginning with City of Boerne v. Flores, 521 U.S. 507 (1997), the Court has elaborated on the appropriate scope of Congress' authority to enforce the 14th Amendment. *Boerne* involved a challenge to the Religious Freedom Restoration Act (RFRA), a statute passed in response to the Court's earlier decision in Employment Division v. Smith, 494 U.S. 872 (1990), which had held that neutral, generally applicable laws may be applied to religious practices even when not supported by a compelling governmental interest. In RFRA, Congress prohibited state and local governments from substantially burdening free exercise even if the burden resulted from a rule of general applicability unless the law was the least restrictive means of furthering a compelling government interest. The Court held that RFRA exceeded Congress' power. While Section 5 of the 14th Amendment gave Congress the power to enact legislation enforcing free exercise rights, that enforcement power was "preventive" or "remedial." As a matter of separation of powers, the Court, and not Congress, had the power to decree the substance of the Constitution's restrictions on the state. In order for a congressional enactment to represent appropriate legislation, the Court required "congruence and proportionality between the injury to be prevented or remedied and the means adopted to that end." RFRA failed that test, the Court concluded, because in proscribing a broad range of state conduct that the 14th Amendment itself would not have prohibited, the Act went far beyond counteracting state laws that were likely to be unconstitutional.

Following *Boerne*, the Court issued a series of opinions in which it held that Congress had exceeded its Section 5 enforcement powers in the 11th Amendment context. In Kimel v. Florida Bd. of Regents, 528 U.S. 62 (2000), the Court held that Congress could not use its Section 5 powers to subject states to suit under the Age Discrimination in Employment Act. Age is not a suspect classification under the Equal Protection Clause. Thus, states were entitled to discriminate on the basis of age as long as their use of age was rationally related to a legitimate state interest. Because this level of scrutiny is extremely deferential to state judgments, states were entitled to use age as a proxy for other characteristics even if it was a somewhat inaccurate proxy. The Court found that the ADEA's broad ban on using race would prohibit substantially more state employment practices than would likely be held unconstitutional under the applicable equal protection, rational basis standard and concluded that the ADEA was "so out of proportion to a ... remedial or preventive object that it cannot be understood as responsive to, or designed to prevent, unconstitutional behavior."

Similarly, in Florida Prepaid Postsecondary Educ. Expense Bd. v. College Savings Bank, 527 U.S. 627 (1999), the Court struck down Congress' attempt to abrogate states' sovereign immunity in the Patent and Plant Variety Protection Remedy Clarification Act because of Congress's failure to identify a pattern of pervasive, unremedied patent infringement by the states. While such a pattern might violate the due process clause—because it would involve deprivation of property without due process—the Court found that the legislative record could not support the claim that the Act responded to a history of widespread and persisting deprivation of constitutional rights of the sort that justified prophylactic Section 5 legislation. Congress's failure to limit the Act's coverage to cases involving arguable constitutional violations or to confine its reach by limiting the remedy to certain types of infringement failed the congruence and proportionality test. While the Act's basic aim of providing a remedy for patent infringement was a proper concern under Article I, that Article did not give Congress the power to abrogate a state's sovereign immunity.

And in Board of Trustees v. Garrett, 531 U.S. 356 (2001), the Court rejected Congress's attempt to abrogate state sovereign immunity in cases brought under Title I of the Americans with Disabilities Act (ADA), which prohibits certain employers, including state governments, from discriminating against otherwise qualified individuals with disabilities and requires these employers to offer "reasonable accommodations to the known physical or mental limitations of an otherwise qualified individual" unless the accommodation would impose an undue hardship. Discrimination against the disabled, like discrimination on the basis of age, triggered "only the minimum 'rational-basis' review applicable to general social and economic legislation," rather than the heightened forms of scrutiny triggered by discrimination against suspect classes. Thus, the *Garrett* Court explained, it might be "entirely rational (and therefore constitutional) for a state employer to conserve scarce financial resources by hiring employees who are able to use existing facilities," rather than accommodating disabled individuals. As in *Kimel*, the Court concluded that the legislative record did not demonstrate a sufficient history and pattern of unconstitutional state behavior to justify abrogating sovereign immunity.

But in Nevada Department of Human Resources v. Hibbs, 538 U.S. 721 (2003), the Court reached the opposite conclusion. *Hibbs* involved a provision of the Family and Medical Leave Act that created a private right of action to seek both equitable relief and money damages against any employer, including a public agency, that interfered with the exercise of the Act's right to take unpaid leave to care for a sick family member. The Court found that the FMLA was an appropriate instance of prophylactic legislation that proscribes facially constitutional conduct in order to prevent and deter unconstitutional conduct. It found that the FMLA was intended to protect the right to be free from gender-based discrimination in the workplace. Unlike discrimination on the basis of disability or age, discrimination on the basis of sex is subject to heightened scrutiny: such classifications must serve "important governmental objectives," and be "substantially related to the achievement of those objectives." The Court concluded that when Congress enacted the FMLA, it had before it a significant record of sex discrimination with respect to the administration of leave benefits by the states that justified the enactment of prophylactic Section 5 legislation. And it concluded that Congress' chosen remedy for that pattern of violations—the FMLA's leave provisions—was congruent and proportional to the targeted violation, because earlier and less intrusive congressional efforts had failed to solve the problem. And unlike the statutes at issue in *Boerne, Kimel,* and *Garrett*, the Court found the FMLA to be narrowly targeted at precisely the employment practice where sex-based overgeneralization had been a problem.

And in Tennessee v. Lane, 541 U.S. 509 (2004), the Court held that although Title I of the Americans with Disabilities Act, which dealt with employment, could not abrogate states' sovereign immunity, Title II of the Act, which forbid exclusion of disabled individuals from participating in or receiving the benefits of "the services, programs or activities of a public entity," could constitutionally be applied to abrogate states' sovereign immunity with respect to damages actions involving the denial of access to the courts.

Writing for the Court, Justice Stevens observed that Title II, unlike Title I, sought not only to enforce the Fourteenth Amendment's prohibition on irrational disability discrimination—a principle enforced by relatively deferential rationality review—but also to enforce a variety of other basic constitutional guarantees, including some, like the right of access to the courts, the infringement of which are subject to heightened judicial scrutiny. The Court held that the record before Congress contained evidence of pervasive unequal treatment of persons with disabilities in the administration of state services and programs, including access to state courts. In particular, the Court pointed to testimony regarding both the failure to make courtrooms accessible to witnesses with physical disabilities and other discrimination within the judicial system against disabled individuals. Faced with this extensive record of disability discrimination, prophylactic legislation requiring states to accommodate disabled individuals in the administration of judicial services and enforcing that requirement through private lawsuits by affected individuals was appropriate. Notably, the Court declined to address the question whether Title II was constitutional in all circumstances:

> [N]othing in our case law requires us to consider Title II, with its wide variety of applications, as an undifferentiated whole. Whatever might be said about Title II's other applications, the question presented in this case is not whether Congress can validly subject the States to private suits for money damages for failing to provide reasonable access to hockey rinks, or even to voting booths, but whether Congress had the power under § 5 to enforce the constitutional right of access to the courts. Because we find that Title II unquestionably is valid § 5 legislation as it applies to the class of cases implicating the accessibility of judicial services, we need go no further.

The Court's decisions regarding congressional power to enforce the 14th amendment through private lawsuits has occasioned voluminous scholarship. For some representative examples, see John T. Noonan, Jr., Narrowing the Nation's Power: The Supreme Court Sides with the States (2002); Evan H. Caminker, "Appropriate" Means–Ends Constraints on Section 5 Powers, 53 Stan. L. Rev. 1127 (2001); Ruth C. Colker and James J. Brudney, Dissing Congress, 100 Mich. L. Rev. 80 (2001); Pamela S. Karlan, Disarming the Private Attorney General, 2003 U. Ill. L. Rev. 183; Robert C. Post, Fashioning the Legal Constitution: Culture, Courts, and Law, 117 Harv. L. Rev. 4 (2003); Ronald D. Rotunda, The Eleventh Amendment, Garrett, and Protection for Civil Rights, 53 Ala. L. Rev. 1183 (2002).

CHAPTER I

42 U.S.C. § 1983

Page 40, add a footnote at the end of Note 2:

    h. The "under color of" clause refers to more than state law. It also refers to action under the "custom" or "usage" of any state. These terms, as they are commonly understood, do not require any form of state action but, in the cases interpreting § 1983, they have been interpreted to mean custom or usage of state officials. Adickes v. S.H. Kress Co., 398 U.S. 144, 166–68 (1970). Custom and usage, however, have a long history as sources of law independent of official action. For an extensive examination of this history and how it bears on the interpretation of § 1983 and the 14th Amendment, see George Rutherglen, Custom and Usage as Action Under Color of State Law: An Essay on the Forgotten Terms of Section 1983, 89 Va. L. Rev. 925 (2003) (arguing that § 1983 was directed against "custom" and "usage" in the sense of pervasive practices, both public and private, that sought to perpetuate the inferior status of blacks in the South).

Page 49, add at the end of footnote a:

    See also Cornelia T.L. Pillard, Taking Fiction Seriously: The Strange Results of Public Officials' Individual Liability Under *Bivens*, 88 Geo. L.J. 65 (1999) (examining the analogous question of *Bivens* actions against federal officers and reporting that "virtually without exception, the government represents or pays for representation of federal officials accused of constitutional violations and pays the costs of judgments or settlements"). For an argument that juries should be told of the prospect of indemnification, see Martin A. Schwartz, Should Juries Be Informed that Municipality Will Indemnify Officer's § 1983 Liability for Constitutional Wrongdoing?, 86 Iowa L. Rev. 1209 (2001).

Page 90, add a footnote at the end of Note 3:

    b. The applicability to governments of general deterrence theory is challenged in Daryl Levinson, Making Government Pay: Markets, Politics, and the Allocation of Constitutional Costs, 67 U. Chi. L. Rev. 345 (2000). Levinson argues that government officers do not necessarily respond to liability rules in the same way as private actors. "Because government actors respond to political, not market, incentives, we should not assume that government will internalize social costs just because it is forced to make a budgetary outlay." Moreover, even if government officers do respond to the prospect of money damages, deterrence will still fail if constitutional violations create benefits for a majority of citizens that outweigh the costs imposed on a few. Levinson's arguments suggest a profound skepticism about the utility of money damages in enforcing constitutional rights.

    These ideas are examined in a symposium in the Georgia Law Review. Included is a Foreword by Thomas A. Eaton, 35 Ga. L. Rev. 837 (2001), and an Afterword by Marshall Shapo, id., at 931. Articles in the symposium include: Myriam E. Gilles, In Defense of Making Government Pay: The Deterrent Effect of Constitutional Tort Remedies, 35 Ga. L. Rev. 845 (2001); Brian J. Serr, Turning Section 1983's Protection of Civil Rights Into an Attractive Nuisance: Extra-Textual Barriers in Municipal Liability Under *Monell*, 35 Ga. L. Rev. 881 (2001); Bernard P. Dauenhauer & Michael L. Wells, Corrective Justice and Constitutional Torts, 35 Ga. L. Rev. 903 (2001). For another response to Levinson, see

Mark R. Brown, Deterring Bully Government: A Sovereign Dilemma, 76 Tul. L. Rev. 149 (2001) (using game theory to argue that government can be deterred by the prospect of damages liability).

Page 92, add a footnote at the end of Note 5:

c. For an analysis that seeks to go beyond the cost-effectiveness of money damages to consider other values that § 1983 actions might have in our constitutional system, see James J. Park, The Constitutional Tort Action as Individual Remedy, 38 Harv. C.R.-C.L.L. Rev. 393 (2003).

Page 112, add new Notes and renumber remaining Notes:

3. *Saucier v. Katz*. Saucier v. Katz, 533 U.S. 194 (2001), was a *Bivens* action challenging a military policeman's use of excessive force in removing a demonstrator protesting at a speech given by Vice President Gore at a military base. The respondent was a protestor who alleged that he was gratuitously shoved when he was being put into a police van.

The district court held that a dispute on a material fact existed concerning whether petitioner had used excessive force. It denied petitioner's claim of qualified immunity, holding that, in the Fourth Amendment context, qualified immunity duplicates the inquiry on the merits into whether the use of force was unreasonable and therefore violative of the Fourth Amendment. The court of appeals affirmed, on the basis of the Supreme Court's earlier opinion in Graham v. Connor, 490 U.S. 386 (1989), which had held that objective reasonableness was the appropriate test for excessive force claim.

The Supreme Court, in an opinion by Justice Kennedy, reversed.

In a suit against an officer for an alleged violation of a constitutional right, the requisites of a qualified immunity defense must be considered in proper sequence. Where the defendant seeks qualified immunity, a ruling on that issue should be made early in the proceedings so that the costs and expenses of trial are avoided where the defense is dispositive. Qualified immunity is "an entitlement not to stand trial or face the other burdens of litigation." Mitchell v. Forsyth, 472 U.S. 511, 526 (1985). The privilege is "an immunity from suit rather than a mere defense to liability; and like an absolute immunity, it is effectively lost if a case is erroneously permitted to go to trial." As a result, "we repeatedly have stressed the importance of resolving immunity questions at the earliest possible stage in litigation." Hunter v. Bryant, 502 U.S. 224, 227 (1991) (per curiam).

A court required to rule upon the qualified immunity issue must consider, then, this threshold question: Taken in the light most favorable to the party asserting the injury, do the facts alleged show the officer's conduct violated a constitutional right? This must be the initial inquiry. Siegert v. Gilley, 500 U.S. 226, 232 (1991). In the course of determining whether a constitutional right was violated on the premises alleged, a court might find it necessary to set forth principles which will become the basis for a holding that a right is clearly established. This is the process for the law's elaboration from case to case, and it is one reason for our insisting upon turning to the existence or nonexistence of a constitutional right as the first inquiry. The law might be deprived of this explanation were a court simply to skip ahead to the question whether the law clearly established that the officer's conduct was unlawful in the circumstances of the case.

If no constitutional right would have been violated were the allegations established, there is no necessity for further inquiries concerning qualified immunity. On the other hand, if a violation could be made out on a favorable view of the parties' submissions, the next, sequential step is to ask whether the right was clearly established. This inquiry, it is vital to note, must be undertaken in light of the specific context of the case, not as a broad general proposition; and it too serves to advance understanding of the law and to allow officers to avoid the burden of trial if qualified immunity is applicable.

In this litigation, for instance, there is no doubt that *Graham v. Connor* clearly establishes the general proposition that use of force is contrary to the Fourth Amendment if it is excessive under objective standards of reasonableness. Yet that is not enough. Rather, we emphasized in *Anderson* "that the right the official is alleged to have violated must have been 'clearly established' in a more particularized, and hence more relevant, sense: The contours of the right must be sufficiently clear that a reasonable official would understand that what he is doing violates that right." 483 U.S. at 640. The relevant, dispositive inquiry in determining whether a right is clearly established is whether it would be clear to a reasonable officer that his conduct was unlawful in the situation he confronted. See Wilson v. Layne, 526 U.S. 603, 615 (1999) ("As we explained in *Anderson*, the right allegedly violated must be defined at the appropriate level of specificity before a court can determine if it was clearly established")....

The Court of Appeals concluded that qualified immunity is merely duplicative in an excessive force case, eliminating the need for the second step where a constitutional violation could be found based on the allegations. In *Anderson*, a warrantless search case, we rejected the argument that there is no distinction between the reasonableness standard for warrantless searches and the qualified immunity inquiry. We acknowledged there was some "surface appeal" to the argument that, because the Fourth Amendment's guarantee was a right to be free from "unreasonable" searches and seizures, it would be inconsistent to conclude that an officer who acted unreasonably under the constitutional standard nevertheless was entitled to immunity because he " 'reasonably' acted unreasonably." This superficial similarity, however, could not overcome either our history of applying qualified immunity analysis to Fourth Amendment claims against officers or the justifications for applying the doctrine in an area where officers perform their duties with considerable uncertainty as to "whether particular searches or seizures comport with the Fourth Amendment." With respect, moreover, to the argument made in *Anderson* that an exception should be made for Fourth Amendment cases, we observed "the heavy burden this argument must sustain to be successful," since "the doctrine of qualified immunity reflects a balance that has been struck 'across the board.'" We held that qualified immunity applied in the Fourth Amendment context just as it would for any other claim of official misconduct.

... *Graham*, in respondent's view, sets forth an excessive force analysis indistinguishable from qualified immunity, rendering the separate immunity inquiry superfluous and inappropriate. Respondent asserts that, like the qualified immunity analysis applicable in other contexts, the excessive force test already affords officers latitude for mistaken beliefs as to the amount of force necessary....

[In *Graham*, we] set out a test that cautioned against the "20/20 vision of hindsight" in favor of deference to the judgment of reasonable officers on the scene. *Graham* sets forth a list of factors relevant to the merits of the constitutional excessive force claim, "requiring careful attention to the facts and circumstances of each particular case, including the severity of the crime at issue, whether the suspect poses an immediate threat to the safety of the officers or others, and whether he is actively resisting arrest or attempting to evade arrest by flight." If an officer reasonably, but mistakenly, believed that a suspect was likely to fight back, for instance, the officer would be justified in using more force than in fact was needed.

The qualified immunity inquiry, on the other hand, has a further dimension. The concern of the immunity inquiry is to acknowledge that reasonable mistakes can be made as to the legal constraints on particular police conduct. It is sometimes difficult for an officer to determine how the relevant legal doctrine, here excessive force, will apply to the factual situation the officer confronts. An officer might correctly perceive all of the relevant facts but have a mistaken understanding as to whether a particular amount of force is legal in those circumstances. If the officer's mistake as to what the law requires is reasonable, however, the officer is entitled to the immunity defense....

The deference owed officers facing suits for alleged excessive force is not different in some qualitative respect from the probable cause inquiry in *Anderson*. Officers can have reasonable, but mistaken, beliefs as to the facts establishing the existence of probable cause or exigent circumstances, for example, and in those situations courts will not hold that they have violated the Constitution. Yet, even if a court were to hold that the officer violated the Fourth Amendment by conducting an unreasonable, warrantless search, *Anderson* still operates to grant officers immunity for reasonable mistakes as to the legality of their actions. The same analysis is applicable in excessive force cases, where in addition to the deference officers receive on the underlying constitutional claim, qualified immunity can apply in the event the mistaken belief was reasonable. . . .

Ultimately, the Supreme Court decided that the petitioner had "substantial grounds" to conclude that he had legitimate justification under the existing law for using the force he did:

A reasonable officer in petitioner's position could have believed that hurrying respondent away from the scene, where the Vice President was speaking and respondent had just approached the fence designed to separate the public from the speakers, was within the bounds of appropriate police responses.

Petitioner did not know the full extent of the threat respondent posed or how many other persons there might be who, in concert with respondent, posed a threat to the security of the Vice President. . . . In carrying out the detention, as it has been assumed the officers had the right to do, petitioner was required to recognize the necessity to protect the Vice President by securing respondent and restoring order to the scene. It cannot be said there was a clearly established rule that would prohibit using the force petitioner did to place respondent into the van to accomplish these objectives.

As for the shove respondent received when he was placed into the van, those same circumstances show some degree of urgency. . . . In the circumstances presented to this officer, which included the duty to protect the safety and security of the Vice President of the United States from persons unknown in number, neither respondent nor the Court of Appeals has identified any case demonstrating a clearly established rule prohibiting the officer from acting as he did, nor are we aware of any such rule. Our conclusion is confirmed by the uncontested fact that the force was not so excessive that respondent suffered hurt or injury. On these premises, petitioner was entitled to qualified immunity, and the suit should have been dismissed at an early stage in the proceedings.

Justice Ginsburg, joined by Justices Stevens and Breyer, concurred in the judgment. She felt that application of the objective reasonableness standard laid out in *Graham* as a matter of substantive Fourth Amendment law was "both necessary, under currently governing precedent, and, in my view, sufficient to resolve cases of this genre." Thus she disapproved of the Court's decision to "tac[k] on to a *Graham* inquiry a second, overlapping objective reasonableness inquiry purportedly demanded by qualified immunity doctrine." She noted that the lower federal courts had recognized that "the same 'objectively reasonable' standard [governs] . . . both the constitutional test of liability and the . . . standard for qualified immunity." Roy v. Inhabitants of City of Lewiston, 42 F.3d 691, 695 (1st Cir.1994); see also Street v. Parham, 929 F.2d 537, 540 (10th Cir.1991) (describing excessive force cases as ones "where the determination of liability and the availability of qualified immunity depend on the same findings"):

> Double counting "objective reasonableness," the Court appears to suggest, is demanded by *Anderson*, which twice restated that qualified immunity shields the conduct of officialdom "across the board." 483 U.S. at 642, 645 (quoting Harlow v. Fitzgerald, 457 U.S. 800, 821 (1982) (Brennan, J., concurring)). As I see it, however, excessive force cases are not meet for *Anderson*'s two-part test. . . .
>
> The Court fears that dispensing with the duplicative qualified immunity inquiry will mean "leaving the whole matter to the jury." Again, experience teaches otherwise. Lower courts, armed with *Graham*'s directions, have not shied away from granting summary judgment to defendant officials in Fourth Amendment excessive force cases where the challenged conduct is objectively reasonable based on relevant, undisputed facts. See, e.g., Wilson v. Spain, 209 F.3d 713, 716 (8th Cir.2000) ("addressing in one fell swoop both [defendant's] qualified immunity and the merits of [plaintiff's] Fourth Amendment [excessive force] claim" and concluding officer's conduct was objectively reasonable in the circumstances, so summary judgment for officer was proper); *Roy*, 42 F.3d at 695 (under single objective reasonableness test, district court properly granted summary judgment for defendant); Wardlaw v. Pickett, 303 U.S. App. D.C. 130, 1 F.3d 1297, 1303–04 (D.C.Cir.1993) (same). Indeed, this very case, as I earlier explained, fits the summary judgment bill. Of course, if an excessive force claim turns on which of two conflicting stories best captures what happened on the street, *Graham* will not permit summary judgment in favor of the defendant official. And that is as it should be. When a plaintiff proffers evidence that the official subdued her with a chokehold even though she complied at all times with his orders, while the official proffers evidence that he used only stern

words, a trial must be had. In such a case, the Court's two-step procedure is altogether inutile....

Is the major practical effect of *Saucier* to reinforce the idea that judges, near the outset of the litigation, rather than juries towards the end, have the power to decide reasonableness? Is that the point?

In Chavez v. Martinez, 538 U.S. 760 (2003), in an opinion announcing the Court's judgment and joined in relevant part by the Chief Justice and Justices O'Connor and Scalia, Justice Thomas offered a gloss on Saucier that illustrates the potential confusion over the relationship of the various parts of the qualified immunity inquiry to one another: "In deciding whether an officer is entitled to qualified immunity, we must first determine whether the officer's alleged conduct violated a constitutional right. If not, the officer is entitled to qualified immunity, and we need not consider whether the asserted right was 'clearly established.'" Strictly speaking, if no constitutional right was violated in the first place, doesn't it make more sense simply to say that the plaintiff has failed to state a claim on which relief can be granted? Is there any need to add that the officer is entitled to qualified immunity?

4. *Groh v. Ramirez.* Groh v. Ramirez, 540 U.S. 551 (2004), involved a clerical error by an ATF agent. Special Agent Groh prepared a detailed affidavit in support of an application for a warrant to search the Ramirez ranch for "automatic firearms or parts to automatic weapons, destructive devices to include but not limited to grenades, grenade launchers, rocket launchers, and any and all receipts pertaining to the purchase or manufacture of automatic weapons or explosive devices or launchers." The same description of the items to be seized appeared on the application, but when he filled out the draft warrant for use by the Magistrate Judge, Agent Groh mistakenly typed in a description of the place to be searched (a two-story blue house) rather than the items to be seized. The Magistrate Judge issued the warrant without noticing the mistake, and ATF agents searched the house. No illegal weaponry was found, and no charges were brought.

Subsequently, Ramirez brought a *Bivens* action seeking damages for illegal search and seizure. At issue were both the legality of the search and the defendant's entitlement to a defense of qualified immunity. Speaking for the Court, Justice Stevens found the search invalid for not "particularly describing ... the persons or things to be seized," as required by the Fourth Amendment. The Court also disallowed qualified immunity: "Given that the particularity requirement is set forth in the text of the Constitution, no reasonable officer could believe that a warrant that plainly did not comply with that requirement was valid."

Four Justices dissented. Justice Thomas, joined by Justice Scalia, thought the search itself not unconstitutional. They reasoned that the rationale behind the particularity requirement had been fully served in this case and that the search was therefore constitutionally reasonable, despite the defective warrant.

Justice Kennedy, joined by the Chief Justice, confined his dissent to qualified immunity. For him, the question was not whether a police officer could reasonably believe that a warrant lacking particular description of the items to be seized was nonetheless valid, but whether, in the circumstances of this case, the officer could reasonably have failed to notice that the description was missing. In Kennedy's words, "[t]he issue in this case is whether an officer can reasonably fail to recognize a clerical error, not whether an officer who recognizes a clerical error can reasonably conclude that a defective warrant is legally valid." Kennedy thought the officer's mistake was reasonable and that he was therefore entitled to qualified immunity.

Page 113, add a footnote at the end of the next to last paragraph in Note 4:

c. For an interesting argument relating this line of analysis to the doctrine of harmless error, see Sam Kamin, Harmless Error and the Rights/Remedies Split, 88 Va.L.Rev. (2002). And for thoughtful criticism of current doctrine on the sequence of decision in qualified immunity cases, see Thomas Healy, The Rise of Unnecessary Constitutional Rulings, 83 N.C.L. Rev. 847 (2005) (arguing, on the basis of an extensive review of lower court decisions, that "unnecessary" merits rulings in qualified immunity cases are unlikely to result in the establishment of new rights).

Page 114, add at the end of the third full paragraph of Note 5:

For illuminating analysis of § 1983 liability in other specialized contexts, see Sheldon Nahmod, From the Courtroom to the Street: Court Orders and Section 1983, 29 Hat. Const'l L.Q.613 (2002) (presenting both theoretical and practical arguments against recognizing quasi-judicial immunity for police officers implementing court orders); Michael Avery, Paying for Silence: The Liability of Police Officers under Section 1983 for Suppressing Exculpatory Evidence, 13 Temple Pol. & C.R. L. Rev. 1 (2003) (examining constitutional tort remedies for police suppression of evidence).

Page 114, add prior to the last paragraph of Note 5:

For criticism of qualified immunity and of the whole scheme of officer liability, see Cornelia T.L. Pillard, Taking Fiction Seriously: The Strange Results of Public Officials' Individual Liability Under *Bivens*, 88 Geo. L.J. 65 (1999).

For criticism of the Court's one-size-fits-all approach to qualified immunity and an argument that constitutional tort liability should take account of the presence or absence of alternative remedies, see John C. Jeffries, Jr., Disaggregating Constitutional Torts, 110 Yale L.J. 259 (2000).

Page 115, add new main case and Notes immediately before *Crawford-El v. Britton*:

Brosseau v. Haugen

Supreme Court of the United States, 2004.
___ U.S. ___, 125 S.Ct. 596.

■ Per Curiam.

Officer Rochelle Brosseau, a member of the Puyallup, Washington, Police Department, shot Kenneth Haugen in the back as he attempted to flee from law enforcement authorities in his vehicle. Haugen subsequently filed this action in the United States District Court for the Western District of Washington pursuant to 42 U.S.C. § 1983. He alleged that the shot fired by Brosseau constituted excessive force and violated his federal constitutional rights. The District Court granted summary judgment to Brosseau after finding she was entitled to qualified immunity. The Court of Appeals for the Ninth Circuit reversed. Following the two-step process set out in Saucier v. Katz, 533 U.S. 194 (2001), the Court of Appeals found, first, that Brosseau had violated Haugen's Fourth Amendment right to be free from excessive force and, second, that the right violated was clearly established and thus Brosseau was not entitled to qualified immunity. Brosseau then petitioned for writ of certiorari, requesting that we review both of the Court of Appeals' determinations. We grant the petition on the second, qualified immunity question and [summarily] reverse.

The material facts, construed in a light most favorable to Haugen, are as follows. On the day before the fracas, Glen Tamburello went to the police station and reported to Brosseau that Haugen, a former crime partner of his, had stolen tools from his shop. Brosseau later learned that there was a felony no-bail warrant out for Haugen's arrest on drug and other offenses. The next morning, Haugen was spray-painting his Jeep Cherokee in his mother's driveway. Tamburello learned of Haugen's whereabouts, and he and cohort Matt Atwood drove a pickup truck to Haugen's mother's house to pay Haugen a visit. A fight ensued, which was witnessed by a neighbor who called 911.

Brosseau heard a report that the men were fighting in Haugen's mother's yard and responded. When she arrived, Tamburello and Atwood were attempting to get Haugen into Tamburello's pickup. Brosseau's arrival created a distraction, which provided Haugen the opportunity to get away. Haugen ran through his mother's yard and hid in the neighborhood. Brosseau requested assistance, and, shortly thereafter, two officers arrived with a K–9 to help track Haugen down....

An officer radioed from down the street that a neighbor had seen a man in her backyard. Brosseau ran in that direction, and Haugen appeared. He ran past the front of his mother's house and then turned and ran into the driveway. With Brosseau still in pursuit, he jumped into the driver's side of the Jeep and closed and locked the door. Brosseau believed that he was running to the Jeep to retrieve a weapon.

Brosseau arrived at the Jeep, pointed her gun at Haugen, and ordered him to get out of the vehicle. Haugen ignored her command and continued to look for the keys so that he could get the Jeep started. Brosseau repeated her commands and hit the driver's side window several times with her handgun, which failed to deter Haugen. On the third or fourth try, the window shattered. Brosseau unsuccessfully attempted to grab the keys and struck Haugen on the head with the barrel and butt of her gun. Haugen, still undeterred, succeeded in starting the Jeep. As the Jeep started or shortly after it began to move, Brosseau jumped back and to the left. She fired one shot through the rear driver's side window at a forward angle, hitting Haugen in the back. She later explained that she shot Haugen because she was " 'fearful for the other officers on foot who [she] believed were in the immediate area, [and] for the occupied vehicles in [Haugen's] path and for any other citizens who might be in the area.' "

Despite being hit, Haugen, in his words, " 'st[ood] on the gas' " ... ; swerved across the neighbor's lawn; and continued down the street. After about a half block, Haugen realized that he had been shot and brought the Jeep to a halt. He suffered a collapsed lung and was airlifted to a hospital. He survived the shooting and subsequently pleaded guilty to the felony of "eluding." Wash. Rev. Code § 46.61.024 (1994). By so pleading, he admitted that he drove his Jeep in a manner indicating "a wanton or wilful disregard for the lives ... of others." He subsequently brought this § 1983 action against Brosseau.

* * *

When confronted with a claim of qualified immunity, a court must ask first [whether the Constitution has been violated]. As the Court of Appeals recognized, the constitutional question in this case is governed by the principles enunciated in Tennessee v. Garner, 471 U.S. 1 (1985), and Graham v. Connor, 490 U.S. 386 (1989). These cases establish that claims of excessive force are to be judged under the Fourth Amendment's "objective reasonableness" standard. Specifically, with regard to deadly force, we explained in *Garner* that it is unreasonable for an officer to "seize an unarmed, nondangerous suspect by shooting him dead." But "[w]here the officer has probably cause to believe that the suspect poses a threat of serious physical harm, either to the officer or to others, it is not constitutionally unreasonable to prevent escape by using deadly force."

We express no view as to the correctness of the Court of Appeals' decision on the constitutional question itself. We believe that, however that question is decided, the Court of Appeals was wrong on the issue of qualified immunity.[3]

Qualified immunity shields an officer from suit when she makes a decision that, even if constitutionally deficient, reasonably misapprehends the law governing the circumstances she confronted.... It is important to emphasize that this inquiry "must be undertaken in light of the specific context of the case, not as a broad proposition." *Saucier v. Katz*, 533 U.S., at 206. As we previously said in this very context:

---

3. We have no occasion in this case to reconsider our instruction in Saucier v. Katz, 533 U.S. 194, 201 (2001), that lower courts decide the constitutional question prior to deciding the qualified immunity question. We exercise our summary reversal procedure here simply to correct a clear misapprehension of the qualified immunity standard.

[T]here is no doubt that *Graham v. Connor*, supra, clearly establishes the general proposition that use of force is contrary to the Fourth Amendment if it is excessive under objective standards of reasonableness. Yet that is not enough. Rather, we emphasized in Anderson v. Creighton, 483 U.S. 635, 640 (1987), "that the right the official is alleged to have violated must have been 'clearly established' in a more particularized, and hence more relevant, sense: The contours of the right must be sufficiently clear that a reasonable official would understand that what he is doing violates that right." . . .

The Court of Appeals acknowledged this statement of law, but then proceeded to find fair warning in the general tests set out in *Graham* and *Garner*. In so doing, it was mistaken. . . .

We therefore turn to ask whether, at the time of Brosseau's actions, it was "clearly established" in this more "particularized" sense that she was violating Haugen's Fourth Amendment right. The parties point us to only a handful of cases relevant to the "situation [Brosseau] confronted": whether to shoot a disturbed felon, set on avoiding capture through vehicular flight, when persons in the immediate area are at risk from that flight.[4] Specifically, Brosseau points us to Cole v. Bone, 993 F.2d 1328 (8th Cir. 1993), and Smith v. Freland, 954 F.2d 343 (6th Cir. 1992).

In these cases, the courts found no Fourth Amendment violation when an officer shot a fleeing suspect who presented a risk to others. *Smith* is closer to this case. There, the officer and suspect engaged in a car chase, which appeared to be at an end when the officer cornered the suspect at the back of a dead-end residential street. The suspect, however, freed his car and began speeding down the street. At this point, the officer fired a shot, which killed the suspect. The court held the officer's decision was reasonable and thus did not violate the Fourth Amendment. It noted that the suspect, like Haugen here, "had proven he would do almost anything to avoid capture" and that he posed a major threat to, among others, the officers at the end of the street.

Haugen points us to Estate of Starks v. Enyart, 5 F.3d 230 (7th Cir. 1993), where the court found summary judgment inappropriate on a Fourth Amendment claim involving a fleeing suspect. There, the court concluded that the threat created by the fleeing suspect's failure to brake when an officer suddenly stepped in front of his just-started car was not a sufficiently grave threat to justify the use of deadly force.

These . . . cases taken together undoubtedly show that this are is one in which the result depends very much on the facts of each case. None of them squarely governs the case here; they do suggest that Brosseau's

---

4. The parties point us to a number of other cases in this vein that postdate the conduct in question. These decisions, of course, could not have given fair notice to Brosseau and are of no use in the clearly established inquiry.

actions fell in the " 'hazy border between excessive and acceptable force.' " *Saucier v. Katz*, 533 U.S., at 206. The cases by no means "clearly establish" that Brosseau's conduct violated the Fourth Amendment.

The judgment of the United States Court of Appeals for the Ninth Circuit is therefore reversed, and the case is remanded for further proceedings consistent with this opinion.

■ JUSTICE BREYER, with whom JUSTICE SCALIA and JUSTICE GINSBURG join, concurring.

I join the Court's opinion but write separately to express my concern about the matter to which the Court refers in footnote 3, namely, the way in which lower courts are required to evaluate claims of qualified immunity under the Court's decision in Saucier v. Katz, 533 U.S. 194 (2001). As the Court notes, *Saucier* requires lower courts to decide (1) the constitutional question prior to deciding (2) the qualified immunity question. I am concerned that the current rule rigidly requires the courts unnecessarily to decide difficult constitutional questions when there is available an easier basis for the decision (e.g., qualified immunity) that will satisfactorily resolve the case before the court. Indeed, when courts' dockets are crowded, a rigid "order of battle" makes little administrative sense and can sometimes lead to a constitutional decision that is effectively insulated from review, see Bunting v. Mellen, 541 U.S. 1019 (2004) (Scalia, J., dissenting from denial of certiorari). For these reasons, I think we should reconsider this issue.

■ JUSTICE STEVENS dissenting.

In my judgment, the answer to the constitutional question presented by this case is clear: Under the Fourth Amendment, it was objectively unreasonable for Officer Brosseau to use deadly force against Kenneth Haugen in an attempt to prevent his escape. What is not clear is whether Brosseau is nonetheless entitled to qualified immunity because it might not have been apparent to a reasonably well trained officer in Brosseau's shoes that killing Haugen to prevent his escape was unconstitutional. In my opinion that question should be answered by a jury. . . .

An officer is entitled to qualified immunity, despite having engaged in constitutionally deficient conduct, if, in doing so, she did not violate "clearly established statutory or constitutional rights of which a reasonable person would have known." Harlow v. Fitzgerald, 457 U.S. 800, 818 (1982). The requirement that the law be clearly established is designed to ensure that officers have fair notice of what conduct is proscribed. See Hope v. Pelzer, 536 U.S. 730, 739 (2002). Accordingly, we have recognized that "general statements of the law are not inherently incapable of giving fair and clear warning," United States v. Lanier, 520 U.S. 259, 271 (1997), and have firmly rejected the notion that "an official action is protected by qualified immunity unless the very action in question has previously been held unlawful." Anderson v. Creighton, 483 U.S. 635, 640 (1987).

Thus, the Court's search for relevant case law applying the Tennessee v. Garner, 471 U.S. 1 (1985), standard to materially similar facts is both unnecessary and ill-advised. See *Hope*, 536 U.S., at 741 ("Although earlier cases involving 'fundamentally similar' facts can provide especially strong support for a conclusion that the law is clearly established, they are not necessary to such a finding").

Rather than uncertainty about the law, it is uncertainty about the likely consequences of Haugen's flight—or, more precisely, uncertainly about how a reasonable officer making the split-second decision to use deadly force would have assessed the foreseeability of a serious accident—that prevents me from answering the question of qualified immunity that this case presents. This is a quintessentially "fact-specific" question, not a question that judges should try to answer "as a matter of law." Although it is preferable to resolve the qualified immunity question at the earliest possible stage of litigation, this preference does not give judges license to take inherently factual questions away from the jury. . . .

In sum, the constitutional limits on an officer's use of deadly force have been well settled in this Court's jurisprudence for nearly two decades, and, in this case, Officer Brosseau acted outside of those clearly delineated bounds. Nonetheless, in my judgment, there is a genuine factual question as to whether a reasonably well-trained officer standing in Brosseau's shoes could have concluded otherwise, and the question plainly falls within the purview of the jury.

For these reasons, I respectfully dissent.

NOTES ON "CLEARLY ESTABLISHED LAW"

1. Required Similarity Between Challenged Conduct and Prior Precedent: *Hope v. Pelzer*. Use of deadly force by police officers—the act challenged in *Brosseau*—is a sufficiently common occurrence that there will be many opportunities for fleshing out the circumstances in which an officer's actions are unreasonable. But how are courts to assess whether the law is "clearly established" in more unusual circumstances?

The Supreme Court addressed that issue in Hope v. Pelzer, 536 U.S. 730 (2002). The case concerned the Alabama Department of Corrections' (ADOC) use of a "hitching post" to punish state prison inmates who refused to work or disrupted work squads. (Alabama was apparently the only state to use this practice.) According to his complaint, Hope was handcuffed to a hitching post on two occasions. The first time, he was attached to the post for two hours. Due to his height, his arms were pinioned above shoulder height and "[w]henever he tried moving his arms to improve his circulation, the handcuffs cut into his wrists, causing pain and discomfort." The second time, Hope was required to remove his shirt before being handcuffed to the post, and he remained at the post for seven hours. He was given water only once or twice, was denied any bathroom breaks, was taunted by guards, and suffered sunburn.

Hope filed a § 1983 suit against three guards involved in the first incident, one of whom was also involved in the second. Both the District Court and the Court of Appeals held that the guards were entitled to qualified immunity. The Court of Appeals agreed with Hope that the alleged conduct would violate the Eighth Amendment. Nonetheless, because the facts in the cases on which Hope relied, "though analogous," were not "materially similar," they did not create clearly established law.

The Supreme Court reversed the grant of qualified immunity. Justice Stevens's opinion for the Court agreed that Alabama's practices violated the Eighth Amendment. Given the facts as alleged by Hope, the guards' actions involved the "unnecessary and wanton infliction of pain" that Whitley v. Albers, 475 U.S. 312 (1986), had held violative of the Cruel and Unusual Punishment Clause. With respect to qualified immunity, the Court held that the Eleventh Circuit's requirement that § 1983 plaintiffs point to a decision involving "materially similar" facts was a "rigid gloss on the qualified immunity standard ... not consistent with our cases." Such a requirement, the Court stated, was not necessary "to ensure that before they are subjected to suit, officers are on notice their conduct is unlawful."

The Court drew a parallel to its decision in United States v. Lanier, 520 U.S. 259 (1997) (discussed at pages 635–37 of the casebook), which involved criminal prosecution under 18 U.S.C. § 242 of a state-court judge who sexually assaulted a number of women. Section 242 makes it a crime for a state official to "willfully" deprive a person of rights protected by the Constitution. Lanier argued that he had not received "fair warning" that his conduct violated the statute because no prior case had held that sexual assaults committed under color of state law violated the Fourth Amendment. The Supreme Court disagreed, noting that it had repeatedly upheld convictions under § 242 despite factual differences between the instant prosecutions and prior precedents:

> Our opinion in *Lanier* thus makes clear that officials can still be on notice that their conduct violates established law even in novel factual circumstances. Indeed, in *Lanier*, we expressly rejected a requirement that previous cases be "fundamentally similar." Although earlier cases involving "fundamentally similar" facts can provide especially strong support for a conclusion that the law is clearly established, they are not necessary to such a finding. The same is true of cases with "materially similar" facts. Accordingly, pursuant to *Lanier* the salient question that the Court of Appeals ought to have asked is whether the state of the law in 1995 gave respondents fair warning that their alleged treatment of Hope was unconstitutional.

The Court held that it did. It pointed to a 1974 court of appeals decision, binding on the Eleventh Circuit, that had held unconstitutional several forms of corporal punishment inflicted within the Mississippi prison system, including "handcuffing inmates to the fence and to cells for long periods of time, ... and forcing inmates to stand, sit or lie on crates, stumps, or otherwise maintain awkward positions for prolonged periods":

> [For] the purpose of providing fair notice to reasonable officers administering punishment for past misconduct, [there is no] reason to draw a constitutional distinction between a practice of handcuffing an inmate to a fence for prolonged periods and handcuffing him to a hitching post for seven hours. The Court of Appeals' conclusion to the contrary exposes the danger of a rigid, overreliance on factual similarity. As the Government submits in its brief amicus curiae: "No reasonable officer could have concluded that the constitutional holding of [Gates v. Collier, 501 F.2d 1291 (5th Cir. 1974)] turned on the fact that inmates were handcuffed to fences or the bars of cells, rather than a specially designed metal bar designated for shackling. If anything, the use of a designated hitching post highlights the constitutional problem." Brief for United States as Amicus Curiae 22. In light of *Gates*, the unlawfulness of the alleged conduct should have been apparent to the respondents.

The Court further viewed the "reasoning, though not the holding" of Ort v. White, 813 F.2d 318 (11th Cir. 1987), as "sen[ding] the same message to reasonable officers in that Circuit." *Ort* had reasoned that while temporary denials of drinking water to inmates who refused to work might be characterized as "necessary coercive measures undertaken to obtain compliance with a reasonable prison rule," denials of water as punishment would raise serious constitutional issues, and would violate the Constitution if they threatened the inmate's health.

> Relevant to the question whether *Ort* provided fair warning to respondents that their conduct violated the Constitution is a regulation promulgated by ADOC in 1993. The regulation ... provides that an activity log should be completed for each ... inmate, detailing his responses to offers of water and bathroom breaks every 15 minutes. Such a log was completed and maintained for petitioner's shackling in May, but the record contains no such log for the seven-hour shackling in June and the record indicates that the periodic offers contemplated by the regulation were not made. The regulation also states that an inmate "will be allowed to join his assigned squad" whenever he tells an officer "that he is ready to go to work." [Findings in an earlier case], as well as the record in this case, indicate that this important provision of the regulation was frequently ignored by corrections officers. If regularly observed, a requirement that would effectively give the inmate the keys to the handcuffs that attached him to the hitching post would have made this case more analogous to the

practice upheld in *Ort*, rather than the kind of punishment *Ort* described as impermissible. A course of conduct that tends to prove that the requirement was merely a sham, or that respondents could ignore it with impunity, provides equally strong support for the conclusion that they were fully aware of the wrongful character of their conduct. . . .

Our conclusion that "a reasonable person would have known," Harlow v. Fitzgerald, 457 U.S. 800, 818 (1982), of the violation is buttressed by the fact that the [United States Department of Justice (DOJ)] specifically advised the ADOC of the unconstitutionality of its practices before the incidents in this case took place. . . . The ADOC replied that it thought the post could permissibly be used "to preserve prison security and discipline." In response, the DOJ informed the ADOC that, "although an emergency situation may warrant drastic action by corrections staff, our experts found that the 'rail' is being used systematically as an improper punishment for relatively trivial offenses. Therefore, we have concluded that the use of the 'rail' is without penological justification." Although there is nothing in the record indicating that the DOJ's views were communicated to respondents, this exchange lends support to the view that reasonable officials in the ADOC should have realized that the use of the hitching post under the circumstances alleged by Hope violated the Eighth Amendment prohibition against cruel and unusual punishment.

The obvious cruelty inherent in this practice should have provided respondents with some notice that their alleged conduct violated Hope's constitutional protection against cruel and unusual punishment. Hope was treated in a way antithetical to human dignity–he was hitched to a post for an extended period of time in a position that was painful, and under circumstances that were both degrading and dangerous.

Justice Thomas, joined by Chief Justice Rehnquist and Justice Scalia, dissented:

In evaluating whether it was clearly established in 1995 that respondents' conduct violated the Eighth Amendment, the Court of Appeals properly noted that "it is important to analyze the facts in [the prior cases relied upon by petitioner where courts found Eighth Amendment violations], and determine if they are materially similar to the facts in the case in front of us." The right not to suffer from "cruel and unusual punishments" is an extremely abstract and general right. In the vast majority of cases, the text of the Eighth Amendment does not, in and of itself, give a government official sufficient notice of the clearly established Eighth

Amendment law applicable to a particular situation. Rather, one must look to case law....

Such cases give government officials the best indication of what conduct is unlawful in a given situation....

Previous litigation over Alabama's use of the restraining bar, however, did nothing to warn reasonable Alabama prison guards that attaching a prisoner to a restraining bar was unlawful, let alone that the illegality of such conduct was clearly established. In fact, the outcome of those cases effectively forecloses petitioner's claim that it should have been clear to respondents in 1995 that handcuffing petitioner to a restraining bar violated the Eighth Amendment....

In the face of these decisions, and the absence of contrary authority, I find it impossible to conclude that respondents either were "plainly incompetent" or "knowingly violating the law" when they affixed petitioner to the restraining bar. Malley v. Briggs, 475 U.S. 335, 341 (1986). A reasonably competent prison guard attempting to obey the law is not only entitled to look at how courts have recently evaluated his colleagues' prior conduct, such judicial decisions are often the only place that a guard can look for guidance, especially in a situation where a State stands alone in adopting a particular policy.

Moreover, if the application of this Court's general Eighth Amendment jurisprudence to the use of a restraining bar was as "obvious" as the Court claims, one wonders how Federal District Courts in Alabama could have repeatedly arrived at the opposite conclusion, and how respondents, in turn, were to realize that these courts had failed to grasp the "obvious."....

The Department of Justice report referenced by the Court does nothing to demonstrate that it should have been clear to respondents that attaching petitioner to a restraining bar violated his Eighth Amendment rights. To begin with, the Court concedes that there is no indication the Justice Department's recommendation that the ADOC stop using the restraining bar was ever communicated to respondents, prison guards in the small town of Capshaw, Alabama. In any event, an extraordinarily well-informed prison guard in 1995, who had read both the Justice Department's report and Federal District Court decisions addressing the use of the restraining bar, could have concluded only that there was a dispute as to whether handcuffing a prisoner to a restraining bar constituted an Eighth Amendment violation, not that such a practice was clearly unconstitutional.

2. Unintended Effects of the *Saucier* Sequencing Requirement: *Bunting v. Mellen.* Note that in *Brosseau*, three Justices expressed concern at the requirement that lower courts invariably adhere to *Saucier*'s requirement of first determining the constitutionality of the defendant's conduct before asking whether the law was clearly established at the time of the defendant's actions. The bases for their concern were illustrated in Bunting v. Mellen, 541 U.S. 1019 (2004). The underlying case concerned a First Amendment challenge by two cadets at the Virginia Military Institute, a state institution of higher education, to the school's practice of conducting a prayer before the cadets' evening meal. The cadets sued Bunting, the Superintendent of VMI, seeking declaratory and injunctive relief, as well as nominal damages. The District Court entered summary judgment in favor of the plaintiffs, awarding them declaratory relief and enjoining Bunting from continuing to sponsor the prayer. But it found that Bunting was entitled to qualified immunity on plaintiffs' damages claims because his arguments were not "so obviously incorrect that a reasonable government official in [his] place should have known that his actions violated [the plaintiffs'] rights under the Establishment Clause."

Both sides appealed—the superintendent challenging the District Court's award of declaratory and injunctive relief, and the cadets challenging the District Court's decision on qualified immunity. In the meantime, the cadets had graduated and Bunting had retired as superintendent. The Court of Appeals therefore vacated as moot the District Court's judgment awarding them declaratory and injunctive relief. With respect to the damages claim, the Court of Appeals affirmed, agreeing with the District Court that the supper prayer violated the Establishment Clause of the First Amendment, but that Bunting was nevertheless entitled to qualified immunity.

Bunting and Peay, the new Superintendent of VMI, petitioned for certiorari, seeking review of the determination that the supper prayer was unconstitutional. The Court denied the petition, but five Justices expressed their views regarding the interaction of the *Saucier* sequencing principle and appellate review. Justice Scalia, joined by the Chief Justice, dissented from the denial of certiorari. He noted that the "*Saucier* constitutional-question-first procedure played a central role in the proceedings below." The Court of Appeals' ruling created the kind of conflict with decisions of other courts of appeals that would normally make the case a strong candidate for certiorari:

> But it is questionable whether Bunting's request for review can be entertained, since he won judgment in the court below. For although the statute governing our certiorari jurisdiction permits application by "any party" to a case in a federal court of appeals, 28 U.S.C. § 1254(1), our practice reflects a "settled refusal" to entertain an appeal by a party on an issue as to which he prevailed. We sit, after all, not to correct errors in dicta; "this Court reviews judgments, not statements in opinions." California

v. Rooney, 483 U.S. 307, 311 (1987) (per curiam) (internal quotation marks omitted).

<u>I think it plain that this general rule should not apply where a favorable judgment on qualified-immunity grounds would deprive a party of an opportunity to appeal the unfavorable (and often more significant) constitutional determination.</u> That constitutional determination is not mere dictum in the ordinary sense, since the whole reason we require it to be set forth (despite the availability of qualified immunity) is to clarify the law and thus make unavailable repeated claims of qualified immunity in future cases....

Not only is the denial of review unfair to the litigant (and to the institution that the litigant represents) but it undermines the purpose served by initial consideration of the constitutional question, which is to clarify constitutional rights without undue delay. See, e.g., Wilson v. Layne, 526 U.S., 603, 609 (1999); County of Sacramento v. Lewis, 523 U.S. 833, 841–42, n.5 (1998)....

This situation should not be prolonged. We should either make clear that constitutional determinations are not insulated from our review (for which purpose this case would be an appropriate vehicle), or else drop any pretense at requiring the ordering in every case.

By contrast, Justice Stevens, joined by Justices Ginsburg and Breyer, voted to deny certiorari in the case and reiterated the view that the "'perceived procedural tangle' described by Justice Scalia's dissent is a byproduct of an unwise judge-made rule under which courts must decide whether the plaintiff has alleged a constitutional violation before addressing the question whether the defendant state actor is entitled to qualified immunity." They would therefore relax the "inflexible rule requiring the premature adjudication of constitutional issues." And they argued further that the Court lacked jurisdiction over the petition for certiorari because Bunting "had retired from his position as Superintendent of VMI, and will suffer no direct injury if VMI is unable to continue the prayer. Thus, there no longer is a live controversy between Bunting and respondents regarding the constitutionality of the prayer. As for the other named petitioner, new Superintendent Peay, there never was a live controversy. Peay was added to the case (apparently in error) after the Court of Appeals issued its decision vacating the District Court's award of injunctive and declaratory relief. At that point, the only issue was Bunting's individual-capacity liability–an issue in which Peay obviously has no interest. VMI itself is not a party."

Several courts of appeals have also discussed the problem caused when a constitutional determination is embedded in a § 1983 suit which the defendant wins on qualified immunity grounds. See, e.g., Kalka v. Hawk, 215 F.3d 90 (D.C. Cir. 2000); Horne v. Coughlin, 191 F.3d 244, 247 (2d Cir. 1999).

Note the interaction of the sequencing issue with another significant aspect of § 1983 doctrine and practice: the non-amenability of states and state-level institutions to suit under § 1983. See Will v. Michigan Dept. of State Police, 491 U.S. 58 (1989). *Will* means that the formal defendants even in cases challenging policy determinations at the state level will always be individual state officials. The articulation of a constitutional rule, however, will strip later officials of any assertion of qualified immunity, since the rule will now be clearly established. The presence of a clear rule is likely to have a strong deterrent effect on future action. Does this mean that state-level entities will frequently be denied any ability to seek effective review? If a proposal like Justice Scalia's were adopted, who would defend the finding of unconstitutionality if the original plaintiff no longer wanted to pursue the lawsuit?

3. The Sources of Clearly Established Law. A decision by the Supreme Court of the United States that particular conduct violates the Constitution "clearly establishes" the law regarding that conduct. And within a particular circuit, a decision by the court of appeals creates clearly established law for purposes of qualified immunity. There is a split among the courts of appeals, however, on whether persuasive authority from other circuits is relevant to the question of qualified immunity. The Eleventh Circuit, for example, categorically refuses to look to out-of-circuit authority on questions of qualified immunity. See Thomas ex rel. Thomas v. Roberts, 323 F.3d 950, 955 (11th Cir. 2003) ("As we have stated, only Supreme Court cases, Eleventh Circuit caselaw, and Georgia Supreme Court caselaw can 'clearly establish' law in this circuit.") The Second Circuit has recently adopted the same approach, though there is also prior circuit authority taking the opposite view. See Moore v. Vega, 371 F.3d 110, 114 (2d Cir. 2004) ("Only Supreme Court and Second Circuit precedent existing at the time of the alleged violation is relevant in deciding whether a right is clearly established."); African Trade & Info. Ctr., Inc. v. Abromaitis, 294 F.3d 355, 361 (2d Cir. 2002) (noting that "our decisions send conflicting signals" on this issue). By contrast, seven other circuits agree that persuasive out-of-circuit authority can, under at least some circumstances, clearly establish a constitutional right. See Owens v. Lott, 372 F.3d 267, 279–80 (4th Cir. 2004) ("[W]e look ordinarily to 'the decisions of the Supreme Court, this court of appeals, and the highest court of the state in which the case arose," but "[w]hen there are no such decisions from courts of controlling authority, we may look to 'a consensus of cases of persuasive authority' from other jurisdictions, if such exists."); McClendon v. City of Columbia, 305 F.3d 314, 331 (5th Cir. 2002) (looking to "cases from our sister circuits" to determine whether the relevant law was clearly established); Walton v. City of Southfield, 995 F.2d 1331, 1336 (6th Cir. 1993) ("In an extraordinary case, it may be possible for the decisions of other courts to clearly establish a principle of law."); Cleveland-Perdue v. Brutsche, 881 F.2d 427, 431 (7th Cir. 1989) (stating that "[i]n the absence of a controlling precedent" the court would "look to all relevant caselaw" in determining whether the law was clearly established); Buckley v. Rogerson, 133 F.3d 1125, 1129 (8th Cir. 1998) ("In the absence of binding precedent, a court should look to all available decisional law, including decisions of state courts, other circuits and district courts."); Boyd v. Benton County, 374 F.3d 773, 781 (9th Cir. 2004) ("[I]n the absence of binding precedent, we look to whatever decisional law is available to ascertain whether the law is clearly established for qualified immunity purposes...."); Peterson v. Jensen, 371 F.3d 1199, 1202 (10th Cir. 2004) ("A right is clearly established ... if the clearly established weight of authority from other circuits found a constitutional violation from similar actions.").

In thinking about how to resolve this conflict, consider the views of Chief Judge Posner in Burgess v. Lowery, 201 F.3d 942, 945 (7th Cir. 2000), that "[t]o rule that until the Supreme Court has spoken, no right of litigants in this circuit can be deemed established before we have decided the issue would discourage anyone from being the first to bring a damages suit in this court; he would be *certain* to be unable to obtain any damages." Compare the restriction in habeas corpus cases, added as part of the Antiterrorism and Effective Death Penalty Act of 1996, that "[a]n application for a writ of habeas corpus ... shall not be granted with respect to any claim that was adjudicated on the merits in State court proceedings unless the adjudication of the claim ... resulted in a decision that was contrary to, or involved an unreasonable application of, clearly established Federal law, as determined by the Supreme Court of the United States." 28 U.S.C. § 2254(d)(1). See also Kinports, Habeas Corpus, Qualified Immunity, and Crystal Balls: Predicting the Course of Constitutional Law, 33 Ariz. L. Rev. 115 (1991) (discussing parallels between the clearly established law inquiries in § 1983 and habeas cases).

Page 129, add a footnote at the end of Note 1:

a. For an endorsement of *Crawford-El*'s rejection of a heightened pleading requirement, see Elaine Korb and Rick Bales, A Permanent Stop Sign: Why Courts Should Yield to the Temptation to Impose Heightened Pleading Standards in § 1983 Cases, 41 Brandeis L.J. 267 (2002).

Page 147, add at the end of Note 2:

In Inyo County v. Paiute–Shoshone Indians of the Bishop Community of the Bishop Colony, 538 U.S. 701 (2003), the Court relied in part on its analysis of the meaning of "person" in *Will* to conclude that an Indian tribe cannot bring suit under § 1983 to vindicate its claimed protection against seizure of tribal records by state law enforcement officers. Based on *Will*, the Court assumed that tribes, like states, are not subject to suit under § 1983. Analogously, the Court concluded that a tribe also is not a "person within the jurisdiction" of the United States for purposes of § 1983. The tribe's claim rested on its assertion of sovereign status. Since § 1983 is designed to secure private rights against government encroachment, it does not reach the type of claim asserted by the tribe.

Page 175, add a new Note:

6. *Correctional Services Corp. v. Malesko.* In Correctional Services Corp. v. Malesko, 534 U.S. 61 (2001), the court extended *Meyer* to private companies acting under color of federal law. Malesko was an inmate in a half-way house operated by Correctional Services Corp. (CSC) under contract with the Federal Bureau of Prisons. He had a heart condition and was given special permission to use the elevator to reach his room on the fifth floor. On one occasion, a CSC employee refused to let him use the elevator. Malesko climbed the stairs and suffered a heart attack. His *Bivens* claims against various individual defendants were dismissed on statute-of-limitations grounds, but the action against the corporation triggered a different statute and was allowed to proceed.

A divided Supreme Court extended the rule of *Meyer* to private corporations acting under color of federal law. Speaking for the Court, the Chief Justice described *Bivens* as an exception to the Court's general reluctance to find private rights of action in the absence of clear legislative authorization. He noted that since *Bivens*, which alleged violations of the Fourth Amendment, the Court had extended its holding only twice—to violations of the Fifth Amendment's Due Process Clause (and its equal protection component) in Davis v. Passman, 442 U.S. 228 (1979), and to violations of the Eight Amendment's Cruel and Unusual Punishments Clause in Carlson v. Green, 446 U.S. 14 (1980). Rehnquist said that the "purpose of *Bivens* is to deter *individual* federal officers from committing constitutional violations" (emphasis added). Permitting lawsuits against entities would undermine this purpose because potential plaintiffs would sue them as deep pockets not entitled to qualified immunity.

The Court also gave additional reasons for refusing to extend *Bivens* to Malesko's suit against CSC. Federal prison inmates can bring *Bivens* actions only against individual officers and not against the United States or the Bureau of Prisons. The Court saw no reason to give Malesko broader federal remedies than he would have had if confined in a federal prison. Moreover, the Court noted that Malesko did not lack for alternative remedies, as the corporation could have been sued for negligence under state law.

Justice Stevens, joined by Justices Souter, Ginsburg, and Breyer, dissented. Stevens argued that the Court's exemption of corporate defendants would allow them to violate rights with impunity. He also argued that lawsuits against private prison corporations would have an important deterrent effect in preventing future Eighth Amendment violations. Whereas the majority compared Malesko to federal prisoners, Stevens compared him to state prisoners, who presumably can sue private prisons under § 1983. See Lugar v. Edmondson Oil Co., 457 U.S. 922 (1982) (permitting § 1983 suits against private corporations acting under color of state law). Unlike state prisoners, Malesko was left without a comparable federal remedy against CSC.

Page 205, add at the end of Note 2:

In addition, two recent symposia address issues of municipal liability from a variety of perspectives. Volume 48 of the DePaul Law Review published a symposium on Municipal Liability in Civil Rights Litigation, with contents as follows: Susan Bandes, Introduction: The Emperor's New Clothes, 48 DePaul L. Rev. 619 (1999); Jack M. Beermann, Municipal Responsibility for Constitutional Torts, id. at 627; Michael J. Gerhardt, Institutional Analysis of Municipal Liability Under Section 1983, id. at 669; Karen M. Blum, Municipal Liability: Derivative or Direct? Statutory or Constitutional? Distinguishing the *Canton* Case from the *Collins* Case, id. at 687; David F. Hamilton, The Importance and Overuse of Policy and Custom Claims: A View from One Trench, id. at 723; G. Flint Taylor, A Litigator's View of Discovery and Proof in Police Misconduct Policy and Practice Cases, id. at 747. Volume 31 of the Urban Lawyer published a symposium on Reconsidering *Monell*'s Limitation on Municipal Liability for Civil Rights Violations, with an introduction by David M. Gelfand, 31 Urb. Law. 395 (1999) and the following articles: Robert J. Kaczorowski, Reflections on *Monell*'s Analysis of the Legislative History of Section 1983, id. at 407; Barbara Kritchevsky, Reexamining *Monell*: Basing Section 1983 Municipal Liability Doctrine on the Statutory Language, id. at 437; Robert E. Manley, Effective But Messy, *Monell* Should Endure, id. at 481; Oscar G. Chase and Arlo Monell Chase, *Monell*: The Story Behind the Landmark, id. at 491; Ronald Turner, Employer Liability for Supervisory Hostile Environment Sexual Harassment: Comparing Title VII's and Section 1983's Regulatory Regimes, id. at 503; Laura Oren, If *Monell* Were Reconsidered: Sexual Abuse and the Scope-of-Employment Doctrine in the Common Law, id. at 527.

Finally, for an interesting recent article that calls for renewed attention to "custom" as a basis of municipal liability, see Myriam E. Gilles, Breaking the Code of Silence: Rediscovering "Custom" in Section 1983 Municipal Liability, 80 B.U. L. Rev. 17 (2000). Gilles focuses particularly on the "police code of silence" as a "custom" that "causes" constitutional violations.

Page 216, add a new Section 4A, as follows:

SECTION 4A: STATE ACTION AND § 1983

Brentwood Academy v. Tennessee Secondary School Athletic Association

Supreme Court of the United States, 2001.
531 U.S. 288.

■ JUSTICE SOUTER delivered the opinion of the Court.

The issue is whether a statewide association incorporated to regulate interscholastic athletic competition among public and private secondary schools may be regarded as engaging in state action when it enforces a rule against a member school. The association in question here includes most public schools located within the State, acts through their representatives, draws its officers from them, is largely funded by their dues and income received in their stead, and has historically been seen to regulate in lieu of the State Board of Education's exercise of its own authority. We hold that the association's regulatory activity may and should be treated as state action owing to the pervasive entwinement of state school officials in the structure of the association, there being no offsetting reason to see the association's acts in any other way.

I

Respondent Tennessee Secondary School Athletic Association (Association) is a not-for-profit membership corporation organized to regulate interscholastic sport among the public and private high schools in Tennessee that belong to it. ... [I]t enjoys the memberships of almost all the State's public high schools (some 290 of them or 84% of the Association's voting membership), far outnumbering the 55 private schools that belong. A member school's team may play or scrimmage only against the team of another member, absent a dispensation.

The Association's rulemaking arm is its legislative council, while its board of control tends to administration. The voting membership of each of these nine-person committees is limited under the Association's bylaws to high school principals, assistant principals, and superintendents elected by the member schools, and the public school administrators who so serve typically attend meetings during regular school hours. Although the Association's staff members are not paid by the State, they are eligible to join the State's public retirement system for its employees. ...

The constitution, bylaws, and rules of the Association set standards of school membership and the eligibility of students to play in interscholastic games. ...

Ever since the Association was incorporated in 1925, Tennessee's State Board of Education (State Board) has (to use its own words) acknowledged the corporation's functions "in providing standards, rules and regulations for interscholastic competition in the public schools of Tennessee." More recently, the State Board cited its statutory authority, Tenn. Code Ann. § 49-1-302, when it adopted language expressing the relationship between the Association and the Board. Specifically, in 1972, it went so far as to adopt a rule expressly "designating" the Association as "the organization to supervise and regulate the athletic activities in which the public junior and senior high schools in Tennessee participate on an interscholastic basis." Tennessee State Board of Education, Administrative Rules and Regulations, Rule 0520-1-2-.26 (1972) (later moved to Rule 0520-1-2-.08).

The Rule provided that "the authority granted herein shall remain in effect until revoked" and instructed the State Board's chairman to "designate a person or persons to serve in an ex-officio capacity on the [Association's governing bodies]." That same year, the State Board specifically approved the Association's rules and regulations, while reserving the right to review future changes. . . . In 1996, however, the State Board dropped the original Rule 0520–1–2–.08 expressly designating the Association as regulator; it substituted a statement "recognizing the value of participation in interscholastic athletics and the role of [the Association] in coordinating interscholastic athletic competition," while "authorizing the public schools of the state to voluntarily maintain membership in [the Association]."

The action before us responds to a 1997 regulatory enforcement proceeding brought against petitioner, Brentwood Academy, a private parochial high school member of the Association. The Association's board of control found that Brentwood violated a rule prohibiting "undue influence" in recruiting athletes, when it wrote to incoming students and their parents about spring football practice. The Association accordingly placed Brentwood's athletic program on probation for four years, declared its football and boys' basketball teams ineligible to compete in playoffs for two years, and imposed a $3,000 fine. When these penalties were imposed, all the voting members of the board of control and legislative council were public school administrators.

Brentwood sued the Association and its executive director in federal court under 42 U.S.C. § 1983, claiming that enforcement of the Rule was state action and a violation of the First and Fourteenth Amendments. . . .

II

A

Our cases try to plot a line between state action subject to Fourteenth Amendment scrutiny and private conduct (however exceptionable) that is not. National Collegiate Athletic Assn. v. Tarkanian, 488 U.S. 179, 191 (1988); Jackson v. Metropolitan Edison Co., 419 U.S. 345, 349 (1974). The judicial obligation is not only to " 'preserve an area of individual freedom by limiting the reach of federal law' and avoid the imposition of responsibility on a State for conduct it could not control," Tarkanian, supra, 488 U.S. at 191 (quoting Lugar v. Edmondson Oil Co., 457 U.S. 922, 936–37 (1982)), but also to assure that constitutional standards are invoked "when it can be said that the State is responsible for the specific conduct of which the plaintiff complains." Blum v. Yaretsky, 457 U.S. 991, 1004 (1982). If the Fourteenth Amendment is not to be displaced, therefore, its ambit cannot be a simple line between States and people operating outside formally governmental organizations, and the deed of an ostensibly private organization or individual is to be treated sometimes as if a State had caused it to be performed. Thus, we say that state action may be found if, though only if, there is such a "close nexus between the State and the challenged action" that seemingly private behavior "may be fairly treated as that of the State itself." *Jackson*, supra, 419 U.S. at 351.[2]

What is fairly attributable is a matter of normative judgment, and the criteria lack rigid simplicity. From the range of circumstances that could point toward the State behind an individual face, no one fact can function as a necessary condition across the board for finding state action; nor is any set of circumstances absolutely sufficient, for there may be some countervailing reason against attributing activity to the government.

Our cases have identified a host of facts that can bear on the fairness of such an attribution. We have, for example, held that a challenged activity may be state action when it results from the State's exercise of "coercive power," *Blum*, supra, 457 U.S. at 1004, when the State provides "significant encouragement, either overt or covert," ibid. or when a private actor operates as a "willful participant in joint activity with the State or its agents," *Lugar*, supra, 457 U.S. at 941. We have treated a nominally private entity as a state actor when it is controlled by an "agency of the State," Pennsylvania v. Board of Directors of City Trusts of Philadelphia, 353 U.S. 230, 231 (1957) (per curiam), when it has been delegated a public function by the State, when it is "entwined with governmental policies" or when government is "entwined in [its] management or control," Evans v. Newton, 382 U.S. 296, 299, 301 (1966).

Amidst such variety, examples may be the best teachers, and examples from our cases are unequivocal in showing that the character of a legal entity is determined neither by its expressly private characterization in statutory law, nor by the failure of the law to acknowledge the entity's inseparability from recognized government officials or agencies. Lebron v. National Railroad Passenger Corporation, 513 U.S. 374 (1995), held that Amtrak was the Government for constitutional purposes, regardless of its congressional designation as private; it was organized under federal law to attain governmental objectives and was directed and controlled by federal appointees. *Pennsylvania v. Board of Directors of City Trusts of Philadelphia*, supra, held the privately endowed Girard College to be a state actor and enforcement of its private founder's limitation of admission to whites attributable to the State, because, consistent with the terms of the settlor's gift, the college's board of directors was a state agency established by state law. Ostensibly the converse situation occurred in *Evans v. Newton*, supra, which held that private trustees to whom a city had transferred a park were nonetheless state actors barred from enforcing racial segregation, since the park served the public purpose of providing community recreation, and "the municipality remained entwined in [its] management [and] control." . . .

---

2. If a defendant's conduct satisfies the state-action requirement of the Fourteenth Amendment, the conduct also constitutes action "under color of state law" for § 1983 purposes. Lugar v. Edmondson Oil Co., 457 U.S. 922, 935 (1982).

B

[T]he "necessarily fact-bound inquiry," *Lugar, supra,* 457 U.S. at 939, leads to the conclusion of state action here. The nominally private character of the Association is overborne by the pervasive entwinement of public institutions and public officials in its composition and workings, and there is no substantial reason to claim unfairness in applying constitutional standards to it.

The Association is not an organization of natural persons acting on their own, but of schools, and of public schools to the extent of 84% of the total. Under the Association's bylaws, each member school is represented by its principal or a faculty member, who has a vote in selecting members of the governing legislative council and board of control from eligible principals, assistant principals and superintendents.

Although the findings and prior opinions in this case include no express conclusion of law that public school officials act within the scope of their duties when they represent their institutions, no other view would be rational, the official nature of their involvement being shown in any number of ways. ... [T]he 290 public schools of Tennessee belonging to [the Association] can sensibly be seen as exercising their own authority to meet their own responsibilities. ... Unlike mere public buyers of contract services, whose payments for services rendered do not convert the service providers into public actors, see Rendell–Baker v. Kohn, 457 U.S. 830, 839–43 (1982), the schools here obtain membership in the service organization and give up sources of their own income to their collective association. The Association thus exercises the authority of the predominantly public schools to charge for admission to their games; the Association does not receive this money from the schools, but enjoys the schools' moneymaking capacity as its own. ...

In sum, ... the Association is an organization of public schools represented by their officials acting in their official capacity to provide an integral element of secondary public schooling. ... Only the 16% minority of private school memberships prevents this entwinement of the Association and the public school system from being total and their identities totally indistinguishable.

To complement the entwinement of public school officials with the Association from the bottom up, the State of Tennessee has provided for entwinement from top down. State Board members are assigned ex officio to serve as members of the board of control and legislative council, and the Association's ministerial employees are treated as state employees to the extent of being eligible for membership in the state retirement system.

It is, of course, true that ... the terms of the State Board's Rule expressly designating the Association as regulator of interscholastic athletics in public schools was deleted in 1996, the year after a Federal District

Court held that the Association was a state actor because its rules were "caused, directed and controlled by the Tennessee Board of Education...."

But the removal of the designation language from Rule 0520–1–2–.08 affected nothing but words.... The most one can say on the evidence is that the State Board once freely acknowledged the Association's official character but now does it by winks and nods.[4]....

C

... The Association places great stress ... on the application of a public function test, as exemplified in Rendell–Baker v. Kohn, 457 U.S. 830 (1982). There, an apparently private school provided education for students whose special needs made it difficult for them to finish high school. The record, however, failed to show any tradition of providing public special education to students unable to cope with a regular school, who had historically been cared for (or ignored) according to private choice. It was true that various public school districts had adopted the practice of referring students to the school and paying their tuition, and no one disputed that providing the instruction aimed at a proper public objective and conferred a public benefit. But we held that the performance of such a public function did not permit a finding of state action on the part of the school unless the function performed was exclusively and traditionally public, as it was not in that case. The Association argues that application of the public function criterion would produce the same result here, and we will assume, arguendo, that it would. But this case does not turn on a public function test, any more than *Rendell–Baker* had anything to do with entwinement of public officials in the special school. ...

D

... Even facts that suffice to show public action (or, standing alone, would require such a finding) may be outweighed in the name of some value at odds with finding public accountability in the circumstances. In Polk County v. Dodson, 454 U.S. 312 (1981), a defense lawyer's actions were deemed private even though she was employed by the county and was acting within the scope of her duty as a public defender. Full-time public employment would be conclusive of state action for some purposes, but not when the employee is doing a defense lawyer's primary job; then, the public defender does "not act on behalf of the State; he is the State's adversary."

---

4. The significance of winks and nods in state-action doctrine seems to be one of the points of the dissenters' departure from the rest of the Court. In drawing the public-private action line, the dissenters would emphasize the formal clarity of the legislative action ..., in preference to our reliance on the practical certainty in this case that public officials will control operation of the Association under its bylaws. ... But if formalism were the sine qua non of state action, the doctrine would vanish owing to the ease and inevitability of its evasion, and for just that reason formalism has never been controlling. For example, a criterion of state action like symbiosis (which the dissenters accept) looks not to form but to an underlying reality.

Polk County, supra, 454 U.S. at 323, n.13. The state-action doctrine does not convert opponents into virtual agents.

The assertion of such a countervailing value is the nub of each of the Association's two remaining arguments, neither of which, however, persuades us. The Association suggests, first, that reversing the judgment here will somehow trigger an epidemic of unprecedented federal litigation. Even if that might be counted as a good reason for a *Polk County* decision to call the Association's action private, the record raises no reason for alarm here. Save for the Sixth Circuit, every Court of Appeals to consider a statewide athletic association like the one here has found it a state actor. . . . No one, however, has pointed to any explosion of § 1983 cases against interscholastic athletic associations in the affected jurisdictions. . . .

Nor do we think there is anything to be said for the Association's contention that there is no need to treat it as a state actor since any public school applying the Association's rules is itself subject to suit under § 1983. . . . If Brentwood's claim were pushing at the edge of the class of possible defendant state actors, an argument about the social utility of expanding that class would at least be on point, but because we are nowhere near the margin in this case, the Association is really asking for nothing less than a dispensation for itself. Its position boils down to saying that the Association should not be dressed in state clothes because other, concededly public actors are; that Brentwood should be kept out of court because a different plaintiff raising a different claim in a different case may find the courthouse open. Pleas for special treatment are hard to sell, although saying that does not, of course, imply anything about the merits of Brentwood's complaint; the issue here is merely whether Brentwood properly names the Association as a § 1983 defendant, not whether it should win on its claim. . . .

■ JUSTICE THOMAS, with whom THE CHIEF JUSTICE, JUSTICE SCALIA, and JUSTICE KENNEDY join, dissenting.

. . . . Like the state-action requirement of the Fourteenth Amendment, the state-action element of 42 U.S.C. § 1983 excludes from its coverage "merely private conduct, however discriminatory or wrongful." American Mfrs. Mut. Ins. Co. v. Sullivan, 526 U.S. 40, 50 (1999). "Careful adherence to the 'state action' requirement" thus "preserves an area of individual freedom by limiting the reach of federal law and federal judicial power." Lugar v. Edmondson Oil Co., 457 U.S. 922, 936 (1982). The state-action doctrine also promotes important values of federalism, "avoiding the imposition of responsibility on a State for conduct it could not control." National Collegiate Athletic Assn. v. Tarkanian, 488 U.S. 179, 191 (1988). . . .

[T]he State of Tennessee has never had any involvement in the particular action taken by the TSSAA in this case: the enforcement of the TSSAA's recruiting rule prohibiting members from using "undue influence" on students or their parents or guardians "to secure or to retain a student for athletic purposes." There is no indication that the State has ever had any interest in how schools choose to regulate recruiting. In fact, the TSSAA's authority to enforce its recruiting rule arises solely from the voluntary membership contract that each member school signs, agreeing to conduct its athletics in accordance with the rules and decisions of the TSSAA. . . .

I am not prepared to say that any private organization that permits public entities and public officials to participate acts as the State in anything or everything it does, and our state-action jurisprudence has never reached that far. The state-action doctrine was developed to reach only those actions that are truly attributable to the State, not to subject private citizens to the control of federal courts hearing § 1983 actions.[a]

NOTES ON THE STATE ACTION DOCTRINE

1. **Introduction.** Section 1983 requires the plaintiff to show that the defendant acted "under color of" state law. As the *Brentwood Academy* Court noted, the question of "under color of" law under § 1983 is essentially the same as the question of state action under the Fourteenth Amendment. For the vast majority of § 1983 claims, this element is straightforward. Questions can arise, however, in two kinds of cases. First, in exact parallel to state-action doctrine, the question can arise whether a private individual or entity should be considered to be acting under color of state law with regard to the practice or conduct giving rise to the litigation. *Brentwood Academy* is such a case. Second, even where the defendant is a public officer, the question can arise whether he or she was acting in a purely private capacity when the wrong was committed. These questions will be examined in turn.

2. **Private Actors as Public Actors.** It has long been settled that private parties engaged in concerted action with government officials may subject themselves to liability under § 1983. See, e.g., Adickes v. S.H. Kress & Co., 398 U.S. 144 (1970) (department store might be liable under § 1983 for its involvement in enforcing state-mandated unconstitutional racial segregation laws against the plaintiff). A more modern question of this sort concerns lawsuits against media defendants who participate in the kind of media ride-alongs at issue in Wilson v. Layne, 526 U.S. 603 (1999), discussed in the casebook at pages 102–10. See generally Sheila M. Lombardi, Note, Media In The Spotlight: Private Parties Liable For Violating the Fourth Amendment, 6 Roger Williams U. L. Rev. 393 (2000) (collecting conflicting cases on this question). Additionally, a private actor or entity will be treated as a governmental insofar as its conduct fulfills a "public

---

a. For commentary on *Brentwood Academy*, see Michael L. Wells, Identifying State Actors in Constitutional Litigation: Reviving the Role of Substantive Context, 26 Cardozo L. Rev. 99 (2004). Wells criticizes the decision as being insufficiently rule-oriented and insufficiently attentive to the substantive constitutional issues at stake.—[Footnote by eds.]

function." As is indicated by Rendell–Baker v. Kohn, 457 U.S. 830 (1982), which is discussed in *Brentwood Academy*, the public function concept has been narrowly construed.

One of the most important contemporary contexts where private actors will be treated as state actors is in the industry of private prisons. See generally Ahmed A. White, Rule of Law and the Limits of Sovereignty: The Private Prison in Jurisprudential Perspective, 38 Am. Crim. L. Rev. 111 (2001); Paul Howard Morris, Note, The Impact of Constitutional Liability on the Privatization Movement After *Richardson v. McKnight*, 52 Vand. L. Rev. 489 (1999). Private prisons are undoubtedly state actors, as their sole authority to confine the inmates assigned to them is the delegation of power from the state. But as been noted in connection with *Richardson v. McKnight*, discussed in the casebook at pages 131–34, private prison guards and presumably the corporations that employ them are not entitled to qualified immunity, but at most to some sort of good-faith defense.

In addition to cases where an officer is clearly off-duty, there are cases that arise when an officer, although technically off-duty, is nonetheless acting in a quasi-police capacity. Consider here the prevalent use of off-duty officers, sometimes even in uniform and even more frequently still carrying service revolvers, acting as private security guards. See generally David A. Sklansky, The Private Police, 46 U.C.L.A. L. Rev. 1165 (1999). Professor Sklansky notes that "an estimated 150,000 police officers moonlight as private security guards, often in police uniform. This practice, too, appears to have escalated sharply; more than half of the officers in many metropolitan police departments now supplement their income with private security work. In a growing number of cases police departments themselves contract to supply their personnel to groups of merchants or residents, and then pay the officers out of the proceeds." Id. at 1176.

Are these officers then acting with "apparent authority" for purposes of § 1983? If so, what about those who are not moonlighting police officers but are employed full-time in the private security industry? Professor Sklansky points out that there are more private security guards in the United States than sworn law enforcement officers and that, in some areas, they perform much of the traditional police job of patrolling neighborhoods. Sklansky canvasses the courts' treatment of private security personnel and notes that, for the most part, courts have refused to find that private "police" are state actors. His article suggests that this result may flow from a concern far removed from the question of liability under § 1983. If private police are engaged in state action, then the exclusionary rules of the Fourth, Fifth, and Sixth Amendments would apply to the products of any searches or questioning they conducted. Consequently, courts are primarily concerned, in declining to find state action, with the general applicability of constitutional protections. The finding of no state action also means, however, that private police also are not liable for damages under § 1983. Professor Sklansky concludes that the main legal limitations on the private police today are [state law-based] tort and criminal doctrines of assault, trespass, and false imprisonment—variants of the same doctrines that once defined the principal boundaries of permissible public policing. Unless the owner has given consent, a security guard's search of private property will generally constitute a trespass. And arrests or detentions not authorized by state law generally will expose a security guard to civil and criminal liability for false imprisonment and, if force is involved, for assault.

Id. at 1183. Although the legal regimes are formally quite different, Sklansky suggests that, at least when it comes to damages liability, there may be several strong parallels: for example, the good-faith defense to common-law claims of false imprisonment resembles qualified immunity in some respects.

3. Public Actors as Private Actors. Not everything a public official does occurs "under color of" law. Public officials have private lives, and the line between state action and private behavior can sometimes be rather fuzzy. One area that has seen substantial litigation as well as scholarly commentary involves the actions of off-duty police officers. Consider, for example, the decision in Parrilla–Burgos v. Hernandez–Rivera, 108 F.3d 445 (1st Cir.1997). The defendant in *Parrilla–Burgos* was an off-duty police officer (indeed, he was on medical leave) who killed another bar patron with his service revolver, which he was required by department policy to carry at all times. The plaintiff's estate brought suit under § 1983. The court of appeals held that the officer had not been acting under color of law because his actions were unrelated to his official duties and clearly lay outside the boundaries of a police officer's actions. One commentator has criticized this approach because it insulates the most egregious forms of off-duty misbehavior from § 1983 liability precisely because such conduct is unrelated to the defendant's official duties. See Seth M. Kean, Note, Municipal Liability for Off–Duty Police Misconduct Under Section 1983: The "Under Color of Law Requirement," 79 B.U.L. Rev. 195, 211–16 (1999).

Parrilla–Burgos may well state the result that other courts would reach on similar facts, but slight factual differences produce different results. For example, in United States v. Tarpley, 945 F.2d 806 (5th Cir.1991), the court held that a deputy sheriff acted under color of law when he assaulted his wife's former lover because the officer claimed special authority from his official status, summoned another police officer for assistance, and used a police car to chase the victim.

One of the most unusual cases of public officers found not to be acting "under color of" state law is discussed in the *Brentwood Academy* opinion. In Polk County v. Dodson, 454 U.S. 312 (1981), the Supreme Court held that a criminal defendant could not sue his public defender under § 1983. *Polk County* is the only case in which the Court held that a public employee, while performing the function for which he or she was paid, is not a state actor. In West v. Atkins, 487 U.S. 42 (1988), the Court refused to extend the *Polk County* rationale to private physicians providing services to prison inmates pursuant to a contract with the state. Unlike public defenders, whose exercise of independent judgment would often lead them to positions that conflicted with the state's interest—thus making it inappropriate to hold the state responsible for their acts—prison physicians, even though they exercised independent medical judgment, were engaged in a fundamentally cooperative relationship with the state to provide the medical care required by the Eighth Amendment.

Does *Polk County* make sense? Particularly in light of the fact that the government is held "responsible" for public defenders' serious shortcomings under established Sixth Amendment case law—that is, a defendant's conviction will be reversed if he shows that he was denied effective assistance of counsel, because the Supreme Court has held that the government bears the responsibility for providing effective assistance to indigent defendants—what problems would arise if public defenders were liable to suit under § 1983?

4. Why It Matters. Why might § 1983 be advantageous in such cases? A person assaulted by an off-duty police officer has a state-law tort claim against the officer. But § 1983 offers several potential substantive and strategic advantages. Most obviously, § 1983 claims can be litigated in federal, as well as state, court regardless of the citizenship of the parties or the amount in controversy. Docket congestion, different jury pools, nonelected judges, and various procedural differences may make federal courts a more plaintiff-friendly forum. Even more importantly, prevailing plaintiffs under § 1983 are entitled to reasonable attorney's fees under 42 U.S.C. § 1988, while state tort plaintiffs are usually subject to the "American rule," under which each party bears its own costs.

Moreover, the presence of a § 1983 claim may increase a plaintiff's chance of recovering significant damages for two additional reasons. First, when the plaintiff establishes that the defendant was acting under color of state law, the effective recovery may be greater if the defendant's employer considers itself bound (or is required by state law) to indemnify the officer for any damages owed the plaintiff. Second, § 1983 plaintiffs can sometimes name the municipality or department that employed the defendant as a defendant under *Monell*, claiming injury resulting from departmental policy. Indeed, the courts of appeals have split on the question whether, even if the defendant *officer* was not acting under color of law—because he was off duty and clearly acting outside his authority—the government can still be held liable because its policies, particularly a failure to train officers properly, were a cause of the injury. Compare, e.g., Pitchell v. Callan, 13 F.3d 545 (2d Cir.1994) (holding that, because an off-duty officer who shot the plaintiff after a night of drinking was not acting under color of law, the plaintiff's claim against the city that employed him necessarily failed) with

Gibson v. City of Chicago, 910 F.2d 1510, 1520 (7th Cir.1990) (holding that, although an officer who had been declared mentally unfit for further duty, but who had kept his service revolver, was not acting under color of law when he shot a neighbor, "the City's policy of allowing a deranged police officer to retain his service revolver and bullets" might be "the state action that deprived [the plaintiff] of his life" and might constitute municipal policy).

Page 235, add at the beginning of footnote a:

For a recent reinterpretation of *Paul*, see Barbara E. Armacost, Race and Reputation: The Real Legacy of *Paul v. Davis*, 85 Va. L. Rev. 569 (1999) (arguing that much of the "scholarly hand-wringing" is misdirected, because most of the claims excluded from due process by *Paul* are redirected to other constitutional "homes").

Page 248, add at the end of Note 5:

5a. *Chavez v. Martinez*. In Chavez v. Martinez, 538 U.S. 760 (2003), the Court revisited the question of substantive due process. Martinez was shot during an altercation with police. While he was being treated in the hospital, he was interrogated by Chavez, a patrol supervisor. Martinez was not given *Miranda* warnings. Although he was never charged with a crime, Martinez filed suit under § 1983, claiming that Chavez's actions violated both his Fifth Amendment right not to be "compelled in any criminal case to be a witness against himself," and his Fourteenth Amendment substantive due process right to be free from coercive questioning. A majority of the Court rejected Martinez's Fifth Amendment claim. Four Justices, in an opinion written by Justice Thomas, concluded as a textual matter that the Fifth Amendment's Self–Incrimination Clause comes into play only if there is a "criminal case" in which an individual faces the prospect of being a "witness" against himself. Mere compulsive questioning does not violate the Constitution. Justice Souter, in an opinion joined by Justice Breyer, concluded that it was unnecessary to recognize a claim for damages under the Fifth Amendment because there was "no reason to believe that the guarantee [against compelled self-incrimination] has been ineffective in all or many of those circumstances in which its vindication has depended on excluding testimonial admissions or barring penalties." But Justice Souter went on to note that "any argument for a damages remedy in this case must depend not on its Fifth Amendment feature but upon the particular charge of outrageous conduct by the police, extending from their initial encounter with Martinez through the questioning by Chavez. That claim, however, if it is to be recognized as a constitutional one that may be raised in an action under § 1983, must sound in substantive due process." An overlapping group of five Justices—Stevens, Kennedy, Souter, Ginsburg, and Breyer—remanded the question whether Martinez could pursue such a claim to the Court of Appeals. Stevens, Kennedy, and Ginsburg would actually have concluded that Chavez's behavior violated the Constitution, but Justice Kennedy nonetheless voted to remand the case because otherwise there would have been no controlling judgment of the Court.

Martinez raises an interesting issue in light of the Court's holding in Graham v. Connor, 490 U.S. 386 (1989), that when there is an explicit textual source of constitutional protection against a particular sort of government behavior, that provision, and not the more generalized notion of substantive due process, should provide the analytic framework for analyzing a plaintiff's claim. In *Graham*, the Court held that because the Fourth Amendment provided explicit constitutional protection against unreasonable "seizures," it should govern claims of excessive use of force in effecting an arrest. The more general protections of substantive due process did not apply. Here, by contrast, although six justices addressed and rejected the claim under the Fifth Amendment, a majority of the Court expressed a willingness to have the claim addressed as a matter of substantive due process.

For discussion of *Graham* and its relationship to substantive due process, see Peter J. Rubin, Square Pegs and Round Holes: Substantive Due Process, Procedural Due Process, and the Bill of Rights, 103 Colum. L. Rev. 833 (2003).

Page 295, add new Notes:

10. Recent Developments. An interesting question concerning the intersection of *Maine v. Thiboutot* and the Supreme Court's increasingly restrictive approach to implied rights of action arose in the aftermath of Alexander v. Sandoval, 532 U.S. 275 (2001). The case involved a private action to enforce disparate-impact regulations promulgated by the Department of Justice under § 602 of Title VI of the 1964 Civil Rights Act. In Cannon v. University of Chicago, 441 U.S. 677 (1979), the Court had held that § 601 of the Act, a provision forbidding racial discrimination in programs receiving federal funds, created an implied right of action in favor of private parties. In *Sandoval*, however, the Court held that § 602 of the Act, authorizing federal agencies to promulgate regulations to "effectuate" the rights guaranteed by Title VI, does *not* create an implied right of action. Enforcement of regulations promulgated under § 602 was therefore limited to the statutorily-specified remedy of cutting off federal funds to the offending program. The Court therefore barred a lawsuit challenging the decision of the Alabama Department of Public Safety to offer drivers' license examinations only in English due to its disparate impact on Spanish speaking applicants.

Can plaintiffs circumvent the lack of a private right of action under § 602 of Title VI by using § 1983? In dissent, Justice Stevens, joined by Justices Souter, Ginsburg, and Breyer suggested that they could:

> [T]o the extent that the majority denies relief to the respondents merely because they neglected to mention 42 U.S.C. § 1983 in framing their Title VI claim, this case is something of a sport.

Litigants who in the future wish to enforce the Title VI regulations against state actors in all likelihood must only reference § 1983 to obtain relief; indeed, the plaintiffs in this case (or other similarly situated individuals) presumably retain the option of re-challenging Alabama's English-only policy in a complaint that invokes § 1983 even after today's decision.

In light of *Sandoval* and Gonzaga University v. Doe, 536 U.S. 273 (2002), discussed in the next note, courts of appeals have generally been hostile to treating regulations as "rights creating" laws the violations of which can support § 1983 lawsuits. The circuits that have confronted the issue recently have taken the position that agency regulations cannot themselves create rights that are not found in the statute itself. See, e.g., Save Our Valley v. Sound Transit, 335 F.3d 932 (9th Cir. 2003); Peters v. Jenney, 327 F.3d 307 (4th Cir. 2003); South Camden Citizens in Action v. New Jersey Dep't. of Envtl. Prot., 274 F.3d 771 (3d Cir. 2001); Kissimmee River Valley Sportsman Ass'n v. City of Lakeland, 250 F.3d 1324 (11th Cir. 2001).

For discussions of the availability of private rights of action post-*Sandoval* and *Gonzaga* and the role of § 1983, see, e.g., Brian D. Galle, Can Federal Agencies Authorize Private Suits Under Section 1983?: A Theoretical Approach, 69 Brooklyn L. Rev. 163 (2003); Pamela S. Karlan, Disarming the Private Attorney General, 2003 U. Ill. L. Rev. 183 ; Bradford C. Mank, Suing Under § 1983: The Future After *Gonzaga University v. Doe*, 39 Hous. L. Rev. 1417 (2003).

11. The Interaction of Section 1983 and Implied Rights of Action. The Supreme Court sought to align the tests for determining when there is an implied right of action and when § 1983 provides an express remedy in Gonzaga University v. Doe, 536 U.S. 273 (2002). The case concerned the Family Educational Rights and Privacy Act of 1974 (FERPA), 20 U.S.C. § 1232g, which prohibits federal funding of schools that permit the release of students' records without written consent. Doe alleged that Gonzaga, a private university in Washington state, violated FERPA by revealing allegations of sexual misconduct by an employee to state officials involved in teacher certification. The employee sued in state court under § 1983, and the state courts agreed that Gonzaga had acted under color of state law in helping the state officials. A jury awarded both compensatory and punitive damages, and the Washington Supreme Court upheld the verdict.

The United States Supreme Court reversed. Chief Justice Rehnquist began by noting that FERPA was enacted under Congress's spending clause power—that is, Congress required privacy of personal information as a condition of receiving federal funds, rather than as a direct legislative command. In Pennhurst State School and Hospital v. Halderman, 451 U.S. 1 (1981), the Court had held that federal funding provisions create individually enforceable rights only when Congress manifests an "unambiguous" intent to create them. Otherwise, the Court stated, the remedy "for state noncompliance with federally imposed conditions is not a private cause of action for noncompliance but rather action by the Federal Government to terminate funds to the State."

The Court recognized that the line of cases extending from *Wright* and *Wilder* through *Artist M.* and *Blessing v. Freestone* had caused "uncertainty" in the lower courts. Some decisions allowed plaintiffs to enforce statutory rights under § 1983 so long as they fell "within the general zone of interest that the statute is intended to protect; something less than what is required for a statute to create rights enforceable directly from the statute itself under an implied private right of action. Fueling this uncertainty is the notion that our implied private right of action cases have no bearing on the standards for discerning whether a statute creates rights enforceable by § 1983." In *Gonzaga University*, the Court rejected this approach:

> We now reject the notion that our cases permit anything short of an unambiguously conferred right to support a cause of action brought under § 1983. Section 1983 provides a remedy only for the deprivation of "rights, privileges, or immunities secured by the Constitution and laws" of the United States. Accordingly, only "rights," not "benefits" or "interests," may be enforced under that section. This being so, we further reject the notion that our implied right of action cases are separate and distinct from our § 1983 cases. To the contrary, our implied right of action cases should guide the determination of whether a statute confers rights enforceable under § 1983.
>
> We have recognized that whether a statutory violation may be enforced through § 1983 "is a different inquiry than that involved in determining whether a private right of action can be implied from a particular statute." *Wilder*, 496 U.S. 498 at 508, n. 9. But the inquiries overlap in one meaningful respect—in either case we must first determine whether Congress intended to create a federal right. Thus we have held that "the question whether Congress ... intended to create a private right of action [is] definitively answered in the negative" where "a statute by its terms grants no private rights to any identifiable class." Touche Ross & Co. v. Redington, 442 U.S. 560, 576 (1979). For a statute to create such private rights, its text must be "phrased in terms of the persons benefited." Cannon v. University of Chicago, 441 U.S. 677, 692, n. 13 (1979). ... But even where a statute is phrased in such explicit rights-creating terms, a plaintiff suing under an implied right of action still must show that the statute manifests an intent "to create not just a private right but also a private remedy." Alexander v. Sandoval, 532 U.S. 275, 286 (2001).

Plaintiffs suing under § 1983 do not have the burden of showing an intent to create a private remedy because § 1983 generally supplies a remedy for the vindication of rights secured by federal statutes. Once a plaintiff demonstrates that a statute confers an individual right, the right is presumptively enforceable by § 1983. But the initial inquiry—determining whether a statute confers any right at all—is no different from the initial inquiry in an implied right of action case, the express purpose of which is to determine whether or not a statute "confers rights on a particular class of persons." California v. Sierra Club, 451 U.S. 287, 294 (1981). . . .

A court's role in discerning whether personal rights exist in the § 1983 context should therefore not differ from its role in discerning whether personal rights exist in the implied right of action context. . . . Both inquiries simply require a determination as to whether or not Congress intended to confer individual rights upon a class of beneficiaries. . . . Accordingly, where the text and structure of a statute provide no indication that Congress intends to create new individual rights, there is no basis for a private suit, whether under § 1983 or under an implied right of action.

The Court found that FERPA did not contain the kind of rights-creating language that could support a § 1983 claim. It did not contain "individually focused terminology"—for example, that "no person shall be subjected to" violations of FERPA. Instead, FERPA, like the provisions at issue in *Blessing*, had an "aggregate focus," referring to institutional policies and requiring that funds recipients "comply substantially." The conclusion that FERPA's nondisclosure provisions do not confer enforceable rights was "buttressed by the mechanism that Congress chose to provide for enforcing those provisions." The Court noted Congress' express direction to the Secretary of Education to "deal with violations" and the extensive administrative complaint structure the Secretary had created and found that "[t]hese administrative procedures squarely distinguish this case from *Wright* and *Wilder*, where an aggrieved individual lacked any federal review mechanism." Finally, the Court pointed to statutory language providing that "except for the conduct of hearings, none of the functions of the Secretary under this section shall be carried out in any of the regional offices" of the Department of Education. 20 U.S.C. § 1232g(g). The legislative history showed that Congress had provided for "centralized review" because of concern that "regionalizing the enforcement of [FERPA] may lead to multiple interpretations. . . ." 120 Cong. Rec. 39863 (1974) (joint statement). "It is implausible," the Court concluded, "to presume that the same Congress nonetheless intended private suits to be brought before thousands of federal-and state-court judges, which could only result in the sort of 'multiple interpretations' the Act explicitly sought to avoid."

Justice Breyer, joined by Justice Souter, concurred in the judgment. They agreed that congressional intent was the key issue in determining whether an individual could bring suit under § 1983, and that FERPA manifested no such intent, but would not have adopted a presumption that Congress intended to create a right only if the text or structure of a statute showed an "unambiguous" intent.

Justice Stevens, joined by Justice Ginsburg, dissented. He argued that the FERPA did contain rights-creating language and satisfied the *Blessing* test. He also disagreed with what he saw as the Court's "needlessly borrowing from cases involving implied rights of action":

> [O]ur implied right of action cases "reflect a concern, grounded in separation of powers, that Congress rather than the courts controls the availability of remedies for violations of statutes." *Wilder*, 496 U.S. 498 at 509, n. 9. However, imposing the implied right of action framework upon the § 1983 inquiry is not necessary: The separation-of-powers concerns present in the implied right of action context "are not present in a § 1983 case," because Congress expressly authorized private suits in § 1983 itself. *Wilder*, 496 U.S. 498 at 509, n. 9.

For discussion of the implications of this case, see Bradford C. Mank, Suing Under Section 1983: The Future After *Gonzaga University v. Doe*, 39 Hous. L. Rev. 1417 (2003); Ralph D. Mawdsley, A Section 1983 Cause of Action Under IDEA? Measuring the Effect of *Gonzaga University v. Doe*, 170 Ed. L. Rep. 425 (2002).

12. *City of Rancho Palos Verdes v. Abrams.* The restrictive approach of *Gonzaga University* was reaffirmed in City of Rancho Palos Verdes v. Abrams, 544 U.S. ___, 125 S.Ct. 1453 (2005). Plaintiff Abrams sued his locality, claiming that the denial of a zoning permit for a radio antenna on his property violated restrictions imposed on localities by the Telecommunications Act of 1996. Writing for a nearly unanimous Court, Justice Scalia began with the familiar admonition that the statute must create individually enforceable rights in the class of beneficiaries to which the plaintiff belongs. That showing, however, creates only a rebuttable presumption that the right is enforceable under § 1983. The presumption is rebutted if the defendant shows that Congress "did not intend" that the newly created right be enforceable under § 1983, and a lack of congressional intent is the "ordinary inference" from a different statutory enforcement scheme. In the case of the Telecommunications Act, individual enforcement is explicitly authorized but on a shorter timetable, arguably without compensatory damages, and certainly without attorneys fees. These differences in remedy precluded application of § 1983, absent legislation indication of a purpose to provide that relief. Justice Breyer, joined by Justices O'Connor, Souter, and Ginsburg, concurred to say that context would sometimes be important in determining whether Congress intended to exclude enforcement under § 1983. Only Justice Stevens dissented.

CHAPTER II

Attorney's Fees

Page 361, prior to Section 2:

Buckhannon Board and Care Home v. West Virginia Department of Health and Human Resources

Supreme Court of the United States, 2001.
532 U.S. 598.

■ CHIEF JUSTICE REHNQUIST delivered the opinion of the Court.

Numerous federal statutes allow courts to award attorney's fees and costs to the "prevailing party." The question presented here is whether this term includes a party that has failed to secure a judgment on the merits or a court-ordered consent decree, but has nonetheless achieved the desired result because the lawsuit brought about a voluntary change in the defendant's conduct. We hold that it does not.

Buckhannon Board and Care Home, Inc., which operates care homes that provide assisted living to their residents, failed an inspection by the West Virginia Office of the State Fire Marshal because some of the residents were incapable of "self-preservation" as defined under state law. ... On October 28, 1997, after receiving cease and desist orders requiring the closure of its residential care facilities within 30 days, Buckhannon Board and Care Home, Inc., on behalf of itself and other similarly situated homes and residents (hereinafter petitioners), brought suit in the United States District Court for the Northern District of West Virginia against the State of West Virginia, two of its agencies, and 18 individuals (hereinafter respondents), seeking declaratory and injunctive relief that the "self-preservation" requirement violated the Fair Housing Amendments Act of 1988 (FHAA), 42 U.S.C. §§ 3601 et seq., and the Americans with Disabilities Act of 1990 (ADA), 42 U.S.C. §§ 12101 et seq.

Respondents agreed to stay enforcement of the cease and desist orders pending resolution of the case and the parties began discovery. In 1998, the West Virginia Legislature enacted two bills eliminating the "self-preservation" requirement, and respondents moved to dismiss the case as moot. The District Court granted the motion, finding that the 1998 legislation had eliminated the allegedly offensive provisions and that there was no indication that the West Virginia Legislature would repeal the amendments.

Petitioners requested attorney's fees as the "prevailing party" under the FHAA, 42 U.S.C. § 3613(c)(2) ("The court, in its discretion, may allow the prevailing party . . . a reasonable attorney's fee and costs"), and ADA, 42 U.S.C. § 12205 ("The court . . ., in its discretion, may allow the prevailing party . . . a reasonable attorney's fee, including litigation expenses, and costs"). Petitioners argued that they were entitled to attorney's fees under the "catalyst theory," which posits that a plaintiff is a "prevailing party" if it achieves the desired result because the lawsuit brought about a voluntary change in the defendant's conduct. Although most Courts of Appeals recognize the "catalyst theory," the Court of Appeals for the Fourth Circuit had rejected it [in an earlier case]. . . . To resolve the disagreement amongst the Courts of Appeals, we granted certiorari, and now affirm.

In the United States, parties are ordinarily required to bear their own attorney's fees—the prevailing party is not entitled to collect from the loser. See Alyeska Pipeline Service Co. v. Wilderness Society, 421 U.S. 240, 247 (1975). Under this "American Rule," we follow "a general practice of not awarding fees to a prevailing party absent explicit statutory authority." Key Tronic Corp. v. United States, 511 U.S. 809, 819 (1994). Congress, however, has authorized the award of attorney's fees to the "prevailing party" in numerous statutes in addition to those at issue here, such as the Civil Rights Act of 1964, 42 U.S.C. § 2000e–5(k), the Voting Rights Act Amendments of 1975, 42 U.S.C. § 1973l(e), and the Civil Rights Attorney's fees Awards Act of 1976, 42 U.S.C. § 1988.[4]

In designating those parties eligible for an award of litigation costs, Congress employed the term "prevailing party," a legal term of art. Black's Law Dictionary 1145 (7th ed. 1999) defines "prevailing party" as "[a] party in whose favor a judgment is rendered, regardless of the amount of damages awarded. . . .—Also termed *successful party*." This view that a "prevailing party" is one who has been awarded some relief by the court can be distilled from our prior cases.

In Hanrahan v. Hampton, 446 U.S. 754, 758 (1980) (per curiam), we reviewed the legislative history of § 1988 and found that "Congress intended to permit the interim award of counsel fees only when a party has prevailed on the merits of at least some of his claims." Our "respect for ordinary language requires that a plaintiff receive at least some relief on the merits of his claim before he can be said to prevail." Hewitt v. Helms, 482 U.S. 755, 760 (1987). We have held that even an award of nominal damages suffices under this test. See Farrar v. Hobby, 506 U.S. 103 (1992).[6]

---

4. We have interpreted these fee-shifting provisions consistently, see Hensley v. Eckerhart, 461 U.S. 424, 433, n. 7 (1983), and so approach the nearly identical provisions at issue here.

6. However, in some circumstances such a "prevailing party" should still not receive an award of attorney's fees. See *Farrar v. Hobby*, supra, at 115–16.

In addition to judgments on the merits, we have held that settlement agreements enforced through a consent decree may serve as the basis for an award of attorney's fees. See Maher v. Gagne, 448 U.S. 122 (1980). Although a consent decree does not always include an admission of liability by the defendant, it nonetheless is a court-ordered "change [in] the legal relationship between [the plaintiff] and the defendant." Texas State Teachers Assn. v. Garland Independent School Dist., 489 U.S. 782, 792 (1989).[7] These decisions, taken together, establish that enforceable judgments on the merits and court-ordered consent decrees create the "material alteration of the legal relationship of the parties" necessary to permit an award of attorney's fees. 489 U.S. at 792–93.

We think, however, the "catalyst theory" falls on the other side of the line from these examples. It allows an award where there is no judicially sanctioned change in the legal relationship of the parties. Even under a limited form of the "catalyst theory," a plaintiff could recover attorney's fees if it established that the "complaint had sufficient merit to withstand a motion to dismiss for lack of jurisdiction or failure to state a claim on which relief may be granted." Brief for United States as Amicus Curiae 27. This is not the type of legal merit that our prior decisions, based upon plain language and congressional intent, have found necessary. . . . A defendant's voluntary change in conduct, although perhaps accomplishing what the plaintiff sought to achieve by the lawsuit, lacks the necessary judicial imprimatur on the change. Our precedents thus counsel against holding that the term "prevailing party" authorizes an award of attorney's fees without a corresponding alteration in the legal relationship of the parties.

. . . We have only awarded attorney's fees where the plaintiff has received a judgment on the merits, see, e.g., *Farrar*, supra, at 112, or obtained a court-ordered consent decree, *Maher*, supra, at 129–30—we have not awarded attorney's fees where the plaintiff has secured the reversal of a directed verdict, see *Hanrahan*, supra, at 759, or acquired a judicial pronouncement that the defendant has violated the Constitution unaccompanied by "*judicial* relief," *Hewitt*, supra, at 760 (emphasis added). Never have we awarded attorney's fees for a nonjudicial "alteration of actual circumstances." While urging an expansion of our precedents on this front, the dissenters would simultaneously abrogate the "merit" requirement of our prior cases and award attorney's fees where the plaintiff's claim "was at least colorable" and "not . . . groundless." We cannot agree that the term "prevailing party" authorizes federal courts to award attorney's fees

---

7. We have subsequently characterized the *Maher* opinion as also allowing for an award of attorney's fees for private settlements. See *Farrar v. Hobby*, supra, at 111; *Hewitt v. Helms*, supra, at 760. But this dicta ignores that *Maher* only "held that fees *may* be assessed . . . after a case has been settled by the entry of a consent decree." Evans v. Jeff D., 475 U.S. 717, 720 (1986). Private settlements do not entail the judicial approval and oversight involved in consent decrees. And federal jurisdiction to enforce a private contractual settlement will often be lacking unless the terms of the agreement are incorporated into the order of dismissal.

to a plaintiff who, by simply filing a nonfrivolous but nonetheless potentially meritless lawsuit (it will never be determined), has reached the "sought-after destination" without obtaining any judicial relief.

Petitioners nonetheless argue that the legislative history of the Civil Rights Attorney's Fees Awards Act supports a broad reading of "prevailing party" which includes the "catalyst theory." We doubt that legislative history could overcome what we think is the rather clear meaning of "prevailing party"—the term actually used in the statute. Since we resorted to such history in *Garland*, 489 U.S. at 790, *Maher*, 448 U.S. at 129, and *Hanrahan*, 446 U.S. at 756–57, however, we do likewise here.

The House Report to § 1988 states that "the phrase 'prevailing party' is not intended to be limited to the victor only after entry of a final judgment following a full trial on the merits," H. R. Rep. No. 94–1558, p. 7 (1976), while the Senate Report explains that "parties may be considered to have prevailed when they vindicate rights through a consent judgment or without formally obtaining relief," S. Rep. No. 94–1011, p. 5 (1976). Petitioners argue that these Reports and their reference to a 1970 decision from the Court of Appeals for the Eighth Circuit, Parham v. Southwestern Bell Telephone Co., 433 F.2d 421 (1970), indicate Congress' intent to adopt the "catalyst theory."[9] We think the legislative history cited by petitioners is at best ambiguous as to the availability of the "catalyst theory" for awarding attorney's fees. Particularly in view of the "American Rule" that attorney's fees will not be awarded absent "explicit statutory authority," such legislative history is clearly insufficient to alter the accepted meaning of the statutory term.

Petitioners finally assert that the "catalyst theory" is necessary to prevent defendants from unilaterally mooting an action before judgment in an effort to avoid an award of attorney's fees. They also claim that the rejection of the "catalyst theory" will deter plaintiffs with meritorious but expensive cases from bringing suit. We are skeptical of these assertions, which are entirely speculative and unsupported by any empirical evidence (e.g., whether the number of suits brought in the Fourth Circuit has declined, in relation to other Circuits, since [that court rejected the catalyst theory]).

---

9. Although the Court of Appeals in *Parham* awarded attorney's fees to the plaintiff because his "lawsuit acted as a catalyst which prompted the [defendant] to take action ... seeking compliance with the requirements of Title VII," 433 F.2d at 429–30, it did so only after finding that the defendant had acted unlawfully, see id. at 426 ("We hold as a matter of law that [plaintiff's evidence] established a violation of Title VII"). Thus, consistent with our holding in *Farrar*, *Parham* stands for the proposition that an enforceable judgment permits an award of attorney's fees. And like the consent decree in *Maher v. Gagne*, supra, the Court of Appeals in *Parham* ordered the District Court to "retain jurisdiction over the matter for a reasonable period of time to insure the continued implementation of the appellee's policy of equal employment opportunities." 433 F.2d at 429. Clearly *Parham* does not support a theory of fee shifting untethered to a material alteration in the legal relationship of the parties as defined by our precedents.

Petitioners discount the disincentive that the "catalyst theory" may have upon a defendant's decision to voluntarily change its conduct, conduct that may not be illegal. "The defendants' potential liability for fees in this kind of litigation can be as significant as, and sometimes even more significant than, their potential liability on the merits," Evans v. Jeff D., 475 U.S. 717, 734 (1986), and the possibility of being assessed attorney's fees may well deter a defendant from altering its conduct.

And petitioners' fear of mischievous defendants only materializes in claims for equitable relief, for so long as the plaintiff has a cause of action for damages, a defendant's change in conduct will not moot the case. Even then, it is not clear how often courts will find a case mooted: "It is well settled that a defendant's voluntary cessation of a challenged practice does not deprive a federal court of its power to determine the legality of the practice" unless it is "absolutely clear that the allegedly wrongful behavior could not reasonably be expected to recur." Friends of Earth, Inc. v. Laidlaw Environmental Services (TOC), Inc., 528 U.S. 167, 189 (2000). If a case is not found to be moot, and the plaintiff later procures an enforceable judgment, the court may of course award attorney's fees. Given this possibility, a defendant has a strong incentive to enter a settlement agreement, where it can negotiate attorney's fees and costs.

We have also stated that "[a] request for attorney's fees should not result in a second major litigation," Hensley v. Eckerhart, 461 U.S. 424, 437 (1983), and have accordingly avoided an interpretation of the fee-shifting statutes that would have "spawned a second litigation of significant dimension," *Garland*, 489 U.S. at 791. Among other things, a "catalyst theory" hearing would require analysis of the defendant's subjective motivations in changing its conduct, an analysis that "will likely depend on a highly factbound inquiry and may turn on reasonable inferences from the nature and timing of the defendant's change in conduct." Brief for United States as Amicus Curiae 28. Although we do not doubt the ability of district courts to perform the nuanced "three thresholds" test required by the "catalyst theory"—whether the claim was colorable rather than groundless; whether the lawsuit was a substantial rather than an insubstantial cause of the defendant's change in conduct; whether the defendant's change in conduct was motivated by the plaintiff's threat of victory rather than threat of expense—it is clearly not a formula for "ready administrability." Burlington v. Dague, 505 U.S. 557, 566 (1992).

Given the clear meaning of "prevailing party" in the fee-shifting statutes, we need not determine which way these various policy arguments cut. In *Alyeska*, 421 U.S. at 260, we said that Congress had not "extended any roving authority to the Judiciary to allow counsel fees as costs or otherwise whenever the courts might deem them warranted." To disregard the clear legislative language and the holdings of our prior cases on the basis of such policy arguments would be a similar assumption of a "roving authority." For the reasons stated above, we hold that the "catalyst theory" is not a permissible basis for the award of attorney's fees under the FHAA, 42 U.S.C. § 3613(c)(2), and ADA, 42 U.S.C. § 12205.

■ JUSTICE SCALIA with whom JUSTICE THOMAS joins, concurring.

I join the opinion of the Court in its entirety, and write to respond at greater length to the contentions of the dissent.

I

"Prevailing party" is not some newfangled legal term invented for use in late–20th-century fee-shifting statutes. . . .

At the time 42 U.S.C. § 1988 was enacted, I know of no case, state or federal, in which—either under a statutory invocation of "prevailing party," or under the common-law rule—the "catalyst theory" was enunciated as the basis for awarding costs. . . . While . . . costs were awarded in actions at law to the "prevailing party," an equity court could award costs "as the equities of the case might require." The other state or state-law cases the dissent cites as awarding costs despite the absence of a judgment all involve a judicial finding—or its equivalent, an acknowledgement by the defendant—of the merits of plaintiff's case. Moreover, the dissent cites not a single case in which this Court—or even any other federal court applying federal law prior to enactment of the fee-shifting statutes at issue here—has regarded as the "prevailing party" a litigant who left the courthouse emptyhanded. If the term means what the dissent contends, that is a remarkable absence of authority.

That a judicial finding of liability was an understood requirement of "prevailing" is confirmed by many statutes that use the phrase in a context that *presumes* the existence of a judicial ruling. See, e.g., 5 U.S.C. § 1221(g)(2) ("if an employee . . . is the prevailing party . . . and the decision is based on a finding of a prohibited personnel practice"); 8 U.S.C. § 1324b(h) (permitting the administrative law judge to award an attorney's fee to the prevailing party "if the losing party's argument is without reasonable foundation in law and fact").

The dissent points out that the Prison Litigation Reform Act of 1995 limits attorney's fees to an amount " 'proportionately related to the court ordered relief for the violation.' " This shows that *sometimes* Congress *does* explicitly "tightly bind fees to judgments," inviting (the dissent believes) the conclusion that "prevailing party" does *not* fasten fees to judgments. That conclusion does not follow from the premise. What this statutory provision demonstrates, *at most*, is that use of the phrase "prevailing party" is not the *only* way to impose a requirement of court-ordered relief. That is assuredly true. But it would be no more rational to reject the normal meaning of "prevailing party" because some statutes produce the same result with different language, than it would be to conclude that, since there are many synonyms for the word "jump," the word "jump" must mean something else.

[W]hen "prevailing party" is used by courts or legislatures in the context of a lawsuit, it is a term of art. It has traditionally—and to my knowledge, prior to enactment of the first of the statutes at issue here, *invariably*—meant the party that wins the suit or obtains a finding (or an admission) of liability. Not the party that ultimately gets his way because his adversary dies before the suit comes to judgment; not the party that gets his way because circumstances so change that a victory on the legal point for the other side turns out to be a practical victory for him; and not the party that gets his way because the other side ceases (for whatever reason) its offensive conduct. If a nuisance suit is mooted because the defendant asphalt plant has gone bankrupt and ceased operations, one would not normally call the plaintiff the prevailing party. And it would make no difference, as far as the propriety of that characterization is concerned, if the plant did not go bankrupt but moved to a new location to avoid the expense of litigation. In one sense the plaintiff would have "prevailed"; but he would not be the prevailing party in the lawsuit. ...

II

The dissent distorts the term "prevailing party" beyond its normal meaning for policy reasons, but even those seem to me misguided. They rest upon the presumption that the catalyst theory applies when *"the suit's merit* led the defendant to abandon the fray, to switch rather than fight on, to accord plaintiff sooner rather than later the principal redress sought in the complaint,"* (emphasis added). What the dissent's stretching of the term produces is ... an award of attorney's fees when the merits of plaintiff's case remain unresolved—when, for all one knows, the defendant only "abandoned the fray" because the cost of litigation—either financial or in terms of public relations—would be too great. In such a case, the plaintiff may have "prevailed" as Webster's defines that term—"gained victory by virtue of strength or superiority." But I doubt it was greater strength in financial resources, or superiority in media manipulation, rather than *superiority in legal merit*, that Congress intended to reward.
...

It could be argued, perhaps, that insofar as abstract justice is concerned, there is little to choose between the dissent's outcome and the Court's: If the former sometimes rewards the plaintiff with a phony claim (there is no way of knowing), the latter sometimes denies fees to the plaintiff with a solid case whose adversary slinks away on the eve of judgment. But it seems to me the evil of the former far outweighs the evil of the latter. There is all the difference in the world between a rule that denies the extraordinary boon of attorney's fees to some plaintiffs who are no less "deserving" of them than others who receive them, and a rule that causes the law to be the very instrument of wrong—exacting the payment of attorney's fees to the extortionist.

It is true that monetary settlements and consent decrees can be extorted as well, and we have approved the award of attorney's fees in cases resolved through such mechanisms. Our decision that the statute makes plaintiff a "prevailing party" under such circumstances was based entirely on language in a House Report, see *Maher v. Gagne*, 448 U.S. at 129, and if this issue were to arise for the first time today, I doubt whether I would agree with that result. But in the case of court-approved settlements and consent decrees, even if there has been no judicial determination of the merits, the outcome is at least the product of, and bears the sanction of, judicial action *in the lawsuit*. There is at least *some* basis for saying that the party favored by the settlement or decree prevailed *in the suit*. Extending the holding of *Maher* to a case in which no judicial action whatever has been taken stretches the term "prevailing party" (and the potential injustice that *Maher* produces) beyond what the normal meaning of that term in the litigation context can conceivably support. ...

III

... The Court today concludes that a party cannot be deemed to have prevailed, for purposes of fee-shifting statutes such as 42 U.S.C. §§ 1988, 3613(c)(2), unless there has been an enforceable "alteration of the legal relationship of the parties." That is the normal meaning of "prevailing party" in litigation, and there is no proper basis for departing from that normal meaning. Congress is free, of course, to revise these provisions—but it is my guess that if it does so it will not create the sort of inequity that the catalyst theory invites, but will require the court to determine that there was at least a substantial likelihood that the party requesting fees would have prevailed.

■ Justice Ginsburg, with whom Justice Stevens, Justice Souter, and Justice Breyer, joint, dissenting.

... The Court's insistence that there be a document filed in court—a litigated judgment or court-endorsed settlement—upsets long-prevailing Circuit precedent applicable to scores of federal fee-shifting statutes. The decision allows a defendant to escape a statutory obligation to pay a plaintiff's counsel fees, even though the suit's merit led the defendant to abandon the fray, to switch rather than fight on, to accord plaintiff sooner rather than later the principal redress sought in the complaint. Concomitantly, the Court's constricted definition of "prevailing party," and consequent rejection of the "catalyst theory," impede access to court for the less well-heeled, and shrink the incentive Congress created for the enforcement of federal law by private attorneys general. ...

I

[Petitioners' original complaint] sought an immediate order stopping defendants from closing Buckhannon' facilities, injunctive relief permanently barring enforcement of the self-preservation requirement, damages, and attorney's fees. . . .

Less than a month after the District Court found that plaintiffs were entitled to a trial, the West Virginia Legislature repealed the [rule petitioners were challenging.] Plaintiffs still allege, and seek to prove, that their suit triggered the statutory repeal. After the rule's demise, defendants moved to dismiss the case as moot, and plaintiffs sought attorney's fees as "prevailing parties" under the FHAA, 42 U.S.C. § 613(c)(2), and the ADA, 42 U.S.C. § 2205. . . .

Prior to 1994, every Federal Court of Appeals (except the Federal Circuit, which had not addressed the issue) concluded that plaintiffs in situations like Buckhannon's . . . could obtain a fee award if their suit acted as a "catalyst" for the change they sought, even if they did not obtain a judgment or consent decree. . . .

In 1994, the Fourth Circuit en banc, dividing 6-to-5, broke ranks with its sister courts. The court declared that, in light of Farrar v. Hobby, 506 U.S. 103 (1992), a plaintiff could not become a "prevailing party" without "an enforceable judgment, consent decree, or settlement." As the Court today acknowledges, and as we have previously observed, the language on which the Fourth Circuit relied was dictum: *Farrar* "involved no catalytic effect"; the issue plainly "was not presented for this Court's decision in *Farrar*." Friends of Earth, Inc. v. Laidlaw Environmental Services (TOC), Inc., 528 U.S. 167, 194 (2000). . . .

The array of federal court decisions applying the catalyst rule suggested three conditions necessary to a party's qualification as "prevailing" short of a favorable final judgment or consent decree. A plaintiff first had to show that the defendant provided "some of the benefit sought" by the lawsuit. Under most Circuits' precedents, a plaintiff had to demonstrate as well that the suit stated a genuine claim, i.e., one that was at least "colorable," not "frivolous, unreasonable, or groundless." Plaintiff finally had to establish that her suit was a "substantial" or "significant" cause of defendant's action providing relief. In some Circuits, to make this causation showing, plaintiff had to satisfy the trial court that the suit achieved results "by threat of victory," not "by dint of nuisance and threat of expense." . . .

II

. . . The Court today detects a "clear meaning" of the term prevailing party that has heretofore eluded the large majority of courts construing those words. "Prevailing party," today's opinion announces, means "one who has been awarded some relief by the court." The Court derives this "clear meaning" principally from Black's Law Dictionary, which defines a "prevailing party," in critical part, as one "in whose favor a judgment is rendered" (quoting Black's Law Dictionary 1145 (7th ed. 1999)).

One can entirely agree with Black's Law Dictionary that a party "in whose favor a judgment is rendered" prevails, and at the same time resist, as most Courts of Appeals have, any implication that *only* such a party may prevail. ... Notably, this Court did not refer to Black's Law Dictionary in Maher v. Gagne, 448 U.S. 122 (1980), which held that a consent decree could qualify a plaintiff as "prevailing." The Court explained:

> The fact that [plaintiff] prevailed through a settlement rather than through litigation does not weaken her claim to fees. Nothing in the language of [42 U.S.C.] § 1988 conditions the District Court's power to award fees on full litigation of the issues or on a judicial determination that the plaintiff's rights have been violated.

The spare "prevailing party" language of the fee-shifting provision applicable in *Maher*, and the similar wording of the fee-shifting provisions now before the Court, contrast with prescriptions that so tightly bind fees to judgments as to exclude the application of a catalyst concept. The Prison Litigation Reform Act of 1995, for example, directs that fee awards to prisoners under § 1988 be "proportionately related to the *court ordered relief* for the violation." 42 U.S.C. § 1997e(d)(1)(B)(i) (1994 ed., Supp. IV) (emphasis added). That statute, by its express terms, forecloses an award to a prisoner on a catalyst theory. But the FHAA and ADA fee-shifting prescriptions, modeled on 42 U.S.C. § 1988 unmodified, do not similarly staple fee awards to "court ordered relief." Their very terms do not foreclose a catalyst theory. ...

Recognizing that no practice set in stone, statute, rule, or precedent dictates the proper construction of modern civil rights fee-shifting prescriptions, I would "assume ... that Congress intends the words in its enactments to carry 'their ordinary, contemporary, common meaning.'" In everyday use, "prevail" means "gain victory by virtue of strength or superiority: win mastery: triumph." Webster's Third New International Dictionary 1797 (1976). There are undoubtedly situations in which an individual's goal is to obtain approval of a judge, and in those situations, one cannot "prevail" short of a judge's formal declaration. In a piano competition or a figure skating contest, for example, the person who prevails is the person declared winner by the judges. However, where the ultimate goal is not an arbiter's approval, but a favorable alteration of actual circumstances, a formal declaration is not essential. Western democracies, for instance, "prevailed" in the Cold War even though the Soviet Union never formally surrendered. Among television viewers, John F. Kennedy "prevailed" in the first debate with Richard M. Nixon during the 1960 Presidential contest, even though moderator Howard K. Smith never declared a winner. See T. White, The Making of the President 1960, pp. 293–94 (1961).

A lawsuit's ultimate purpose is to achieve actual relief from an opponent. Favorable judgment may be instrumental in gaining that relief. Generally, however, "the judicial decree is not the end but the means. At the end of the rainbow lies not a judgment, but some action (or cessation of action) by the defendant...." Hewitt v. Helms, 482 U.S. 755, 761 (1987). On this common understanding, if a party reaches the "sought-after destination," then the party "prevails" regardless of the "route taken." Hennigan v. Ouachita Parish School Bd., 749 F.2d 1148, 1153 (5th Cir. 1985).

Under a fair reading of the FHAA and ADA provisions in point, I would hold that a party "prevails" in "a true and proper sense" when she achieves, by instituting litigation, the practical relief sought in her complaint....

III

As the Courts of Appeals have long recognized, the catalyst rule suitably advances Congress' endeavor to place private actions, in civil rights and other legislatively defined areas, securely within the federal law enforcement arsenal....

Under the catalyst rule that held sway until today, plaintiffs who obtained the relief they sought through suit on genuine claims ordinarily qualified as "prevailing parties," so that courts had discretion to award them their costs and fees. Persons with limited resources were not impelled to "wage total law" in order to assure that their counsel fees would be paid. They could accept relief, in money or of another kind, voluntarily proffered by a defendant who sought to avoid a recorded decree. And they could rely on a judge then to determine, in her equitable discretion, whether counsel fees were warranted and, if so, in what amount.[10]

Congress appears to have envisioned that very prospect. The Senate Report on the 1976 Civil Rights Attorney's Fees Awards Act states: "For purposes of the award of counsel fees, parties may be considered to have prevailed when they vindicate rights through a consent judgment or *without formally obtaining relief.*" S. Rep. No. 94–1011, at 5 (emphasis added). In support, the Report cites cases in which parties recovered fees in the absence of any court-conferred relief. The House Report corroborates: "After a complaint is filed, a defendant might voluntarily cease the unlawful practice. *A court should still award fees* even though it might conclude, as a matter of equity, that *no formal relief,* such as an injunction, is needed." H. R. Rep. No. 94–1558, at 7 (emphases added). These Reports ...

---

10. Given the protection furnished by the catalyst rule, aggrieved individuals were not left to worry, and wrongdoers were not led to believe, that strategic maneuvers by defendants might succeed in averting a fee award. Apt here is Judge Friendly's observation construing a fee-shifting statute kin to the provisions before us: "Congress clearly did not mean that where a [Freedom of Information Act] suit had gone to trial and developments have made it apparent that the judge was about to rule for the plaintiff, the Government could abort any award of attorney fees by an eleventh hour tender of information." Vermont Low Income Advocacy Council v. Usery, 546 F.2d 509, 513 (2d Cir. 1976) (interpreting 5 U.S.C. § 552(a)(4)(E), allowing a complainant who "substantially prevails" to earn an attorney's fee).

are hardly ambiguous. ... Congress, I am convinced, understood that " 'victory' in a civil rights suit is typically a practical, rather than a strictly legal matter." Exeter–West Greenwich Regional School Dist. v. Pontarelli, 788 F.2d 47, 51 (1st Cir.1986) (citation omitted).

The Court features a case cited by the House as well as the Senate in the Reports on § 1988, Parham v. Southwestern Bell Tel. Co., 433 F.2d 421 (8th Cir.1970). The Court deems *Parham* consistent with its rejection of the catalyst rule, alternately because the Eighth Circuit made a "finding that the defendant had acted unlawfully," and because that court ordered the District Court to " 'retain jurisdiction over the matter ... to insure the continued implementation of the [defendant's] policy of equal employment opportunities.' " Congress did not fix on those factors, however: Nothing in either Report suggests that judicial findings or retention of jurisdiction is essential to an award of fees. ...

IV

The Court identifies several "policy arguments" that might warrant rejection of the catalyst rule. A defendant might refrain from altering its conduct, fearing liability for fees as the price of voluntary action. Moreover, rejection of the catalyst rule has limited impact: Desisting from the challenged conduct will not render a case moot where damages are sought, and even when the plaintiff seeks only equitable relief, a defendant's voluntary cessation of a challenged practice does not render the case moot "unless it is 'absolutely clear that the allegedly wrongful behavior could not reasonably be expected to recur' " (quoting *Friends of Earth, Inc.*, 528 U.S. at 189). Because a mootness dismissal is not easily achieved, the defendant may be impelled to settle, negotiating fees less generous than a court might award. Finally, a catalyst rule would "require analysis of the defendant's subjective motivations," and thus protract the litigation.

The Court declines to look beneath the surface of these arguments, placing its reliance, instead, on a meaning of "prevailing party" that other jurists would scarcely recognize as plain. Had the Court inspected the "policy arguments" listed in its opinion, I doubt it would have found them impressive.

In opposition to the argument that defendants will resist change in order to stave off an award of fees, one could urge that the catalyst rule may lead defendants promptly to comply with the law's requirements: the longer the litigation, the larger the fees. Indeed, one who knows noncompliance will be expensive might be encouraged to conform his conduct to the legal requirements before litigation is threatened. No doubt, a mootness dismissal is unlikely when recurrence of the controversy is under the defendant's control. But, as earlier observed, why should this Court's fee-shifting rulings drive a plaintiff prepared to accept adequate relief, though out-of-court and unrecorded, to litigate on and on? And if the catalyst rule leads defendants to negotiate not only settlement terms but also allied counsel fees, is that not a consummation to applaud, not deplore?

As to the burden on the court, is it not the norm for the judge to whom the case has been assigned to resolve fee disputes (deciding whether an award is in order, and if it is, the amount due), thereby clearing the case from the calendar? If factfinding becomes necessary under the catalyst rule, is it not the sort that "the district courts, in their factfinding expertise, deal with on a regular basis"? Might not one conclude overall, as Courts of Appeals have suggested, that the catalyst rule "saves judicial resources," by encouraging "plaintiffs to discontinue litigation after receiving through the defendant's acquiescence the remedy initially sought"?

The concurring opinion adds another argument against the catalyst rule: That opinion sees the rule as accommodating the "extortionist" who obtains relief because of "greater strength in financial resources, or superiority in media manipulation, rather than superiority in legal merit." This concern overlooks both the character of the rule and the judicial superintendence Congress ordered for all fee allowances. The catalyst rule was auxiliary to fee-shifting statutes whose primary purpose is "to promote the vigorous enforcement" of the civil rights laws. *Christiansburg Garment Co.*, 434 U.S. at 422. To that end, courts deemed the conduct-altering catalyst that counted to be the substance of the case, not merely the plaintiff's atypically superior financial resources, media ties, or political clout. And Congress assigned responsibility for awarding fees not to automatons unable to recognize extortionists, but to judges expected and instructed to exercise "discretion." So viewed, the catalyst rule provided no berth for nuisance suits or "thinly disguised forms of extortion," Tyler v. Corner Constr. Corp., 167 F.3d 1202, 1206 (8th Cir.1999) (citation omitted).[12]

V

As to our attorney fee precedents, the Court correctly observes, "we have never had occasion to decide whether the term 'prevailing party' allows an award of fees under the 'catalyst theory,'" and "there is language in our cases supporting both petitioners and respondents." It bears emphasis, however, that in determining whether fee shifting is in order, the Court in the past has placed greatest weight not on any "judicial imprimatur," but on the practical impact of the lawsuit.[13] In *Maher v.*

---

12. ... The concurring opinion ... states that a prevailing party must obtain relief *"in the lawsuit."* One can demur to that elaboration of the statutory text and still adhere to the catalyst rule. Under the rule, plaintiff's suit raising genuine issues must trigger the defendant's voluntary action; plaintiff will not prevail under the rule if defendant "ceases ... [his] offensive conduct" by dying or going bankrupt. A behavior-altering event like dying or bankruptcy occurs outside the lawsuit; a change precipitated by the lawsuit's claims and demand for relief is an occurrence brought about "through" or "in" the suit.

13. To qualify for fees in any case, we have held, relief must be real. See Rhodes v. Stewart, 488 U.S. 1, 4 (1988) (per curiam) (a plaintiff who obtains a formal declaratory

Gagne, supra, in which the Court held fees could be awarded on the basis of a consent decree, the opinion nowhere relied on the presence of a formal judgment. Some years later, in *Hewitt v. Helms*, supra, the Court suggested that fees might be awarded the plaintiff who "obtained relief without [the] benefit of a formal judgment." 482 U.S. at 760. The Court explained: "If the defendant, under the pressure of the lawsuit, pays over a money claim before the judicial judgment is pronounced," or "if the defendant, under pressure of [a suit for declaratory judgment], alters his conduct (or threatened conduct) towards the plaintiff," i.e., conduct "that was the basis for the suit, the plaintiff will have prevailed." I agree, and would apply that analysis to this case.

The Court posits a " 'merit' requirement of our prior cases." *Maher*, however, affirmed an award of attorney's fees based on a consent decree that "did not purport to adjudicate [plaintiff's] statutory or constitutional claims." 448 U.S. at 126 n.8. The decree in *Maher* "explicitly stated that 'nothing [therein was] intended to constitute an admission of fault by either party.' " Ibid. The catalyst rule, in short, conflicts with none of "our prior *holdings*."[14]

* * *

judgment, but gains no real "relief whatsoever," is not a "prevailing party" eligible for fees); *Hewitt v. Helms*, 482 U.S. at 761 (an interlocutory decision reversing a dismissal for failure to state a claim, although stating that plaintiff's rights were violated, does not entitle plaintiff to fees; to "prevail," plaintiff must gain relief of "substance," i.e., more than a favorable "judicial statement that does not affect the relationship between the plaintiff and the defendant").

14. The Court repeatedly quotes passages from *Hanrahan v. Hampton*, 446 U.S. at 757–58, stating that to "prevail," plaintiffs must receive relief "on the merits." Nothing in *Hanrahan*, however, declares that relief "on the merits" requires a "judicial imprimatur." As the Court acknowledges, *Hanrahan* concerned an interim award of fees, after plaintiff succeeded in obtaining nothing more than reversal of a directed verdict. At that juncture, plaintiff had obtained no change in defendant's behavior, and the suit's ultimate winner remained undetermined. There is simply no inconsistency between *Hanrahan*, denying fees when a plaintiff might yet obtain no real benefit, and the catalyst rule, allowing fees when a plaintiff obtains the practical result she sought in suing. Indeed, the harmony between the catalyst rule and *Hanrahan* is suggested by *Hanrahan* itself; like Maher v. Gagne, 448 U.S. 122, 129 (1980), *Hanrahan* quoted the Senate Report recognizing that parties may prevail "through a consent judgment *or* without formally obtaining relief." 446 U.S. at 757 (quoting S. Rep. No. 94–1011, at 5) (emphasis added). *Hanrahan* also selected for citation the influential elaboration of the catalyst rule in *Nadeau v. Helgemoe*, 581 F.2d at 279–81. See 446 U.S. at 757.

The Court additionally cites Texas State Teachers Assn. v. Garland Independent School Dist., 489 U.S. 782 (1989), which held, unanimously, that a plaintiff could become a "prevailing party" without obtaining relief on the "central issue in the suit." Id. at 790. *Texas State Teachers* linked fee awards to a "material alteration of the legal relationship of the parties," id. at 792–93, but did not say, as the Court does today, that the change must be "court-ordered." The parties' legal relationship does change when the defendant stops engaging in the conduct that furnishes the basis for plaintiff's civil action, and that action, which both parties would otherwise have litigated, is dismissed.

The decision with language most unfavorable to the catalyst rule, Farrar v. Hobby,

The Court states that the term "prevailing party" in fee-shifting statutes has an "accepted meaning." If that is so, the "accepted meaning" is not the one the Court today announces. It is, instead, the meaning accepted by every Court of Appeals to address the catalyst issue before our 1987 decision in *Hewitt*, and disavowed since then only by the Fourth Circuit. A plaintiff prevails, federal judges have overwhelmingly agreed, when a litigated judgment, consent decree, out-of-court settlement, or the defendant's voluntary, postcomplaint payment or change in conduct in fact affords redress for the plaintiff's substantial grievances.

When this Court rejects the considered judgment prevailing in the Circuits, respect for our colleagues demands a cogent explanation. Today's decision does not provide one. The Court's narrow construction of the words "prevailing party" is unsupported by precedent and unaided by history or logic. Congress prescribed fee-shifting provisions like those included in the FHAA and ADA to encourage private enforcement of laws designed to advance civil rights. Fidelity to that purpose calls for court-awarded fees when a private party's lawsuit, whether or not its settlement is registered in court, vindicates rights Congress sought to secure. I would so hold and therefore dissent from the judgment and opinion of the Court.

Page 373, add at the end of the Note on Risk Enhancement:

For another sophisticated economic analysis of risk enhancement and alternatives, see Richard Craswell, Deterrence and Damages: The Multiplier Principle and Its Alternatives, 97 Mich. L. Rev. 2185 (1999) (concluding that the traditional multiplier can achieve optimal deterrence "only if the multiplier is calculated on a case-by-case basis" and undertaking analysis of more plausible alternatives).

Page 403, add a new Note:

NOTE ON TAXATION OF ATTORNEY'S FEES

Section 1988(b) provides, in pertinent part, that courts may "allow the prevailing party . . . a reasonable attorney's fee." As the opinion in *Jeff D.* suggests, the entitlement to fees is vested in the litigant, not in the attorney. In the 1990s, an issue arose concerning the tax consequences of this allocation. Is the portion of an award payable as attorney's fees included in the litigant's adjusted gross income? In many cases, the additional income would in any event be offset by a miscellaneous itemized deduction, but such deductions are not available under the Alternative

506 U.S. 103 (1992), does not figure prominently in the Court's opinion—and for good reason, for *Farrar* "involved no catalytic effect." *Farrar* held that a plaintiff who sought damages of $17 million, but received damages of $1, was a "prevailing party" nonetheless not entitled to fees. 506 U.S. at 113–16. In reinforcing the link between the right to a fee award and the "degree of success obtained," id. at 114 (quoting *Hensley v. Eckerhart*, 461 U.S. at 436), *Farrar*'s holding is consistent with the catalyst rule.

Minimum Tax. For taxpayers subject to the AMT, inclusion of attorney's fees in the litigant's taxable income can have a major impact on tax liability.

In Commissioner of Internal Revenue v. Banks, 541 U.S. 958 (2005), the Supreme Court confronted the closely analogous question of a litigant's tax liability for the portion of a settlement or judgment paid to the attorney as a contingent fee. The Court held that, "as a general rule, when a litigant's recovery constitutes income, the litigant's income includes the portion of the recovery paid to the attorney as a contingent fee." The Court, however, noted at least a possibility that court-ordered fee awards might be treated differently.

In any event, the issue is not likely to have continuing significance. The American Jobs Creation Act of 2004 added § 62(a)(19) to the Internal Revenue Code. That amendment allows a taxpayer, whether or not subject to the AMT, to deduct "attorney's fees and court costs paid by, or on behalf of, the taxpayer in connection with any action involving a claim of unlawful discrimination." Elsewhere, "unlawful discrimination" is defined to include any law "providing for the enforcement of civil rights." It seems likely that this provision covers all, or almost all, cases of attorney's fees under § 1988. The statute is not retroactive and therefore had no application to *Banks*.

CHAPTER III

ADMINISTRATION OF THE CIVIL RIGHTS ACTS: INTERSECTIONS OF STATE AND FEDERAL LAW

Page 418, add a footnote at the end of the first paragraph of Note 1:

a. The Prison Litigation Reform Act imposes an exhaustion requirement on § 1983 suits "brought with respect to prison conditions ... by a prisoner confined in any jail, prison, or other correctional facility." No such actions can be brought "until such administrative remedies as are available are exhausted." 42 U.S.C. § 1997e(a). For consideration of what should happen "when a prisoner makes a misstep in the course of exhaustion," see Kermit Roosevelt III, Exhaustion under the Prison Litigation Reform Act: The Consequence of Procedural Error, 52 Emory L.J. 1771 (2003).

Page 419, add a footnote at the end of Note 1:

a. There are some § 1983 actions for which Congress has required exhaustion of administrative remedies. The Prison Litigation Reform Act provides that "[n]o action shall be brought with respect to prison conditions under [§ 1983] by a prisoner confined in any jail, prison, or other correctional facility until such administrative remedies as are available are exhausted." 42 U.S.C. § 1997e. In Booth v. Churner, 532 U.S. 731 (2001), and Porter v. Nussle, 534 U.S. 516 (2002), the Court gave this provision an expansive reading. In *Booth*, the Court held that § 1997e demands exhaustion of administrative remedies even when the prisoner seeks only damages and that remedy is not available in the grievance process. In *Porter*, the Court held that exhaustion is required for all lawsuits by inmates, including those that involve particular episodes rather than general conditions. An allegation of excessive force by prison guards was thus construed to be a claim about "prison conditions." The Court saw no congressional intent to "bisect the universe of prison suits" into those requiring exhaustion and those allowing by-pass of administrative remedies.

Page 437, add a new Note:

3a. *Nelson v. Campbell.* Nelson v. Campbell, 541 U.S. 637 (2004), involved the following problem:

> Three days before his scheduled execution by lethal injection, petitioner David Nelson filed a civil rights action in District Court, pursuant to 42 U.S.C. § 1983, alleging that the use of a "cutdown" procedure to access his veins would violate the Eighth Amendment. Petitioner, who had already filed one unsuccessful federal habeas application, sought a stay of execution so that the District Court could consider the merits of his constitutional claim. The question before us is whether § 1983 is an appropriate vehicle

for petitioner's Eighth Amendment claim seeking a temporary stay and permanent injunctive relief.

The Circuit Court held that the claim sounded in habeas, and dismissed because it was a repetitive application that fit no exception allowing it to go forward. "Thus," the Supreme Court noted, "the 11th Circuit held that petitioner was without recourse to challenge the constitutionality of the cut-down procedure in Federal District Court."

In an opinion by Justice O'Connor, the Supreme Court held unanimously that the petitioner's § 1983 claim could go forward. Because petitioner had compromised veins due to years of drug abuse, unusual medical procedures were necessary in order to carry out the execution. Petitioner's claim carefully stated that he was not objecting to the fact of execution by legal injection, but only to the particular "cut-down" procedure by which it was proposed to be administered.[b] The Court responded:

> We have not yet had occasion to consider whether civil rights suits seeking to enjoin the use of a particular method of execution—e.g., lethal injection or electrocution—fall within the core of federal habeas corpus or, rather, whether they are properly viewed as challenges to the conditions of a condemned inmate's death sentence. Neither the "conditions" nor the "fact or duration" label is particularly apt. A suit seeking to enjoin a particular means of effectuating a sentence of death does not directly call into question the "fact" or "validity" of the sentence itself—by simply altering its method of execution, the State can go forward with the sentence. On the other hand, imposition of the death penalty presupposes a means of carrying it out. In a State such as Alabama, where the legislature has established lethal injection as the preferred method of execution, a constitutional challenge seeking to permanently enjoin the use of lethal injection may amount to a challenge to the fact of the sentence itself. A finding of unconstitutionality would require statutory amendment or variance, imposing significant costs on the State and the administration of its penal system. And while it makes little sense to talk of the "duration" of a death sentence, a State retains a significant interest in meting out a sentence of death in a timely fashion.

---

b. At one point, petitioner was told that "prison personnel would ... make a 2-inch incision in petitioner's arm or leg; the procedure would take place one hour before the scheduled execution; and only local anesthesia would be used. There was no assurance that a physician would perform or even be present for the procedure." By contrast, petitioner submitted an affidavit from a reputable physician to the effect that "the cut-down is a dangerous and antiquated medical procedure to be performed only by a trained physician in a clinical environment with the patient under deep sedation. In light of safer and less-invasive contemporary means of venous access, [the Doctor] concluded that 'there is no comprehensible reason for the State of Alabama to be planning to employ the cut-down procedure to obtain intravenous access, unless there exists an intent to render the procedure more painful and risky than it otherwise needs to be.'"

We need not reach here the difficult question of how to categorize method-of-execution claims generally. Respondents at oral argument conceded that § 1983 would be an appropriate vehicle for an inmate who is not facing execution to bring a "deliberate indifference" challenge to the constitutionality of the cut-down procedure if used to gain venous access for purposes of providing medical treatment. Tr. of Oral Arg. 40 ("I don't disagree ... that a cut-down occurring for purposes of venous access, wholly divorced from an execution, is indeed a valid conditions of confinement claim"); see also Estelle v. Gamble, 429 U.S. 97, 104 (1976) ("We therefore conclude that deliberate indifference to serious medical needs of prisoners constitutes the 'unnecessary and wanton infliction of pain' proscribed by the Eighth Amendment"). We see no reason on the face of the complaint to treat petitioner's claim differently solely because he has been condemned to die.

Respondents counter that, because the cut-down is part of the execution procedure, petitioner's challenge is, in fact, a challenge to the fact of his execution. They offer the following argument: A challenge to the use of lethal injection as a method of execution sounds in habeas; venous access is a necessary prerequisite to, and thus an indispensable part of, any lethal injection procedure; therefore, a challenge to the State's means of achieving venous access must be brought in a federal habeas application. Even were we to accept as given respondents' premise that a challenge to lethal injection sounds in habeas, the conclusion does not follow. That venous access is a necessary prerequisite does not imply that a particular means of gaining such access is likewise necessary. Indeed, the gravamen of petitioner's entire claim is that use of the cut-down would be *gratuitous*. Merely labeling something as part of an execution procedure is insufficient to insulate it from a § 1983 attack.

If as a legal matter the cut-down were a statutorily mandated part of the lethal injection protocol, or if as a factual matter petitioner were unable or unwilling to concede acceptable alternatives for gaining venous access, respondents might have a stronger argument that success on the merits, coupled with injunctive relief, would call into question the death sentence itself. But petitioner has been careful throughout these proceedings, in his complaint and at oral argument, to assert that the cut-down, as well as the warden's refusal to provide reliable information regarding the cut-down protocol, are *wholly unnecessary* to gaining venous access. Petitioner has alleged alternatives that, if they had been used, would have allowed the State to proceed with the execution as scheduled. App. 17 (complaint) (proffering as "less invasive, less painful, faster, cheaper, and safer" the alternative

> procedure of "percutaneous central line placement"); id., at 37–38 (affidavit of Dr. Mark Heath) (describing relative merits of the cut-down and percutaneous central line placement). No Alabama statute requires use of the cut-down and respondents have offered no duly-promulgated regulations to the contrary.
>
> If on remand and after an evidentiary hearing the District Court concludes that use of the cut-down procedure as described in the complaint is necessary for administering the lethal injection, the District Court will need to address the broader question, left open here, of how to treat method-of-execution claims generally. An evidentiary hearing will in all likelihood be unnecessary, however, as the State now seems willing to implement petitioner's proposed alternatives. See Tr. of Oral Arg. 45–46 ("I think there is no disagreement here that percutaneous central line placement is the preferred method and will, in fact, be used, a cut-down to be used only if actually necessary").
>
> We note that our holding here is consistent with our approach to civil rights damages actions, which, like method-of-execution challenges, fall at the margins of habeas. Although damages are not an available habeas remedy, we have previously concluded that a § 1983 suit for damages that would "necessarily imply" the invalidity of the fact of an inmate's conviction, or "necessarily imply" the invalidity of the length of an inmate's sentence, is not cognizable under § 1983 unless and until the inmate obtains favorable termination of a state, or federal habeas, challenge to his conviction or sentence. Heck v. Humphrey, 512 U.S. 477, 487 (1994); Edwards v. Balisok, 520 U.S. 641, 648 (1997). . . . In the present context, focusing attention on whether petitioner's challenge to the cut-down procedure would *necessarily* prevent Alabama from carrying out its execution both protects against the use of § 1983 to circumvent any limits imposed by the habeas statute and minimizes the extent to which the fact of a prisoner's imminent execution will require differential treatment of his otherwise cognizable § 1983 claims.

The Court also addressed the propriety of a stay of execution in contexts such as this, and emphasized the narrowness of its holding:

> Respondents argue that a decision to reverse the judgment of the 11th Circuit would open the floodgates to all manner of method-of-execution challenges, as well as last minute stay requests. But, because we do not here resolve the question of how to treat method-of-execution claims generally, our holding is extremely limited.
>
> Moreover, as our previous decision in Gomez v. United States Dist. Court for Northern Dist. of Cal., 503 U.S. 653 (1992) (per curiam), makes clear, the mere fact that an inmate states a

cognizable § 1983 claim does not warrant the entry of a stay as a matter of right. *Gomez* came to us on a motion by the State to vacate a stay entered by an en banc panel of the Court of Appeals for the Ninth Circuit that would have allowed the District Court time to consider the merits of a condemned inmate's last-minute § 1983 action challenging the constitutionality of California's use of the gas chamber. We left open the question whether the inmate's claim was cognizable under § 1983, but vacated the stay nonetheless. The inmate, Robert Alton Harris, who had already filed four unsuccessful federal habeas applications, waited until the 11th hour to file his challenge despite the fact that California's method of execution had been in place for years: "This claim could have been brought more than a decade ago. There is no good reason for this abusive delay, which has been compounded by last-minute attempts to manipulate the judicial process. A court may consider the last-minute nature of an application to stay execution in deciding whether to grant equitable relief."

A stay is an equitable remedy, and "[e]quity must take into consideration the State's strong interest in proceeding with its judgment and ... attempt[s] at manipulation." Thus, before granting a stay, a district court must consider not only the likelihood of success on the merits and the relative harms to the parties, but also the extent to which the inmate has delayed unnecessarily in bringing the claim. Given the State's significant interest in enforcing its criminal judgments, there is a strong equitable presumption against the grant of a stay where a claim could have been brought at such a time as to allow consideration of the merits without requiring entry of a stay.

Finally, the ability to bring a § 1983 claim, rather than a habeas application, does not entirely free inmates from substantive or procedural limitations. The Prison Litigation Reform Act of 1995 (Act) imposes limits on the scope and duration of preliminary and permanent injunctive relief, including a requirement that, before issuing such relief, "[a] court shall give substantial weight to any adverse impact on ... the operation of a criminal justice system caused by the relief." 18 U.S.C. § 3626(a)(1); accord, § 3626(a)(2). It requires that inmates exhaust available state administrative remedies before bringing a § 1983 action challenging the conditions of their confinement. 110 Stat. 1321–71, 42 U.S.C. § 1997e(a) ("No action shall be brought with respect to prison conditions under section 1983 of this title, or any other Federal law, by a prisoner confined in any jail, prison, or other correctional facility until such administrative remedies as are available are exhausted"). The Act mandates that a district court "shall," on its own motion, dismiss "any action brought with respect to prison conditions under section 1983 of this title ... if the court is satisfied that the action is frivolous, malicious, fails to state a claim upon which relief can be granted, or seeks monetary relief from a defendant who is immune from relief." § 1997e(c)(1). Indeed, if the claim is frivolous on its face, a district court may dismiss the suit before the plaintiff has exhausted his state remedies. § 1997e(c)(2).

Page 524, add a new Section 7 entitled "The Tax Injunction Act as a Limit on § 1983 Suits" at the end of Chapter 3:

Hibbs v. Winn

Supreme Court of the United States, 2004.
542 U.S. 88.

■ JUSTICE GINSBURG delivered the opinion of the Court.

Arizona law authorizes income-tax credits for payments to organizations that award educational scholarships and tuition grants to children attending private schools. See Ariz.Rev.Stat. Ann. § 43–1089 (West Supp. 2003). Plaintiffs below, respondents here, brought an action in federal court challenging § 43–1089, and seeking to enjoin its operation, on Establishment Clause grounds. The question presented is whether the Tax Injunction Act (TIA or Act), 28 U.S.C. § 1341, which prohibits a lower federal court from restraining "the assessment, levy or collection of any tax under State law," bars the suit. Plaintiffs-respondents do not contest their own tax liability. Nor do they seek to impede Arizona's receipt of tax revenues. Their suit, we hold, is not the kind § 1341 proscribes.

In decisions spanning a near half century, courts in the federal system, including this Court, have entertained challenges to tax credits authorized by state law, without conceiving of § 1341 as a jurisdictional barrier. On this first occasion squarely to confront the issue, we confirm the authority federal courts exercised in those cases.

It is hardly ancient history that States, once bent on maintaining racial segregation in public schools, and allocating resources disproportionately to benefit white students to the detriment of black students, fastened on tuition grants and tax credits as a promising means to circumvent Brown v. Board of Education, 347 U.S. 483 (1954). The federal courts, this Court among them, adjudicated the ensuing challenges, instituted under 42 U.S.C. § 1983, and upheld the Constitution's equal protection requirement. [Citations omitted.]

In the instant case, petitioner Hibbs, Director of Arizona's Department of Revenue, argues, in effect, that we and other federal courts were wrong in those civil-rights cases. The TIA, petitioner maintains, trumps § 1983; the Act, according to petitioner, bars all lower federal-court interference with state tax systems, even when the challengers are not endeavoring to avoid a tax imposed on them, and no matter whether the State's revenues would be raised or lowered should the plaintiffs prevail. The alleged jurisdictional bar, which petitioner asserts has existed since the TIA's enactment in 1937, was not even imagined by the jurists in the pathmarking civil-rights cases just cited, or by the defendants in those cases, litigants with every interest in defeating federal-court adjudicatory authority. Our prior decisions command no respect, petitioner urges, because they constitute mere "sub silentio holdings." We reject that assessment.

We examine in this opinion both the scope of the term "assessment" as used in the TIA, and the question whether the Act was intended to insulate state tax laws from constitutional challenge in lower federal courts even when the suit would have no negative impact on tax collection. Concluding that this suit implicates neither § 1341's conception of assessment nor any of the statute's underlying purposes, we affirm the judgment of the Court of Appeals.

I

Plaintiffs-respondents, Arizona taxpayers, filed suit in the United States District Court for the District of Arizona, challenging Ariz.Rev.Stat. Ann. § 43–1089 (West Supp.2003) as incompatible with the Establishment Clause. Section 43–1089 provides a credit to taxpayers who contribute money to "school tuition organizations" (STOs). An STO is a nonprofit organization that directs moneys, in the form of scholarship grants, to students enrolled in private elementary or secondary schools. STOs must disburse as scholarship grants at least 90 percent of contributions received, may allow donors to direct scholarships to individual students, may not allow donors to name their own dependents, must designate at least two schools whose students will receive funds, and must not designate schools that "discriminate on the basis of race, color, handicap, familial status or national origin." STOs are not precluded by Arizona's statute from designating schools that provide religious instruction or that give admissions preference on the basis of religion or religious affiliation. When taxpayers donate money to a qualified STO, § 43–1089 allows them, in calculating their Arizona tax liability, to credit up to $500 of their donation (or $625 for a married couple filing jointly).

In effect, § 43–1089 gives Arizona taxpayers an election. They may direct $500 (or, for joint-return filers, $625) to an STO, or to the Arizona Department of Revenue. As long as donors do not give STOs more than their total tax liability, their $500 or $625 contributions are costless.

The Arizona Supreme Court, by a 3-to-2 vote, rejected a facial challenge to § 43–1089 before the statute went into effect. That case took the form of a special discretionary action invoking the court's original jurisdiction. [This decision], it is undisputed, has no preclusive effect on the instant as-applied challenge to § 43–1089 brought by different plaintiffs.

Respondents' federal-court complaint against the Director of Arizona's Department of Revenue (Director) alleged that § 43–1089 "authorizes the formation of agencies that have as their sole purpose the distribution of

State funds to children of a particular religious denomination or to children attending schools of a particular religious denomination." Respondents sought injunctive and declaratory relief, and an order requiring STOs to pay funds still in their possession "into the state general fund."

The Director moved to dismiss the action, relying on the TIA, which reads in its entirety:

> The district courts shall not enjoin, suspend or restrain the assessment, levy or collection of any tax under State law where a plain, speedy and efficient remedy may be had in the courts of such State.

The Director did not assert that a federal-court order enjoining § 43–1089 would interfere with the State's tax levy or collection efforts. He urged only that a federal injunction would restrain the "assessment" of taxes "under State law." Agreeing with the Director, the District Court held that the TIA required dismissal of the suit.

The Court of Appeals for the Ninth Circuit reversed.... We granted certiorari in view of the division of opinion on whether the TIA bars constitutional challenges to state tax credits in federal court. We now affirm the judgment of the Ninth Circuit.

II

Before reaching the merits of this case, we must address respondents' contention that the Director's petition for certiorari was jurisdictionally untimely under 28 U.S.C. § 2101(c) and our Rules. [The Court held the petition timely.]

III

To determine whether this litigation falls within the TIA's prohibition, it is appropriate, first, to identify the relief sought. Respondents seek prospective relief only. Specifically, their complaint requests "injunctive relief prohibiting [the Director] from allowing taxpayers to utilize the tax credit authorized by A.R.S. § 43–1089 for payments made to STOs that make tuition grants to children attending religious schools, to children attending schools of only one religious denomination, or to children selected on the basis of their religion." Respondents further ask for a "declaration that A.R.S. § 43–1089, on its face and as applied," violates the Establishment Clause "by affirmatively authorizing STOs to use State income-tax revenues to pay tuition for students attending religious schools or schools that discriminate on the basis of religion." Finally, respondents seek "[a]n order that [the Director] inform all [such] STOs that ... all funds in their possession as of the date of this Court's order must be paid into the state general fund." Taking account of the prospective nature of the relief requested, does respondents' suit, in 28 U.S.C. § 1341's words, seek to "enjoin, suspend or restrain the assessment, levy or collection of any tax under State law"? The answer to that question turns on the meaning of the term "assessment" as employed in the TIA.¹

As used in the Internal Revenue Code (IRC), the term "assessment" involves a "recording" of the amount the taxpayer owes the Government. 26 U.S.C. § 6203. The "assessment" is "essentially a bookkeeping notation." Laing v. United States, 423 U.S. 161, 170 n.13 (1976). Section 6201(a) of the IRC authorizes the Secretary of the Treasury "to make . . . assessments of all taxes . . . imposed by this title." An assessment is made "by recording the liability of the taxpayer in the office of the Secretary in accordance with rules or regulations prescribed by the Secretary." § 6203.³

We do not focus on the word "assessment" in isolation, however. Instead, we follow "the cardinal rule that statutory language must be read in context [since] a phrase gathers meaning from the words around it." General Dynamics Land Systems, Inc. v. Cline, 540 U.S. ___, ___ (2004). In § 1341 and tax law generally, an assessment is closely tied to the collection of a tax, i.e., the assessment is the official recording of liability that triggers levy and collection efforts.

The rule against superfluities complements the principle that courts are to interpret the words of a statute in context. See 2A N. Singer, Statutes and Statutory Construction § 46.06, pp. 181–86 (rev. 6th ed. 2000) ("A statute should be construed so that effect is given to all its provisions, so that no part will be inoperative or superfluous, void or insignificant. . . ."). If, as the Director asserts, the term "assessment," by itself, signified "[t]he entire plan or scheme fixed upon for charging or taxing," the TIA would not need the words "levy" or "collection"; the term "assessment," alone, would do all the necessary work.

Earlier this Term, in United States v. Galletti, 541 U.S. ___ (2004), the Government identified "two important consequences" that follow from the IRS' timely tax assessment: "[T]he IRS may employ administrative enforcement methods such as tax liens and levies to collect the outstanding tax"; and "the time within which the IRS may collect the tax either administratively *or* by a 'proceeding in court' is extended [from 3 years] to 10 years after the date of assessment." The Government . . . made clear in briefing *Galletti* that, under the IRC definition, the tax "assessment" serves as the trigger for levy and collection efforts. The Government did

---

1. State taxation, for § 1341 purposes, includes local taxation.

3. The term "assessment" is used in a variety of ways in tax law. In the property-tax setting, the word usually refers to the process by which the taxing authority assigns a taxable value to real or personal property. To calculate the amount of property taxes owed, the tax assessor multiplies the assessed value by the appropriate tax rate. Income taxes, by contrast, are typically self-assessed in the United States. As anyone who has filed a tax return is unlikely to forget, the taxpayer, not the taxing authority, is the first party to make the relevant calculation of income taxes owed. The word "self-assessment," however, is not a technical term; as IRC § 6201(a) indicates, the Internal Revenue Service executes the formal act of income-tax assessment.

not describe the term as synonymous with the entire plan of taxation. Nor did it disassociate the word "assessment" from the company ("levy or collection") that word keeps.[4] Instead, and in accord with our understanding, the Government related "assessment" to the term's collection-propelling function.

IV

Congress modeled § 1341 upon earlier federal "statutes of similar import," laws that, in turn, paralleled state provisions proscribing "actions in State courts to enjoin the collection of State and county taxes." S.Rep. No. 1035, 75th Cong., 1st Sess., 1 (1937) (hereinafter S. Rep.). In composing the TIA's text, Congress drew particularly on an 1867 measure, sometimes called the Anti–Injunction Act (AIA), which bars "any court" from entertaining a suit brought "for the purpose of restraining the assessment or collection of any [federal] tax." Act of Mar. 2, 1867, ch. 169, § 10, 14 Stat. 475, now codified at 26 U.S.C. § 7421(a). See Jefferson County v. Acker, 527 U.S. 423, 434–35 (1999). While § 7421(a) "apparently has no recorded legislative history," Bob Jones Univ. v. Simon, 416 U.S. 725, 736 (1974), the Court has recognized, from the AIA's text, that the measure serves twin purposes: It responds to "the Government's need to assess and collect taxes as expeditiously as possible with a minimum of preenforcement judicial interference"; and it " 'require[s] that the legal right to the disputed sums be determined in a suit for refund,' " ibid.[5] Lower federal courts have similarly comprehended § 7421(a). See, e.g., McGlotten v. Connally, 338 F.Supp. 448, 453–454 (D.D.C. 1972) (three-judge court) (§ 7421(a) does not bar action seeking to enjoin income-tax exemptions to fraternal orders that exclude nonwhites from membership, for in such an action, plaintiff "does not contest the amount of his own tax, nor does he seek to limit the amount of tax revenue collectible by the United States"); Tax Analysts and Advocates v. Shultz, 376 F.Supp. 889, 892 (D.D.C.1974) (§ 7421(a) does not bar challenge to IRS revenue ruling allowing contributors to political candidate committees to avoid federal gift tax on contributions in excess of $3,000 ceiling; while § 7421(a) "precludes suits to restrain the assessment or collection of taxes," the proscription does not apply when "plaintiffs seek not to restrain the Commissioner from collecting taxes, but rather to *require* him to collect *additional* taxes according to the mandates of the law." (emphases in original)).

---

4. The dissent is of two minds in this regard. On the one hand, it twice suggests that a proper definition of the term "assessment," for § 1341 purposes, is "the entire plan or scheme fixed upon for charging or taxing." On the other hand, the dissent would disconnect the word from the enforcement process ("levy or collection") that "assessment" sets in motion.

5. That Congress had in mind challenges to assessments triggering collections, i.e., attempts to prevent the collection of revenue, is borne out by the final clause of 26 U.S.C. § 7421(a), added in 1966: "whether or not such person is the person *against whom* such tax was assessed" (emphasis added).

Just as the AIA shields federal tax collections from federal-court injunctions, so the TIA shields state tax collections from federal-court restraints. In both 26 U.S.C. § 7421(a) and 28 U.S.C. § 1341, Congress directed taxpayers to pursue refund suits instead of attempting to restrain collections. Third-party suits not seeking to stop the collection (or contest the validity) of a tax *imposed on plaintiffs,* as *McGlotten* and *Tax Analysts* explained, were outside Congress' purview. The TIA's legislative history is not silent in this regard. The Act was designed expressly to restrict "the jurisdiction of the district courts of the United States over suits relating to the collection of State taxes." S. Rep., p. 1.

Specifically, the Senate Report commented that the Act had two closely related, state-revenue-protective objectives: (1) to eliminate disparities between taxpayers who could seek injunctive relief in federal court—usually out-of-state corporations asserting diversity jurisdiction—and taxpayers with recourse only to state courts, which generally required taxpayers to pay first and litigate later; and (2) to stop taxpayers, with the aid of a federal injunction, from withholding large sums, thereby disrupting state government finances. In short, in enacting the TIA, Congress trained its attention on taxpayers who sought to avoid paying their tax bill by pursuing a challenge route other than the one specified by the taxing authority. Nowhere does the legislative history announce a sweeping congressional direction to prevent "federal-court interference with all aspects of state tax administration." Brief for Petitioner 20.[7]

The understanding of the Act's purposes and legislative history set out above underpins this Court's previous applications of the TIA. In California v. Grace Brethren Church, 457 U.S. 393 (1982), for example, we recognized that the principal purpose of the TIA was to "limit drastically" federal-court interference with "the collection of [state] taxes." True, the Court referred to the disruption of "state tax administration," but it did so specifically in relation to the "the collection of revenue." The complainants in *Grace Brethren Church* were several California churches and religious schools. They sought federal-court relief from an unemployment compensation tax that state law imposed on them. Their federal action, which bypassed state remedies, was exactly what the TIA was designed to ward off. The Director and the dissent endeavor to reconstruct *Grace Brethren Church* as precedent for the proposition that the TIA totally immunizes from lower federal-court review "all aspects of state tax administration, and not just interference with the collection of revenue." The endeavor is

---

7. The language of the TIA differs significantly from that of the Johnson Act, which provides in part: "The district courts shall not enjoin, suspend or restrain *the operation of, or compliance with,*" public-utility rate orders made by state regulatory bodies. 28 U.S.C. § 1342 (emphasis added). The TIA does not prohibit interference with "the operation of, or compliance with" state tax laws; rather, § 1341 proscribes interference only with those aspects of state tax regimes that are needed to produce revenue—i.e., assessment, levy, and collection.

unavailing given the issue before the Court in *Grace Brethren Church* and the context in which the words "state tax administration" appear.

The Director invokes several other decisions alleged to keep matters of "state tax administration" entirely free from lower federal-court "interference." Like *Grace Brethren Church,* all of them fall within § 1341's undisputed compass: All involved plaintiffs who mounted federal litigation to avoid paying state taxes (or to gain a refund of such taxes). Federal-court relief, therefore, would have operated to reduce the flow of state tax revenue. See Arkansas v. Farm Credit Servs. of Central Ark., 520 U.S. 821, 824 (1997) (corporations chartered under federal law claimed exemption from Arkansas sales and income taxation); National Private Truck Council, Inc. v. Oklahoma Tax Comm'n, 515 U.S. 582, 584 (1995) (action seeking to prevent Oklahoma from collecting taxes State imposed on nonresident motor carriers); Fair Assessment in Real Estate Assn., Inc. v. McNary, 454 U.S. 100, 105–06 (1981) (taxpayers, alleging unequal taxation of real property, sought, inter alia, damages measured by alleged tax overassessments); Rosewell v. LaSalle National Bank, 450 U.S. 503, 510 (1981) (state taxpayer, alleging her property was inequitably assessed, refused to pay state taxes).[8]

Our prior decisions are not fairly portrayed cut loose from their secure, state-revenue-protective moorings. See, e.g., *Grace Brethren Church*, 457 U.S., at 410 ("If federal declaratory relief were available to test state tax assessments, state tax administration might be thrown into disarray, and *taxpayers might escape the ordinary procedural requirements imposed by state law.* During the pendency of the federal suit *the collection of revenue under the challenged law might be obstructed, with consequent damage to the State's budget, and perhaps a shift to the State of the risk of taxpayer insolvency.*") (emphases added).[9]

In sum, this Court has interpreted and applied the TIA only in cases Congress wrote the Act to address, i.e., cases in which state taxpayers seek federal-court orders enabling them to avoid paying state taxes. We have read harmoniously the § 1341 instruction conditioning the jurisdictional bar on the availability of "a plain, speedy and efficient remedy" in state

8. Petitioner urges, and the dissent agrees, that the TIA safeguards another vital state interest: the authority of state courts to determine what state law means. Respondents, however, have not asked the District Court to interpret any state law—there is no disagreement as to the meaning of Ariz.Rev. Stat. Ann. § 43–1089 (West Supp.2003), only about whether, as applied, the State's law violates the Federal Constitution. That is a question federal courts are no doubt equipped to adjudicate.

9. We note, furthermore, that this Court has relied upon "principles of comity," Brief for Petitioner 26, to preclude original federal-court jurisdiction only when plaintiffs have sought district-court aid in order to arrest or countermand state tax collection. See Fair Assessment in Real Estate Assn., Inc. v. McNary, 454 U.S. 100, 107–08 (1981) (Missouri taxpayers sought damages for increased taxes caused by alleged overassessments); Great Lakes Dredge & Dock Co. v. Huffman, 319 U.S. 293, 296–99 (1943) (plaintiffs challenged Louisiana's unemployment compensation tax).

court. The remedy inspected in our decisions was not one designed for the universe of plaintiffs who sue the State. Rather, it was a remedy tailor-made for taxpayers. See, *e.g., Rosewell*, 450 U.S., at 528 ("Illinois' legal remedy that provides property owners paying property taxes under protest a refund without interest in two years is a 'plain, speedy and efficient remedy' under the [TIA]"); *Grace Brethren Church*, 457 U.S., at 411 ("[A] state-court remedy is 'plain, speedy and efficient'" only if it "provides the taxpayer with a 'full hearing and judicial determination' at which she may raise any and all constitutional objections to the tax.").[10]

V

In other federal courts as well, § 1341 has been read to restrain state taxpayers from instituting federal actions to contest their liability for state taxes, but not to stop third parties from pursuing constitutional challenges to tax benefits in a federal forum. Relevant to the distinction between taxpayer claims that would reduce state revenues and third-party claims that would enlarge state receipts, Seventh Circuit Judge Easterbrook wrote trenchantly:

> Although the district court concluded that § 1341 applies to any federal litigation touching on the subject of state taxes, neither the language nor the legislative history of the statute supports this interpretation. The text of § 1341 does not suggest that federal courts should tread lightly in issuing orders that might allow local governments to raise additional taxes. The legislative history ... shows that § 1341 is designed to ensure that federal courts do not interfere with states' collection of taxes, so long as the taxpayers have an opportunity to present to a court federal defenses to the imposition and collection of the taxes. The legislative history is filled with concern that federal judgments were emptying state coffers and that corporations with access to the diversity jurisdiction could obtain remedies unavailable to resident taxpayers. *There was no articulated concern about federal courts' flogging state and local governments to collect additional taxes.*
> Dunn v. Carey, 808 F.2d 555, 558 (7th Cir. 1986) (emphasis added).

[Discussion of other lower federal court decisions has been omitted. Also omitted is discussion of "numerous federal-court decisions—including decisions of this Court reviewing lower federal-court judgments—[that]

---

10. Far from "ignor[ing]" the "plain, speedy and efficient remedy" proviso, as the dissent charges, we agree that this "codified exception" is key to a proper understanding of the Act. The statute requires the State to provide *taxpayers* with a swift and certain remedy when they resist tax collections. An action dependent on a court's discretion, for example, would not qualify as a fitting taxpayer's remedy.

have reached the merits of third-party constitutional challenges to tax benefits without mentioning the TIA."][12]

* * *

In a procession of cases not rationally distinguishable from this one, no Justice or member of the bar of this Court ever raised a § 1341 objection that, according to the petitioner in this case, should have caused us to order dismissal of the action for want of jurisdiction. [Citations omitted,] Consistent with the decades-long understanding prevailing on this issue, respondents' suit may proceed without any TIA impediment.[13]

For the reasons stated, the judgment of the United States Court of Appeals for the Ninth Circuit is

Affirmed.

■ JUSTICE STEVENS, concurring.

In Part IV of his dissent, Justice Kennedy observes that "years of unexamined habit by litigants and the courts" do not lessen this Court's obligation correctly to interpret a statute. It merits emphasis, however, that prolonged congressional silence in response to a settled interpretation of a federal statute provides powerful support for maintaining the status quo. In statutory matters, judicial restraint strongly counsels waiting for Congress to take the initiative in modifying rules on which judges and litigants have relied. In a contest between the dictionary and the doctrine of stare decisis, the latter clearly wins. The Court's fine opinion, which I join without reservation, is consistent with these views.

■ JUSTICE KENNEDY, with whom THE CHIEF JUSTICE, JUSTICE SCALIA, and JUSTICE THOMAS join, dissenting.

In this case, the Court shows great skepticism for the state courts' ability to vindicate constitutional wrongs. Two points make clear that the Court treats States as diminished and disfavored powers, rather than merely applies statutory text. First, the Court's analysis of the Tax Injunction Act (TIA or Act), 28 U.S.C. § 1341, contrasts with a literal reading of its terms. Second, the Court's assertion that legislative histories support the conclusion that "[t]hird-party suits not seeking to stop the collection

---

12. In school desegregation cases, as a last resort, federal courts have asserted authority to direct the imposition of, or increase in, local tax levies, even in amounts exceeding the ceiling set by state law. See Missouri v. Jenkins, 495 U.S. 33, 57 (1990); Liddell v. Missouri, 731 F.2d 1294, 1320 (8th Cir. 1984) (en banc); cf. Griffin v. School Bd. of Prince Edward Cty., 377 U.S. 218, 233 (1964). Controversial as such a measure may be, see Jenkins, 495 U.S., at 65–81 (Kennedy, J., concurring in part and concurring in judgment), it is noteworthy that § 1341 was not raised in those cases by counsel, lower courts, or this Court on its own motion.

13. In confirming that cases of this order may be brought in federal court, we do not suggest that "state courts are second rate constitutional arbiters." Instead, we underscore that adjudications of great moment discerning no § 1341 barrier cannot be written off as reflecting nothing more than "unexamined custom" or unthinking "habit."

(or contest the validity) of a tax *imposed on plaintiffs* ... were outside Congress' purview" in enacting the TIA and the anti-injunction provision on which the TIA was modeled is not borne out by those sources, as previously recognized by the Court. In light of these points, today's holding should probably be attributed to the concern the Court candidly shows animates it. See [passages] noting it was the federal courts that "upheld the Constitution's equal protection requirement" when States circumvented Brown v. Board of Education, 347 U.S. 483 (1954), by manipulating their tax laws. The concern, it seems, is that state courts are second rate constitutional arbiters, unequal to their federal counterparts. State courts are due more respect than this. Dismissive treatment of state courts is particularly unjustified since the TIA, by express terms, provides a federal safeguard: The Act lifts its bar on federal court intervention when state courts fail to provide "a plain, speedy, and efficient remedy." § 1341.

In view of the TIA's text, the congressional judgment that state courts are qualified constitutional arbiters, and the respect state courts deserve, I disagree with the majority's superseding the balance the Act strikes between federal and state court adjudication. I agree with the majority that the petition for certiorari was timely under 28 U.S.C. § 2101(c), and so submit this respectful dissent on the merits of the decision.

I

Today is the first time the Court has considered whether the TIA bars federal district courts from granting injunctive relief that would prevent States from giving citizens statutorily mandated state tax credits. There are cases, some dating back almost 50 years, which proceeded as if the jurisdictional bar did not apply to tax credit challenges; but some more recent decisions have said the bar is applicable. Compare, e.g., Mueller v. Allen, 463 U.S. 388 (1983); Committee for Public Ed. & Religious Liberty v. Nyquist, 413 U.S. 756 (1973); Griffin v. School Bd. of Prince Edward Cty., 377 U.S. 218 (1964), with, e.g., ACLU Foundation of La. v. Bridges, 334 F.3d 416 (5th Cir. 2003); In re Gillis, 836 F.2d 1001 (6th Cir. 1988). While unexamined custom favors the first position, the statutory text favors the latter. In these circumstances a careful explanation for the conclusion is necessary; but in the end the scope and purpose of the Act should be understood from its terms alone.

The question presented—whether the TIA bars the District Court from granting injunctive relief against the tax credit—requires two inquiries. First, the term assessment, as used in § 1341, must be defined. Second, we must determine if an injunction prohibiting the Director from allowing the credit would enjoin, suspend, or restrain an assessment.

The word assessment in the TIA is not isolated from its use in another federal statute. The TIA was modeled on the anti-injunction provision of the Internal Revenue Code (Code), 26 U.S.C. § 7421(a). That provision specifies, and has specified since 1867, that federal courts may not restrain or enjoin an "assessment or collection of any [federal] tax." The meaning of the term assessment in this Code provision is discernible by reference to other Code sections.

Chapter 63 of Title 26 addresses the subject of assessments and sheds light on the meaning of the term in the Code. Section 6201(a) first instructs that "[t]he Secretary [of the Internal Revenue Service] is . . . required to make the . . . assessments of all taxes . . . imposed by this title . . ." Further it provides, "[t]he Secretary shall assess all taxes determined by the taxpayer or by the Secretary . . ." Section 6203 in turn sets forth a method for making an assessment: "The assessment shall be made by recording the liability of the taxpayer in the office of the Secretary."

Taken together, the provisions of Title 26 establish that an assessment, as that term is used in § 7421(a), must at the least encompass the recording of a taxpayer's ultimate tax liability. This is what the taxpayer owes the Government. See also Laing v. United States, 423 U.S. 161, 170 n.13 (1976) ("The 'assessment,' essentially a bookkeeping notation, is made when the Secretary or his delegate establishes an account against the taxpayer on the tax rolls"). Whether the Secretary or his delegate (today, the Commissioner) makes the recording on the basis of a taxpayer's self-reported filing form or instead chooses to rely on his own calculation of the taxpayer's liability (*e.g.,* via an audit) is irrelevant. The recording of the liability on the Government's tax rolls is itself an assessment.

The TIA was modeled on the anti-injunction provision; it incorporates the same terminology employed by the provision; and it employs that terminology for the same purpose. It is sensible, then, to interpret the TIA's terms by reference to the Code's use of the term. Cf. Lorillard v. Pons, 434 U.S. 575, 581 (1978) ("[W]here, as here, Congress adopts a new law incorporating sections of a prior law, Congress normally can be presumed to have had knowledge of the interpretation given to the incorporated law, at least insofar as it affects the new statute"). The Court of Appeals, which concluded that an assessment was the official estimate of the value of income or property used to calculate a tax or the imposition of a tax on someone, placed principal reliance for its interpretation on a dictionary definition. That was not entirely misplaced; but unless the definition is considered in the context of the prior statute, the advantage of that statute's interpretive guidance is lost.

Furthermore, the court defined the term in an unusual way. It relied on a dictionary that was unavailable when the TIA was enacted; it relied not on the definition of the term under consideration, "assessment," but on the definition of the term's related verb form, "assess"; and it examined only a portion of that terms' definition. In the dictionary used by the Court of Appeals, the verb is defined in two ways not noted by the court. One of the alternative definitions is quite relevant—"(2) to fix or determine the amount of (damages, a tax, a fine, etc.)." Further,

Had [the panel] looked in a different lay dictionary, [it] would have found a definition contrary to the one it preferred, such as "the entire plan or scheme fixed upon for charging or taxing." ... Had the panel considered tax treatises and law dictionaries ... it would have found much in accord with this broader definition.... Even the federal income tax code supports a broad reading of "assessment." Winn v. Killian, 321 F.3d 911, 912 (9th Cir. 2003) (Kleinfeld, J., dissenting from denial of rehearing en banc).

Guided first by the Internal Revenue Code, an assessment under § 1341, at a minimum, is the recording of taxpayers' liability on the State's tax rolls. The TIA, though a federal statute that must be interpreted as a matter of federal law, operates in a state-law context. In this respect, the Act must be interpreted so as to apply evenly to the 50 various state-law regimes and to the various recording schemes States employ. It is therefore irrelevant whether state officials record taxpayer liabilities with their own pen in a specified location, by collecting and maintaining taxpayers' self-reported filing forms, or in some other manner. The recordkeeping that equates to the determination of taxpayer liability on the State's tax rolls is the assessment, whatever the method. The Court seems to agree with this.

The dictionary definition of assessment provides further relevant information. Contemporaneous dictionaries from the time of the TIA's enactment define assessment in expansive terms. They would broaden any understanding of the term, and so the Act's bar. See, e.g., Webster's New International Dictionary 139 (1927) (providing three context relevant definitions for the term assessment: It is the act of apportioning or determining an amount to be paid; a valuation of property for the purpose of taxation; or the entire plan or scheme fixed upon for charging or taxing). See also United States v. Galletti, 541 U.S. 114 (2004) (noting that under the Code the term assessment refers not only to recordings of tax liability but also to "the calculation ... of a tax liability," including self-calculation done by the taxpayer). The Court need not decide the full scope of the term assessment in the TIA, however. For present purposes, a narrow definition of the term suffices. Applying the narrowest definition, the TIA's literal text bars district courts from enjoining, suspending, or restraining a State's recording of taxpayer liability on its tax rolls, whether the recordings are made by self-reported taxpayer filing forms or by a State's calculation of taxpayer liability.

The terms "enjoin, suspend, or restrain" require little scrutiny. No doubt, they have discrete purposes in the context of the TIA; but they also have a common meaning. They refer to actions that restrict assessments to varying degrees. It is noteworthy that the term "enjoin" has not just its meaning in the restrictive sense but also has meaning in an affirmative sense. The Black's Law Dictionary current at the TIA's enactment gives as a definition of the term, "to require; command; positively direct." Black's Law Dictionary 663 (3d ed.1933). That definition may well be implicated here, since an order invalidating a tax credit would seem to command States to collect taxes they otherwise would not collect. The parties, however, proceed on the assumption that enjoin means to bar. It is unobjectionable for the Court to make the assumption too, leaving the broader definition for later consideration.

Respondents argue the TIA does not bar the injunction they seek because even after the credit is enjoined, the Director will be able to record and enforce taxpayers' liabilities. In fact, respondents say, with the credit out of the way the Director will be able to record and enforce a higher level of liability and so profit the State. ("The amount of tax payable by some taxpayers would increase, but that can hardly be characterized as an injunction or restraint of the assessment process"). The argument, however, ignores an important part of the Act: "under State law." 28 U.S.C. § 1341 ("The district courts shall not enjoin, suspend or restrain the assessment . . . of any tax under State law"). The Act not only bars district courts from enjoining, suspending, or restraining a State's recording of taxpayer liabilities altogether; but it also bars them from enjoining, suspending, or restraining a State from recording the taxpayer liability that state law mandates.

Section 43–1089 is state law. It is an integral part of the State's tax statute; it is reflected on state tax forms; and the State Supreme Court has held that it is part of the calculus necessary to determine tax liability. A recording of a taxpayer's liability under state law must be made in accordance with § 43–1089. The same can be said with respect to each and every provision of the State's tax law. To order the Director not to record on the State's tax rolls taxpayer liability that reflects the operation of § 43–1089 (or any other state tax law provision for that matter) would be to bar the Director from recording the correct taxpayer liability. The TIA's language bars this relief and so bars this suit.

The Court tries to avoid this conclusion by saying that the recordings that constitute assessments under § 1341 must have a "collection-propelling function" and that the recordings at issue here do not have such a function. See also footnote 4 ("[T]he dissent would disconnect the word [assessment] from the enforcement process"). That is wrong. A recording of taxpayer liability on the State's tax rolls of course propels collection. In most cases the taxpayer's payment will accompany his filing, and thus will accompany the assessment so that no literal collection of moneys is necessary. As anyone who has paid taxes must know, however, if owed payment were not included with the tax filing, the State's recording of one's liability on the State's rolls would certainly cause subsequent collection efforts, for the filing's recording (i.e., the assessment) would propel collection by establishing the State's legal right to the taxpayer's moneys.

II

The majority offers prior judicial interpretations of the Code's similarly worded anti-injunction provision to support its contrary conclusions about the statutory text. That this Court and other federal courts have allowed nontaxpayer suits challenging tax credits to proceed in the face of the anti-injunction provision is not at all controlling. Those cases are quite distinguishable. Had the plaintiffs in those cases been barred from suit, there would have been no available forum at all for their claims. See McGlotten v. Connally, 338 F.Supp. 448, 453–54 (D.D.C.1972) (three-judge court) ("The preferred course of raising [such tax exemption and deduction] objections in a suit for refund is not available. In this situation we cannot read the statute to bar the present suit"). See also Tax Analysts and Advocates v. Shultz, 376 F.Supp. 889, 892 (D.D.C.1974) ("Since plaintiffs are not seeking to restrain the collection of taxes, and since they cannot obtain relief through a refund suit, [26 U.S.C.] § 7421(a) does not bar the injunctive relief they seek"). The Court ratified those decisions only insofar as they relied on this limited rationale as the basis for an exception to the statutory bar on adjudication. . . .

In contrast to the anti-injunction provision, the TIA on its own terms ensures an adequate forum for claims it bars. The TIA specially exempts actions that could not be heard in state courts by providing an exception for instances "where a plain, speedy, and efficient remedy may [not] be had in the courts of [the] State." 28 U.S.C. § 1341. . . . The practical effect is that a literal reading of the TIA provides for federal district courts to stand at the ready where litigants encounter legal or practical obstacles to challenging state tax credits in state courts. And this Court, of course, stands at the ready to review decisions by state courts on these matters.

The Court does not discuss this codified exception, yet the clause is crucial. It represents a congressional judgment about the balance that should exist between the respect due to the States (for both their administration of tax schemes and their courts' interpretation of tax laws) and the need for constitutional vindication. To ignore the provision is to ignore that Congress has already balanced these interests.

Respondents admit they would be heard in state court. Indeed a quite similar action previously was heard there. As a result, the TIA's exception does not apply. To proceed as if it does is to replace Congress' balancing of the noted interests with the Court's.

III

The Court and respondents further argue that the TIA's policy purposes and relatedly the federal anti-injunction provision's policy purposes (as discerned from legislative histories) justify today's holding. The two Acts, they say, reflect a unitary purpose: "In both . . . Congress directed taxpayers to pursue refund suits instead of attempting to restrain [tax] collections." See also [the Court's statement] that the Act's underlying purpose is to bar suits by "taxpayers who sought to avoid paying their tax bill." This purpose, the Court and respondents say, shows that the Act was not intended to foreclose relief in challenges to tax credits. The proposition rests on the premise that the TIA's sole purpose is to prevent district court orders that would decrease the moneys in state fiscs. Because the legislative histories of the Acts are not carefully limited in the manner that this reading suggests, the policy argument against a literal application of the Act's terms fails.

Taking the federal anti-injunction provision first, as has been noted before, "[its] history expressly reflects the congressional desire that all injunctive suits against the tax collector be prohibited." South Carolina v. Regan, 465 U.S. 367, 387 (1984) (O'Connor, J., concurring in judgment). The provision responded to "the grave dangers which accompany intrusion of the injunctive power of the courts into the administration of the revenue." Id., at 388. It "generally precludes judicial resolution of all abstract tax controversies," whether brought by a taxpayer or a nontaxpayer. Id., at 392. Thus, the provision's object is not just to bar suits that might "interrupt 'the process of collecting . . . taxes,'" but "[s]imilarly, the language and history evidence a congressional desire to prohibit courts from restraining any aspect of the tax laws' administration." Id., at 399.

The majority's reading of the TIA's legislative history is also inconsistent with the interpretation of this same history in the Court's earlier cases. The Court has made clear that the TIA's purpose is not only to protect the fisc but also to protect the State's tax system administration and tax policy implementation. California v. Grace Brethren Church, 457 U.S. 393 (1982), is a prime example.

In *Grace Brethren Church* the Court held that the TIA not only bars actions by individuals to stop tax collectors from collecting moneys (i.e., injunctive suits) but also bars declaratory suits. The Court explained that permitting declaratory suits to proceed would "defea[t] the principal purpose of the Tax Injunction Act: 'to limit drastically federal district court jurisdiction to interfere with so important a local concern as the collection of taxes.'" It continued:

> If federal declaratory relief were available to test state tax assessments, state tax administration might be thrown into disarray, and taxpayers might escape the ordinary procedural requirements imposed by state law. During the pendency of the federal suit the collection of revenue under the challenged law might be obstructed, with consequent damage to the State's budget, and perhaps a shift to the State of the risk of taxpayer insolvency. Moreover, federal constitutional issues are likely to turn on questions of state tax law, which, like issues of state regulatory law, are more properly heard in the state courts.

While this, of course, demonstrates that protecting the state fisc from damage is part of the TIA's purpose, it equally shows that actions that would throw the "state tax administration . . . into disarray" also implicate the Act and its purpose. The Court's concern with preventing administrative disarray puts in context its explanation that the TIA's principal concern is to limit federal district court interference with the "collection of taxes." The phrase, in this context, refers to the operation of the whole tax collection system and the implementation of entire tax policy, not just a part of it. While an order interfering with a specific collection suit disrupts one of the most essential aspects of a State's tax system, it is not the only way in which federal courts can disrupt the State's tax system:

> [T]he legislative history of the Tax Injunction Act demonstrates that Congress worried not so much about the form of relief available in the federal courts, as about divesting the federal courts of jurisdiction to interfere with state tax administration. *Grace Brethren Church*, supra, at 409 n.22.

The Court's decisions in Fair Assessment in Real Estate Assn., Inc. v. McNary, 454 U.S. 100 (1981), National Private Truck Council, Inc. v. Oklahoma Tax Comm'n, 515 U.S. 582 (1995) *(NPTC)*, and *Rosewell*, supra, make the same point. Though the majority says these cases support its holding because they "involved plaintiffs who mounted federal litigation to avoid paying state taxes," the language of these cases is too clear to be ignored and is contrary to the Court's holding today. In *Fair Assessment,* the Court observed that "[t]he [TIA] 'has its roots in equity practice, in principles of federalism, and in recognition of the imperative need of a State to administer its own fiscal operations.' This last consideration was [its] principal motivating force." In *NPTC*, the Court said, "Congress and this Court repeatedly have shown an aversion to federal interference with state tax administration. The passage of the [TIA] in 1937 is one manifestation of this aversion." [*NPTC* also summed] up this aversion, generated also from principles of comity and federalism, as creating a "background presumption that federal law generally will not interfere with administration of state taxes." In *Rosewell,* the Court described the Act's language as "broad" and "prophylactic" [and also said that] the TIA was "passed to limit federal-court interference in state tax matters."

The Act is designed to respect not only the administration of state tax systems but also state court authority to say what state law means. "[F]ederal constitutional issues are likely to turn on questions of state tax law, which, like issues of state regulatory law, are more properly heard in the state courts." *Grace Brethren Church*, supra, at 410. This too establishes that the TIA's purpose is not solely to ensure that the State's fisc is not decreased. There would be only a diminished interest in allowing state courts to say what the State's tax statutes mean if the Act protected just the state fisc. The TIA protects the responsibility of the States and their courts to administer their own tax systems and to be accountable to the citizens of the State for their policies and decisions. The majority objects that "there is no disagreement to the meaning of" state law in this case. As an initial matter, it is not clear that this is a fair conclusion. The litigation in large part turns on what state law requires and whether the product of those requirements violates the Constitution. More to the point, however, even if there were no controversy about the statutory framework the Arizona tax provision creates, the majority's ruling has implications far beyond this case and will most certainly result in federal courts in other States and in other cases being required to interpret state tax law in order to complete their review of challenges to state tax statutes.

Our heretofore consistent interpretation of the Act's legislative history to prohibit interference with state tax systems and their administration accords with the direct, broad, and unqualified language of the statute. The Act bars all orders that enjoin, suspend, or restrain the assessment of any tax under state law. In effecting congressional intent we should give full force to simple and broad proscriptions in the statutory language.

Because the TIA's language and purpose are comprehensive, arguments based on congressional silence on the question whether the TIA applies to actions that increase moneys a state tax system collects are of no moment. Whatever weight one gives to legislative histories, silence in the legislative record is irrelevant when a plain congressional declaration exists on a matter. "[W]hen terms are unambiguous we may not speculate on probabilities of intention." Merchants' Insurance Co. v. Ritchie, 72 U.S. (5 Wall.) 541, 545 (1867). Here, Congress has said district courts are barred from disrupting the State's tax operations. It is immaterial whether the State's collection is raised or lowered. A court order will thwart and replace the State's chosen tax policy if it causes either result. No authority supports the proposition that a State lacks an interest in reducing its citizens' tax burden. It is a troubling proposition for this Court to proceed on the assumption that the State's interest in limiting the tax burden on its citizens to that for which its law provides is a secondary policy, deserving of little respect from us.

IV

The final basis on which both the majority and respondents rest is that years of unexamined habit by litigants and the courts alike have resulted in federal courts' entertaining challenges to state tax credits. While we should not reverse the course of our unexamined practice lightly, our obligation is to give a correct interpretation of the statute. We are not obliged to maintain the status quo when the status quo is unfounded. The exercise of federal jurisdiction does not and cannot establish jurisdiction. See United States v. L.A. Tucker Truck Lines, Inc., 344 U.S. 33, 37–38 (1952): "[T]his Court is not bound by a prior exercise of jurisdiction in a case where it was not questioned and it was passed sub silentio." In this respect, the present case is no different than Federal Election Comm'n v. NRA Political Victory Fund, 513 U.S. 88 (1994). The case presented the question whether we had jurisdiction to consider a certiorari petition filed by the Federal Election Commission (FEC), and not by the Solicitor General on behalf of the FEC. The Court held that it lacked jurisdiction. Though that answer seemed to contradict the Court's prior practices, the Court said:

Nor are we impressed by the FEC's argument that it has represented itself before this Court on several occasions in the past without any question having been raised about its authority to do so.... The jurisdiction of this Court was challenged in none of these actions, and therefore the question is an open one before us.

See also Will v. Michigan Dept. of State Police, 491 U.S. 58, 63 n.4 (1989) (" '[T]his Court has never considered itself bound when a subsequent case finally brings the jurisdictional issue before us.' Hagans v. Lavine, 415 U.S. 528, 535 n.5 (1974)"). These cases make clear that our failure to consider a question hardly equates to a thing's being decided. As a consequence, I would follow the statutory language.

* * *

After today's decision, "[n]ontaxpaying associations of taxpayers, and most other nontaxpayers, will now be allowed to sidestep Congress' policy against [federal] judicial resolution of abstract [state] tax controversies." *Regan*, 465 U.S., at 394 (O'Connor, J., concurring in judgment). This unfortunate result deprives state courts of the first opportunity to hear such cases and to grant the relief the Constitution requires.

For the foregoing reasons, with respect, I dissent.

CHAPTER IV

Additional Reconstruction Legislation

Page 540, add at the end of Note 5:

For a reassessment of the entire history of the Civil Rights Act of 1866, from its initial enactment to its recent amendment in 1991, see George Rutherglen, The Improbable History of Section 1981: Clio Still Bemused and Confused, 2003 Sup. Ct. Rev. 303. This study concludes that the Act was originally intended to protect the right to full participation in public life regardless of race and that it prohibits any systematic form of discrimination that denies this right, whether by government or by private individuals. The Act was therefore correctly interpreted in *Jones v. Mayer* to reach private discrimination that does not involve state action under the 14th Amendment. Although *Jones v. Mayer* may have gone too far in interpreting the Act to prohibit all forms of private discrimination, no matter how isolated or insignificant, this interpretation of the Act was adopted by Congress in the Civil Rights Act of 1991.

Page 571, add at the end of Note 3:

Legislation subsequent to *Johnson v. Railway Express Agency, Inc.* has complicated the analysis of the appropriate statute of limitations applicable to claims under section 1981. A new federal catch-all statute of limitations, 28 U.S.C. § 1658, creates a four-year limitation period for claims under federal statutes enacted after 1990 if those statutes do not themselves contain a limitation period. In Jones v. R.R. Donnelley & Sons Co., 541 U.S. 369 (2004), the Supreme Court held that certain claims under § 1981 were governed by this new four-year limitation period. In particular, this new limitation period applies to claims under § 1981(b) for "performance, modification, and termination of contracts" that were not recognized before this provision was added to the statute by the Civil Rights Act of 1991. For purposes of the new statute of limitations, these claims arise under a federal statute enacted after 1990.

Page 591, add at the end of Note 2:

The Civil Rights Act of 1991 did not put to rest all doubts about the scope of § 1981. Some courts have suggested that a contract of employment terminable-at-will does not support a claim for discriminatory discharge under § 1981. According to these decisions, such a contract does not create a genuine contractual relationship that can be the subject of a § 1981 claim because it does not impose any restriction on either party's power to terminate the employment relationship. See, e.g., Gonzalez v. Ingersoll Milling Machine Co., 133 F.3d 1025, 1035 (7th Cir.1998) (dictum); Moorer v. Grumman Aerospace Corp., 964 F.Supp. 665 (E.D.N.Y.1997). The majority of courts, however, have rejected this reasoning on the common-sense ground that a contract terminable at will is still a contract. See Perry v. Woodward, 199 F.3d 1126, 1133–34 (10th Cir.1999). See also Harry Hutchinson, The Collision of Employment-at-Will, Section 1981 & *Gonzalez*: Discharge, Consent and Contract Sufficiency, 3 U. Pa. J. Lab. & Empl. L. 207 (2001); Joanna L. Grossman, Making a Federal Case Out of It: Section 1981 and At–Will Employment, 67 Brook. L. Rev. 329 (2001).

In the opposite direction, some courts have held that the Civil Rights Acts of 1981 creates a cause of action for private violations of the "equal benefit clause" in the original version of § 1981. See Chapman v. Higbee Co., 319 F.3d 825 (6th Cir. 2003) (en banc) (and cases cited). This provision was a statutory predecessor of the Equal Protection Clause of the 14th Amendment. It is now found in § 1981(a) and it is now protected from "impairment by nongovernmental discrimination" by § 1981(c). Does this mean that Congress has effectively repealed the state action requirement as it applies to some aspects of the Equal Protection Clause? Does it have the power to do so? See George Rutherglen, The Improbable History of Section 1981: Clio Still Bemused and Confused, 2003 Sup. Ct. Rev. 303, 303–04, 347–48; Jeremy Deese, Case Note: Civil Rights—42 U.S.C. section 1981—Scope of the Equal Benefit Clause, 71 Tenn. L. Rev. 199 (2003).

Page 612, add to end of Note 2:

The circuits are in conflict over the effect of the Civil Rights Act of 1991 on the holding in *Jett*. The Ninth Circuit, as well as a district court in the First Circuit, have held that § 1981(c) created a cause of action against governmental defendants separate from the cause of action under § 1983. Federation of African American Contractors v. City of Oakland, 96 F.3d 1204, 1209, 1214 (9th Cir.1996); Powell v. City of Pittsfield, 143 F.Supp.2d 94 (D.Mass.2001). The Eleventh Circuit has held, to the contrary, that § 1981(c) does not add to the remedies available under § 1983. Butts v. Volusia County, 222 F.3d 891, 894 (11th Cir.2000). See also Anne-Marie G. Harris, Shopping While Black: Applying 42 U.S.C. Section 1981 to Cases of Consumer Racial Profiling, 23 B.C. Third World L.J. 1 (2003); Florence Wagman Roisman, The Impact of the Civil Rights Act of 1866 on Racially Discriminatory Donative Transfers, 53 Ala. L. Rev. 463 (2002).

CHAPTER V

MODERN CIVIL RIGHTS LEGISLATION: LAWS AGAINST SEX DISCRIMINATION

Page 654, substitute for the last paragraph of Note 4:

Lower court decisions after *Dothard* have not followed its lenient approach to the evidence necessary to establish a BFOQ. Even in cases involving prison guards, they have required some form of more specific evidence. E.g., United States v. Gregory, 818 F.2d 1114, (4th Cir. 1987); see Torres v. Wisconsin Department of Health & Social Services, 859 F.2d 1523 (7th Cir. 1988) (en banc), cert. denied, 489 U.S. 1017, 1082 (1989) (empirical studies and other forms of objective evidence not required). These cases have also involved arguments that limiting guards to a single sex was necessary to safeguard the inmates' privacy. Such arguments have also been raised by inmates asserting that their constitutional right to privacy was violated by comprehensive surveillance and contact from guards of the opposite sex. Bonitz v. Fair, 804 F.2d 164 (1st Cir. 1986); Forts v. Ward, 621 F.2d 1210 (2d Cir. 1980). Even outside of prisons, it is mainly in cases involving such issues of privacy that the courts have applied the BFOQ to justify sex-based exclusions from particular jobs. E.g., Fesel v. Masonic Home of Delaware, Inc., 447 F.Supp. 1346 (D. Del. 1978), aff'd per curiam, 591 F.2d 1334 (3d Cir. 1979) (nurse at retirement home); Jennings v. New York State Office of Mental Health, 786 F.Supp. 376 (S.D.N.Y.), aff'd, 977 F.2d 731 (2d Cir. 1992) (per curiam) (personal care of mentally ill). And even in such cases, employers have not always succeeded in establishing a BFOQ. See Olsen v. Marriott International, Inc., 75 F.Supp.2d 1052, 1070–75 (D. Ariz. 1999) (no BFOQ for massage therapist).

For a comprehensive review of the BFOQ exception and the theory of sex discrimination generally see Kimberly A. Yuracko, Private Nurses and Playboy Bunnies: Explaining Permissible Sex Discrimination, 92 Cal. L. Rev. 147 (2004). For an analysis of the BFOQ arguing that it should be drastically limited, see Sharon M. McGowan, The Bona Fide Body: Title VII's Last Bastion of Intentional Sex Discrimination, 12 Colum. J. Gender & L. 77 (2003).

Page 655, add at the end of Note 5:

The interpretation of the caps in § 1981a had led to a conflict among the circuits on the question whether awards of "front pay" under Title VII were to be included in determining the amount of monetary relief subject to these caps. "Front pay" is compensation for lost pay awarded from the date of judgment forward, usually to the time when the plaintiff is restored to a position comparable to the one discriminatorily denied to her. Because it involves a prediction of future employment decisions, front pay is necessarily more speculative than back pay, which clearly is excluded from the caps in § 1981a. Awards of front pay, in this respect, more closely resemble an award of damages subject to the caps. The Supreme Court nevertheless held in Pollard v. E.I. du Pont de Nemours & Co., 532 U.S. 843 (2001), that awards of front pay fall outside the caps because they are a form of equitable relief authorized by the original remedial provisions in Title VII, 42 U.S.C. § 2000e–5(g).

Page 681, add at the end of Note 2:

The difficulty of establishing "severe or pervasive" harassment based on a single comment or joke was indirectly addressed by the Supreme Court in Clark County School District v. Breeden, 532 U.S. 268 (2001) (per curiam). That case concerned a claim of retaliation for complaining about an alleged incident of sexual harassment involving the reaction of two co-workers to a remark reportedly made by a prospective applicant for employment, whose file was under evaluation by the plaintiff (a woman) and by two male co-workers. The co-workers chuckled in response to a crude description of sexual activity made by the applicant and contained in his application file, all in the presence of the plaintiff. The Supreme Court, summarily reversing the decision below, held that their reaction to this comment could not reasonably form the basis for a complaint of sexual harassment and that, accordingly, the plaintiff had no claim of retaliation for protesting about their behavior to her employer. The plaintiff, according to the Court, had protested what was, "at worst an 'isolated inciden[t]' that cannot be considered 'extremely serious' as our cases require."

Page 683, add at the end of Note 3:

The law of sexual harassment continues to generate scholarly commentary. For a valuable collection of articles on this subject, see DIRECTIONS IN SEXUAL HARASSMENT LAW (Catharine A. MacKinnon and Reva B. Siegel, eds., 2004). There are many other articles as well: Gregory A. Bullman, Abuse of Female Sweatshop Laborers: Another Form of Sexual Harassment That Does Not Fit Neatly Into the Judiciary's Current Understanding of Discrimination Because of Sex, 78 Ind. L.J. 1019 (2003); Jennifer Ann Drobac, Sex and the Workplace: Consenting Adolescents and a Conflict of Laws, 79 Wash. L. Rev. 471 (2004); Alan R. Kabat, How (Not) to Litigate a Sexual Harassment Class Action, 9 Lab. Law. 129 (2003); Elizabeth A. Hoffmann, Selective Sexual Harassment Differential Treatment of Similar Groups of

Women Workers, 28 Law & Hum. Behav. 29 (2004); Martin Katz, Re-Considering Attraction in Sexual Harassment, 79 Ind. L.J. 101 (2004); Rosalie Berger Levinson, Parsing the Meaning of "Adverse Employment Action" in Title VII Disparate Treatment, Sexual Harassment, and Retaliation Claims: What Should Be Actionable Wrongdoing? 56 Okla. L. Rev. 623 (2003); Anna–Maria Marshall, Injustice Frames, Legality, and the Everyday Construction of Sexual Harassment, 28 Law & Soc. Inquiry 659 (2003); Amy, Oppenheimer, Investigating Workplace Harassment and Discrimination, 29 Employee Rel. L.J. 56 (2004); Elissa L. Perry, Carol T. Kulik & Anne C. Bourhis, The Reasonable Woman Standard Effects on Sexual Harassment Court Decisions, 28 Law & Hum. Behav. 9 (2004); Nan Stein, Bullying or Sexual Harassment? The Missing Discourse of Rights in an Era of Zero Tolerance, 45 Ariz. L. Rev. 783 (2003); e christi cunningham, Preserving Normal Heterosexual Male Fantasy: The "Severe or Pervasive" Missed–Interpretation of Sexual Harassment in the Absence of a Tangible Job Consequence, 1999 U. Chi. Legal F. 199; Eric Schnapper, Some of Them Still Don't Get It: Hostile Work Environment Litigation in the Lower Courts, 1999 U. Chi. Legal F. 277; Ann Juliano & Stewart J. Schwab, The Sweep of Sexual Harassment Cases, 86 Cornell L. Rev. 548 (2001); Brian Lehman, The Equal Protection Problem in Sexual Harassment Doctrine, 10 Colum. J. Gender & L. 125 (2000); Beth A. Quinn, The Paradox of Complaining: Law, Humor, and Harassment in the Everyday Work World, 25 Law & Soc. Inquiry 1151 (2000); Richard A. Posner, Employment Discrimination: Age Discrimination and Sexual Harassment, 19 Int'l Rev. L. & Econ. 421 (1999); Gertrud M. Fremling & Richard A. Posner, Status Signaling and the Law, with Particular Application to Sexual Harassment, 147 U. Pa. L. Rev. 1069 (1999); Cheryl L. Anderson, "Thinking Within the Box": How Proof Models Are Used to Limit the Scope of Sexual Harassment Law, 19 Hofstra Lab. & Emp. L.J. 125 (2001); L. Camille Herbert, Sexual Harassment as Discrimination "Because of Sex": Have We Come Full Circle?, 27 Ohio N.U.L. Rev. 439 (2001); G. Roger King, Sexual Harassment Claims in the New Millennium: A Litigator's Point of View, 27 Ohio N.U.L. Rev. 539 (2001); Anne Lawton, Tipping the Scales of Justice in Sexual Harassment Law, 27 Ohio N.U.L. Rev. 517 (2001); Lucetta Pope, Everything You Ever Wanted to Know About Sexual Harassment But Were Too Politically Correct to Ask (or, the Use and Abuse of "But For" Analysis in Sexual Harassment Law Under Title VII, 30 Sw. U.L. Rev. 253 (2001)); Vicki Schultz, Talking About Harassment, 9 J. L. & Policy 417 (2001); Catharine A. MacKinnon, The Logic of Experience: Reflections on the Development of Sexual Harassment Law 90 Geo. L.J. 813 (2002); Theresa M. Beiner, Let the Jury Decide: The Gap Between What Judges and Reasonable People Believe Is Sexually Harassing, 75 S. Cal. L. Rev. 791 (2002); David S. Schwartz, When is Sex Because of Sex? The Causation Problem in Sexual Harassment Law, 150 U. Pa. L. Rev. 1697 (2002); Vicki Schultz, The Sanitized Workplace, 112 Yale L.J. 2061 (2003); Kelly Cahill Timmons, Sexual Harassment and Disparate Impact:

Should Non–Targeted Workplace Sexual Conduct Be Actionable Under Title VII, 81 Neb. L. Rev. 1152 (2003); Henry L. Chambers, Jr. (Un)welcome Conduct and the Sexually Hostile Environment, 53 Ala. L. Rev. 733 (2002); Judith J. Johnson, License to Harass Women: Requiring Hostile Environment Sexual Harassment to Be "Severe or Pervasive" Discriminates Among "Terms and Conditions" of Employment, 62 Md. L. Rev. 85 (2003); Martha S. West, Preventing Sexual Harassment: The Federal Courts' Wake-Up Call for Women, 68 Brook. L. Rev. 457 (2002); Vivien Toomey Montz, Shifting Paramets: An Examination of Recent Changes in the Baseline of Actionable Conduct for Hostile Working Environment Sexual Harassment, 3 Geo. J. Gender & L. 809 (2002); Theresa M. Beiner, Gender Myths v. Working Realities: Using Social Science to Reformulate Sexual Harassment Law (NYU Press 2005); Camille L. Hebert, The Disparate Impact of Sexual Harassment: Does Motive Matter?, 53 U. Kan. L. Rev. 341 (2005); Linda Kelly Hill, The Feminist Misspeak of Sexual Harassment, 57 Fla. L. Rev. 133 (2005).

For additional articles on the First Amendment issues raised by the law of sexual harassment, see David E. Bernstein, Defending the First Amendment From Antidiscrimination Laws, 2 N.C. L. Rev. 223 (2003); Andrea Meryl Kirshenbaum, Hostile Environment Sexual Harassment Law and the First Amendment: Can the Two Peacefully Coexist?, 12 Tex. J. Women & L. 67 (2002); Robert Austin Ruescher, Saving Title VII: Using Intent to Distinguish Harassment from Expression, 23 Rev. Litig. 349 (2004); Kingsley R. Browne, Zero Tolerance for the First Amendment: Title VII's Regulation of Employee Speech, 27 Ohio N.U.L. Rev. 563 (2001); Richard Allen Olmstead, Comment, In Defense of the Indefensible: Title VII Hostile Environment Claims Unconstitutionally Restrict Free Speech, 27 Ohio N.U.L. Rev. 691 (2001); Debra D. Burke, Workplace Harassment: A Proposal for a Bright Line Test Consistent with the First Amendment, 21 Hofstra Lab. & Emp. L.J. 591 (2004); Eugene Volokh, Speech as Conduct: Generally Applicable Laws, Illegal Courses of Conduct, Situation-Altering Utterances, and the Uncharted Zones, 90 Cornell L. Rev. ___ (2005).

Page 688, add at the end of Note 4:

(iii) *Pennsylvania State Police v. Suders.* A third decision of the Supreme Court clarified when "tangible employment action" could be found, preventing the employer from invoking the defense recognized in *Burlington Industries* and *Faragher*. In Pennsylvania State Police v. Suders, 542 U.S. 129 (2004), the plaintiff alleged that she had been forced out of her job because of a hostile environment created by her supervisors and that such a "constructive discharge" amounted to a tangible employment action. The Supreme Court agreed with her, but only in part, holding that some, but not all, instances of constructive discharge amounted to tangible employment actions. In particular, when a plaintiff is forced to leave her job because of official acts of the employer, such as a demotion or a reduction in pay, a tangible employment action has taken place. Otherwise, when the constructive discharge results from the actions of co-workers or from informal conduct of a supervisor, the employer has not engaged in a tangible employment action and can therefore take advantage of the defense to liability.

For a discussion of constructive discharges, with particular reference to claims of sexual harassment, see Martha Chamallas, Title VII's Midlife Crisis: The Case of Constructive Discharge, 77 S. Cal. L. Rev. 307 (2004).

Page 689, add to Note 6 at the bottom of the page:

The judges of the lower federal courts are divided on the question of when the employer's affirmative defense to claims of sexual harassment has been made out under *Ellerth* and *Faragher*. The opinions in Indest v. Freeman Decorating, Inc., 164 F.3d 258 (5th Cir.1999), 168 F.3d 795 (5th Cir.1999), are illustrative. In this case, Judge Jones would have held that the employer made out the defense simply by establishing the first element identified in *Ellerth* and *Faragher*: that it took "reasonable care to prevent and correct promptly any sexually harassing behavior," even if the plaintiff acted reasonably in reporting the harassing conduct. 164 F.3d at 266 (opinion of Jones, J.). Judge Weiner concurred in the judgment for the employer, but he would have read *Ellerth* and *Faragher* literally to require both elements of the defense to be established: reasonable action by the employer and unreasonable action by the harassed employee. 168 F.3d at 796 (Weiner, J., specially concurring). A third judge in the case, perhaps bewildered by this unexpected problem, simply concurred in the result without opinion.

In conflict with this decision, the Tenth Circuit has held that an employer was not entitled to a jury instruction precluding employer liability if it had promptly and appropriately responded to the plaintiff's complaint of sexual harassment. Harrison v. Eddy Potash, 248 F.3d 1014 (10th Cir.2001).

Other cases have questioned the application of *Ellerth* and *Faragher* to claims of sexual harassment by co-employees. For one case holding that they do not apply and that the employer is liable only for its own negligence, see Quinn v. Green Tree Credit Corp., 159 F.3d 759, 766–67 (2d Cir.1998).

Page 691, add at the end of Note 8:

For an analysis of the implication of *Jones v. Clinton* for the law of sexual harassment, see Barbara Palmer, Judith Baer, Amy Jasperson, and Jacqueline DeLaat, Low–Life–Sleazy–Big–Haired Trailer–Park Girl v. The President: The Paula Jones Case and the Law of Sexual Harassment, 9 Am. U. Gender Soc. Pol'y & L. 283 (2001).

Page 692, add at the end of Note 9:

For further analysis of *Burlington Industries* and *Faragher* see Steven H. Aden, "Harm in Asking": A Reply to Eugene Scalia and an Analysis of the Paradigm Shift in the Supreme Court's Title VII Sexual Harassment Jurisprudence, 8 Temp. Pol. & Civ. Rts. L. Rev. 477 (1999); Philip K. Lyon & Bruce H. Phillips, Faragher v. City of Boca Raton and Burlington Industries, Inc. v. Ellerth: Sexual Harassment Under Title VII Reaches Adolescence, 29 U. Mem. L. Rev. 601 (1999); Ronald Turner, Employer Liability for Supervisory Hostile Environment Sexual Harassment: Comparing Title VII's and Section 1983's Regulatory Regimes, 31 Urb. Law. 503 (1999); Timothy Bland & David P. Knox, EEOC's Guidance on Vicarious Liability for Supervisory Harassment: Are the Courts Following the EEOC's Lead? 30 U. Mem. L. Rev. 793 (2000); B. Glenn George, If You're Not Part of the Solution, You're Part of the Problem: Employer Liability for Sexual Harassment, 13 Yale J.L. & Feminism 133 (2001); Michael Taylor, Let's Talk About Sex: A Clarification of Employer Liability for Supervisor Sexual Harassment Under Title VII, 27 Ohio N.U.L. Rev. 607 (2001); John H. Marks, Smoke, Mirrors, and the Disappearance of "Vicarious" Liability: The Emergence of a Dubious Summary–Judgment Safe Harbor for Employers Whose Supervisory Personnel Commit Hostile Environment Workplace Harassment, 38 Hous. L. Rev. 1401 (2002); Joanna L. Grossman, The Culture of Compliance: The Final Triumph of Form over Substance in Sexual Harassment Law, 26 Harv. Women's L.J. 3 (2003); Paula J. Dalley, All in a Day's Work: Employers' Vicarious Liability for Sexual Harassment, 104 W. Va. L. Rev. 517 (2002); Susan Grover, After *Ellerth*: The Tangible Employment Action in Sexual Harassment Analysis, 35 U. Mich. J.L. Reform 809 (2002); Lea B. Vaughn, The Customer Is Always Right ... Not! Employer Liability for Third Party Sexual Harassment, 9 Mich. J. Gender & L. 1 (2002); Nancy R. Mansfield & Joan T. A. Gabel, An Analysis of the *Burlington* and *Faragher* Affirmative Defense: When Are Employers Liable?, 19 Lab. Law. 107 (2003); Kelly Collins Woodford and Harry A. Rissetto, Tangible Employment Action: What Did the Supreme Court Really Mean in *Faragher* and *Ellerth*?, 19 Lab. Law. 63 (2003); Margaret S. Stockdale, Susan Bisom-Rapp, Maureen O'Connor & Barbara A. Gutek, Coming to Terms with Zero Tolerance Sexual Harassment Policies, 4 J. Forensic Psych. Prac. 65 (2004).

Page 697, add at the end of Note 2:

Several circuits have now held that *Oncale* does not protect employees from discrimination on the basis of sexual preference. Simonton v. Runyon, 232 F.3d 33, 35 (2d Cir.2000); Higgins v. New Balance Athletic Shoe, Inc., 194 F.3d 252, 259 (1st Cir.1999). Another circuit has held that *Oncale* does not allow claims against an "equal opportunity" harasser who engages in the same harassment of men and women, whether or not with bisexual overtones. Holman v. Indiana, 211 F.3d 399, 404 (7th Cir.2000).

Are these decisions affected by the changing constitutional law prohibiting discrimination against gays? The Court's decision striking down laws prohibiting consensual sex among homosexuals in the privacy of the home was decided solely under the Due Process Clause, based on the absence of any rational relationship between such laws and any legitimate state interest. Lawrence v. Texas, 539 U.S. 558 (2003). Only Justice O'Connor would have decided the case on the ground that such laws discriminate against gays in violation of the Equal Protection Clause. Although not directly related to Title VII—or, apart from Justice O'Connor, even to a claim of discrimination—would this decision have any effect on the background principles used to interpret Title VII? Does it shed any light on what constitutes discrimination on the basis of sex under that statute?

The extension of *Oncale* to sexual harassment of all kinds has generated increasing scholarly commentary. Brian Lehman, Why Title VII Should Prohibit All Workplace Sexual Harassment, 12 Yale J.L. & Feminism 225 (2000); Ronald Turner, The Unenvisaged Case, Interpretive Progression, and the Justiciability of Title VII Same–Sex Sexual Harassment Claims, 7 Duke J. Gender L. & Pol'y 57 (2000); Mary Coombs, Title VII and Homosexual Harassment After Oncale: Was It a Victory? 6 Duke J. Gender L. & Pol'y 113 (1999); Marianne C. Del Po, The Thin Line Between Love and Hate: Same–Sex Sexual Harassment, 40 Santa Clara L. Rev. 1–26 (1999); Francis Achampong, The Evolution of Same–Sex Hostile–Environment Sexual Harassment Law: A Critical Examination of the Latest Developments in Workplace Sexual Harassment Litigation, 73 St. John's L. Rev. 701 (1999); Ramona Paetzold, Same–Sex Sexual Harassment, Revisited: The Aftermath of Oncale v. Sundowner Offshore Services, Inc., 3 Employee Rts. & Employ. Pol'y J. 251 (1999); Kirin Dosanjh, Calling on Oncale: Federal Courts' Post–Oncale Approach to the "Evidentiary Routes" to Discriminatory Intent in Title VII Same–Sex Harassment Claims, 33 Urb. Law. 547 (2001); Dawn Macready, Statutory Construction as a Means of Judicial Restraint on Government: A case Study in Bisexual Harassment Under Title VII, 27 Ohio N.U.L. Rev. 659 (2001); Tamanna Quereshi and Anthony Vaupel, Comment, Should Sexual Harassment Based Upon Sexual Orientation be Covered by Title VII or Prohibited?, 27 Ohio N.U.L. Rev. 679 (2001); Mary Ann Connell & Donna Euben, Evolving Law in Same-Sex Sexual Harassment and Sexual Orientation Discrimination, 31 J. Coll. & U.L. 193 (2004); Philip McGough, Same-Sex Harassment: Do Either Price Waterhouse or Oncale Support the Ninth Circuit's Holding in Nichols v. Azteca Restaurant Enterprises, Inc. that Same-Sex Harassment Based on Failure to Conform to Gender Stereotypes is Actionable?, 22 Hofstra Lab. & Emp. L.J. 206 (2004); Ronald Turner, Title VII and the Inequality–Enhancing Effects of the Bisexual and Equal Opportunity Harasser Defenses, 7 U. Pa. J. Lab. & Emp. L. 341 (2005).

Page 701, add a new Note:

4. *Alexander v. Sandoval.* The ability of private litigants to bring claims under Title VI, and by inference, under Title IX, was further restricted by Alexander v. Sandoval, 532 U.S. 275 (2001). As discussed more fully in this supplement (in Note 10 to be added to page 295 of the casebook), this case held that private litigants could not bring claims of disparate impact based on regulations issued under Title VI, reasoning that such a private right of action could only be based on the statutory language rather than on regulations issued under the statute. The Court did not reach the question whether the regulations prohibiting practices with discriminatory effects were themselves valid. It concluded only there was no implied private right action to enforce such regulations. Finding no such basis in the statutory language of Title VI, the Court dismissed the plaintiff's claim. This holding seemingly applies as well to claims under Title IX, to the extent that regulations under that statute prohibit practices with discriminatory effects. For instance, the regulations governing sex discrimination in intercollegiate athletics might be construed to prohibit practices with discriminatory effects, and to that extent, be open to the argument that Title IX provides no private right of action for violation of their terms.

5. *Barnes v. Gorman.* Imposing further restrictions on claims by private plaintiffs, the Supreme Court barred the award of punitive damages on implied rights of action under statutes modeled on Title VI. As in *Alexander v. Sandoval*, the reasoning in this decision plainly reaches claims under Title IX. The specific case, Barnes v. Gorman, 536 U.S. 181 (2002), concerned a claim under Title II of the Americans with Disabilities Act, which requires recipients of funds not to discriminate against the disabled, on the model of the prohibition against racial discrimination in Title VI. The plaintiff in this case, like a private plaintiff under Title IX, asserted an implied right of action based on the defendant's obligation not to discriminate. With particular reference to the remedies made available to under Title IX in *Franklin v. Gwinnett County Public Schools*, the Court stated that "*Franklin*, however, did not describe the scope of 'appropriate relief.' We take up this question today." The Court therefore plainly intended its decision to bar the recovery of punitive damages by private plaintiffs under Title IX.

Page 715, add a new Note and renumber the remaining Notes:

3. **Jackson v. Birmingham Board of Education.** The range of claims under Title IX was further expanded by Jackson v. Birmingham Board of Education, 544 U.S. ___, 125 S.Ct. 1497 (2005), which recognized a claim for retaliation by a public school teacher who complained about sex discrimination in a high school's athletic program. The Supreme Court emphasized that the school district was on notice that it could be held liable for retaliation based on prior judicial decisions such as *Cannon* and *Gebser* and on longstanding regulations prohibiting retaliation. Because the case came up on a motion to dismiss for failure to state a claim, the plaintiff still had to prove retaliation on remand, and in particular, that his coaching duties were terminated because of his complaints about sex discrimination.

For a discussion of this case that anticipated the Supreme Court's ultimate decision, see Bradford C. Mank, Are Anti–Retaliation Regulations in Title VI or Title IX Enforceable in a Private Right of Action: Does Sandoval or Sullivan Control this Question?, 35 Seton Hall L. Rev. 47 (2004).

Page 734, add to citations in Note 4:

Karen Michaelis, Title IX and Same–Gender Sexual Harassment: School District Liability for Damages, 2000 B.Y.U. Educ. & L.J. 47; Patricia Romano Davis v. Monroe County Board of Education: Title IX Recipients' "Head in the Sand" Approach to Peer Sexual Harassment May Incur Liability, 30 J.L. & Educ. 63 (2001); Ivan E. Bodensteiner, Peer Harassment—Interference with an Equal Educational Opportunity in Elementary and Secondary Schools, 79 Neb. L. Rev. 1 (2000); Meredith Rich–Chappell, Child's Play or Sex Discrimination?: School Liability for Peer Sexual Harassment Under Title IX, 3 J. Gender Race & Just. 311 (1999); Julie Davies, Assessing Institutional Responsibility for Sexual Harassment in Education, 77 Tul. L. Rev. 387 (2002); Nancy Hogshead–Makar & Sheldon Elliot Steinbach, Intercollegiate Athletics' Unique Environment for Sexual Harassment Claims: Balancing the Realities of Athletics with Preventing Potential Claims, 13 Marq. Sports L. Rev. 173 (2003); Neal Hutchens, The Legal Effect of College and University Policies Prohibiting Romantic Relationships Between Students and Professors, 32 J.L. & Educ. 411 (2003). See also Diane Heckman, Is Notice Required in a Title IX Athletic Action Not Involving Sexual Harassment?, 14 Marq. Sports L. Rev. 175 (2003).

Several articles and symposia have offered an overall evaluation of Title IX on the occasion of the thirtieth anniversary of its enactment, among them Catherine Pieronek, Title IX Beyond Thirty: A Review of Recent Developments, 30 J. Coll. & Univ. L. 75 (2003); Richard A. Epstein, Foreword—"Just do It!": Title IX as a Threat to University Autonomy, 101 Mich. L. Rev. 1365 (2003); Symposium, Title IX Women, Athletics and the Law (with foreword by Paula A. Monopoli and articles by William C. Duncan, Jocelyn Samuels and Suzanne Sangree), 3 Margins L.J. 209 (2003); Symposium, Title IX at Thirty (with articles by Ted Leland, Karen Peters, Jocelyn Samuels, Kristen Galles, and Martha Burk), 14 Marq. Sports L. Rev. 1 (2003). For a criticism of grievance procedures on sexual assault on college campuses, see Michelle J. Anderson, The Legacy of the Prompt Complaint Requirement, Corroboration Requirement, and Cautionary Instructions on Campus Sexual Assault, 84 B.U. L. Rev. 945 (2004).

Page 734, add a new Note:

5. ***United States v. Morrison.*** The Violence Against Women Act of 1994 created an additional remedy for severe forms of sexual harassment in the form of a private right of action for any victim of "a crime of violence motivated by gender." 42 U.S.C. § 13981. The Act contains an elaborate definition of such crimes, essentially including felonies that pose a serious risk of physical injury and that are "committed because of gender or on the basis of gender, and due, at least in part, to an animus based on the victim's gender." The defendant need not have been charged with or convicted of such a crime to be liable under the act and a plaintiff, upon proof of the crime, is entitled to the full range of legal and equitable remedies.

In United States v. Morrison, 529 U.S. 598 (2000), the Supreme Court held § 13981 unconstitutional because it was beyond the powers of Congress under the Commerce Clause and § 5 of the Fourteenth Amendment. The case itself concerned allegations brought by a student at Virginia Polytechnic Institute against two fellow students. When her university grievances did not result in punishment of the students, she sued them under § 13981 and the university under Title IX. The district court dismissed all of her claims, but the court of appeals affirmed only the dismissal of the claims under § 13981, remanding a claim of hostile environment sexual harassment under Title IX. Without considering the Title IX claim, the Supreme Court affirmed the dismissal of the claims under § 13981.

The Court found no basis for the statute under the Commerce Clause, relying on its decision in United States v. Lopez, 514 U.S. 549 (1995), which declared unconstitutional a federal statute prohibiting knowing possession of firearms in or near schools:

> As we observed in *Lopez*, modern Commerce Clause jurisprudence has "identified three broad categories of activity that Congress may regulate under its commerce power. . . . First, Congress may regulate the use of the channels of interstate commerce. . . . Second, Congress is empowered to regulate and protect the instrumentalities of interstate commerce, or persons or things in interstate commerce, even though the threat may come only from intrastate activities. . . . Finally, Congress' commerce authority includes the power to regulate those activities having a substantial relation to interstate commerce, . . . i.e., those activities that substantially affect interstate commerce." 514 U.S., at 558–559.
>
> Petitioners do not contend that these cases fall within either of the first two of these categories of Commerce Clause regulation. They seek to sustain § 13981 as a regulation of activity that substantially affects interstate commerce. Given § 13981's focus on gender-motivated violence wherever it occurs (rather than violence directed at the instrumentalities of interstate commerce, interstate markets, or things or persons in interstate commerce), we agree that this is the proper inquiry. . . .

The Court then identified four further factors that determine whether a federal statute regulates an activity substantially affects interstate commerce: first, whether the federal statute has "to do with 'commerce' or any sort of economic enterprise, however broadly one might define those terms"; second, whether it contains "an express jurisdictional element which might limit its reach to a discrete set of [activities] that additionally have an explicit connection with or effect on interstate commerce"; third, whether the statute "contains express congressional findings regarding the effects upon interstate commerce ..."; and fourth, how strong the link is between the regulated activity and a substantial effect on interstate commerce. In *Morrison*, the Court found only the third of these requirements to be satisfied and, by itself, insufficient to sustain the statute:

> In contrast with the lack of congressional findings that we faced in *Lopez*, § 13981 *is* supported by numerous findings regarding the serious impact that gender-motivated violence has on victims and their families. But the existence of congressional findings is not sufficient, by itself, to sustain the constitutionality of Commerce Clause legislation. As we stated in *Lopez*, " '[S]imply because Congress may conclude that a particular activity substantially affects interstate commerce does not necessarily make it so.' " 514 U.S., at 557 n.2, (quoting Hodel v. Virginia Surface Mining & Reclamation Ass'n, Inc., 452 U.S. 264, 311 (1981) (Rehnquist, J., concurring in judgment)). Rather, " '[w]hether particular operations affect interstate commerce sufficiently to come under the constitutional power of Congress to regulate them is ultimately a judicial rather than a legislative question, and can be settled finally only by this Court.' " 514 U.S., at 557 n.2, (quoting Heart of Atlanta Motel, Inc. v. United States, 379 U.S. 241, 273 (1964) (Black, J., concurring)).
>
> In these cases, Congress' findings are substantially weakened by the fact that they rely so heavily on a method of reasoning that we have already rejected as unworkable if we are to maintain the Constitution's enumeration of powers. Congress found that gender-motivated violence affects interstate commerce
>
>> by deterring potential victims from traveling interstate, from engaging in employment in interstate business, and from transacting with business, and in places involved in interstate commerce; ... by diminishing national productivity, increasing medical and other costs, and decreasing the supply of and the demand for interstate products.
>
> H.R. Conf. Rep. No. 103–711, at 385, U.S.Code Cong. & Admin.News 1994, pp. 1803, 1853. Accord, S.Rep. No. 103–138, at 54. Given these findings and petitioners' arguments, the concern that we expressed in *Lopez* that Congress might use the Commerce Clause to completely obliterate the Constitution's distinction between national and local authority seems well founded. The reasoning that petitioners advance seeks to follow the but-for causal chain from the initial occurrence of violent crime (the suppression of which has always been the prime object of the States' police

power) to every attenuated effect upon interstate commerce. If accepted, petitioners' reasoning would allow Congress to regulate any crime as long as the nationwide, aggregated impact of that crime has substantial effects on employment, production, transit, or consumption. Indeed, if Congress may regulate gender-motivated violence, it would be able to regulate murder or any other type of violence since gender-motivated violence, as a subset of all violent crime, is certain to have lesser economic impacts than the larger class of which it is a part.

The Court also held that the statute fell outside the power conferred by § 5 of the Fourteenth Amendment, which provides that "Congress shall have power to enforce, by appropriate legislation, the provisions of this [amendment]." The latter provisions, and particularly the Equal Protection Clause, applies only to state action. The only state action invoked in support of § 13981 came by way of congressional findings that state courts were systematically biased against the victims of gender-motivated violence and so did not afford them full relief for their injuries. No state action, however, was necessarily involved in the conduct giving rise to liability under the statute, as evidenced by the purely private action alleged against the two students in *Morrison* itself. As the Court emphasized:

[T]he language and purpose of the Fourteenth Amendment place certain limitations on the manner in which Congress may attack discriminatory conduct. These limitations are necessary to prevent the Fourteenth Amendment from obliterating the Framers' carefully crafted balance of power between the States and the National Government. Foremost among these limitations is the time-honored principle that the Fourteenth Amendment, by its very terms, prohibits only state action. "[T]he principle has become firmly embedded in our constitutional law that the action inhibited by the first section of the Fourteenth Amendment is only such action as may fairly be said to be that of the States. That Amendment erects no shield against merely private conduct, however discriminatory or wrongful." Shelley v. Kraemer, 334 U.S. 1, 13 and n. 12 (1948).

Shortly after the Fourteenth Amendment was adopted, we decided two cases interpreting the Amendment's provisions, United States v. Harris, 106 U.S. 629 (1883), and the Civil Rights Cases, 109 U.S. 3 (1883). In *Harris*, the Court considered a challenge to § 2 of the Civil Rights Act of 1871. That section sought to punish "private persons" for "conspiring to deprive any one of the equal protection of the laws enacted by the State." 106 U.S., at 639. We concluded that this law exceeded Congress' § 5 power because the law was "directed exclusively against the action of private persons, without reference to the laws of the State, or their administration by her officers." Id., at 640. In so doing, we reemphasized our statement from Virginia v. Rives, 100 U.S. 313, 318 (1879), that " 'these provisions of the fourteenth amendment have reference to State action exclusively, and not to any action of private individuals.' " *Harris*, supra, at 639, (misquotation in Harris).

We reached a similar conclusion in the *Civil Rights Cases*. In those consolidated cases, we held that the public accommodation provisions of the Civil Rights Act of 1875, which applied to purely private conduct, were beyond the scope of the § 5 enforcement power. 109 U.S., at 11 ("Individual invasion of individual rights is not the subject-matter of the [Fourteenth] [A]mendment"). . . .

Petitioners alternatively argue that, unlike the situation in the *Civil Rights Cases*, here there has been gender-based disparate treatment by state authorities, whereas in those cases there was no indication of such state action. There is abundant evidence, however, to show that the Congresses that enacted the Civil Rights Acts of 1871 and 1875 had a purpose similar to that of Congress in enacting § 13981: There were state laws on the books bespeaking equality of treatment, but in the administration of these laws there was discrimination against newly freed slaves. . . .

But even if that distinction were valid, we do not believe it would save § 13981's civil remedy. For the remedy is simply not "corrective in its character, adapted to counteract and redress the operation of such prohibited [s]tate laws or proceedings of [s]tate officers." *Civil Rights Cases*, 109 U.S., at 18. Or, as we have phrased it in more recent cases, prophylactic legislation under § 5 must have a "congruence and proportionality between the injury to be prevented or remedied and the means adopted to that end." Florida Prepaid Postsecondary Ed. Expense Bd. v. College Savings Bank, 527 U.S. 627, 639 (1999). Section 13981 is not aimed at proscribing discrimination by officials which the Fourteenth Amendment might not itself proscribe; it is directed not at any State or state actor, but at individuals who have committed criminal acts motivated by gender bias.

Justice Thomas concurred in the Court's opinion on the ground that it correctly applied the standards from *Lopez* on the scope of the Commerce Clause, but he wrote separately to express his dissatisfaction with allowing Congress to regulate any activity with "substantial effects" on interstate commerce.

For precisely the opposite reason, Justices Souter dissented, joined by three other justices. He relied on the sufficiency of the congressional findings of extensive violence against women and its effect on interstate commerce, applying a deferential standard to legislation enacted under the Commerce Clause:

Our cases, which remain at least nominally undisturbed, stand for the following propositions. Congress has the power to legislate with regard to activity that, in the aggregate, has a substantial effect on interstate commerce. See Wickard v. Filburn, 317 U.S. 111, 124–28 (1942); Hodel v. Virginia Surface Mining & Reclamation Assn., 452 U.S. 264, 277 (1981). The fact of such a substantial effect is not an issue for the courts in the first instance, but for the Congress, whose institutional capacity for gathering evidence and taking testimony far exceeds ours. By passing legislation, Congress indicates its conclusion, whether explicitly or not, that facts support its exercise of the commerce power. The business of the courts is to review the congressional assessment, not for soundness but simply for the rationality of concluding that a jurisdictional basis exists in fact. See ibid. Any explicit findings that Congress chooses to make, though not dispositive of the question of rationality, may advance judicial review by identifying factual authority on which Congress relied. . . .

Justice Breyer also dissented, emphasizing the difficulty of distinguishing between regulation of economic and noneconomic activity according to the Court's opinion. He also relied upon the steps that Congress took in the legislative process to protect the interest of the states:

> I would also note that Congress, when it enacted the statute, followed procedures that help to protect the federalism values at stake. It provided adequate notice to the States of its intent to legislate in an "are[a] of traditional state regulation." And in response, attorneys general in the overwhelming majority of States (38) supported congressional legislation, telling Congress that "[o]ur experience as Attorneys General strengthens our belief that the problem of violence against women is a national one, requiring federal attention, federal leadership, and federal funds."

The decision in *Morrison*, although it continues a trend of restricting congressional power, leaves both Title VII and Title IX with ample support in congressional power. Because Title VII covers employment, it directly regulates economic activity, one of the critical elements to sustain federal legislation based on its effects on interstate commerce. Moreover, insofar as Title VII regulates employment by state and local government, it also satisfies the state action requirement for congressional authority under § 5 of the Fourteenth Amendment. Title IX relies on yet another source of congressional authority, the spending power of Article I, § 8, cl. 1. Title IX's coverage is limited to schools that receive federal funds, unlike the coverage of anyone who engages in crimes of sexual violence in *Morrison*. In *Gebser v. Lago Vista Independent School District*, 524 U.S. 274 (1998) (main case at p. 701), the Supreme Court emphasized the basis of the statute in the spending power, a decision that makes sense only on the assumption that Congress can validly attach conditions on the receipt of federal funds. Indeed, *Morrison* itself involved a claim under Title IX that was not considered by the Supreme Court but that was remanded by the court of appeals for reconsideration by the district court.

For discussions of the implications of *Morrison*, see Robert C. Post & Reva B. Siegel, Essay, Equal Protection by Law: Federal Antidiscrimination Legislation After *Morrison* and *Kimel*, 110 Yale L.J. 441 (2000); Ronald D. Rotunda, The Eleventh Amendment, *Garrett*, and Protection for Civil Rights, 53 Ala. L. Rev. 1183 (2002); John Alan Doran & Christopher Michael Mason, Disproportionate Incongruity: State Sovereign Immunity and the Future of Federal Employment Discrimination Law, 2003 L. Rev. Mich. St. U. Det. C.L. 1.

6. Nevada Department of Human Resources v. Hibbs. The significance of *Morrison* was further limited by Nevada Department of Human Resources v. Hibbs, 538 U.S. 721 (2003), a decision upholding the Family and Medical Leave Act, 29 U.S.C. §§ 2601–19 (FMLA), as an exercise of congressional power under Section 5 of the 14th Amendment. The FMLA requires employers above a certain size, including state governments, to allow their employees to take unpaid leave, for periods up to 12 weeks, in order to take care of their own medical problems or situations involving immediate family members. The plaintiff in *Hibbs* worked for the State of Nevada and was terminated after he had taken leave to care for his ailing wife. He sued the state under the FMLA, alleging that he was entitled to more leave than he was actually granted, and the state raised a defense of immunity under the 11th Amendment.

The Court held that Congress had validly abrogated this immunity by enacting the FMLA, in part, under Section 5 of the Fourteenth Amendment. The Court reasoned that the act was aimed at preventing sex discrimination through "prophylactic legislation that proscribes facially constitutional conduct, in order to prevent and deter unconstitutional conduct." The FMLA itself did not prohibit sex discrimination by state employers, which was already prohibited by Title VII. Congress, instead, enacted a prohibition against otherwise neutral leave policies, relying on findings that "stereotype-based beliefs about the allocation of family duties remained firmly rooted, and employers' reliance on them in establishing discriminatory leave policies remained widespread." The FMLA thus satisfied the test of "congruence and proportionality" between the means chosen by Congress under Section 5 of the 14th Amendment and the prohibition against sex discrimination under Section 1.

This holding does not directly contradict the reasoning in *Morrison*, since the crucial issues in that case were not contested in *Hibbs*. First, there was no question that the substantive provisions of the FMLA were constitutional, since the act plainly fell within the power of Congress to regulate employment practices under the Commerce Clause. The state therefore was required to grant leave according to the terms of the act and could be forced, even by private individuals, to comply with the act through injunctions seeking prospective relief against state officers. The only question was whether private individuals could sue the state for damages. Second, the presence of state action also could not be doubted, since the plaintiff in *Hibbs* was a state employee and the lawsuit only involved the actions of state officials. In *Morrison*, by contrast, the plaintiff was victimized by the actions of private individuals.

Nevertheless, some tension remains between the two decisions, particularly in the deference accorded by the Supreme Court to the findings made by Congress of potential violations of the 14th Amendment by the states. The pervasive practice of employers in denying leave to care for family members, which formed the basis for the congressional finding of de facto discrimination against women, could not be attributed only to the state in its capacity as one employer among others. As the dissenting opinions pointed out, the evidence available to Congress on the issue of state action in sponsoring discrimination against women was, in the end, no stronger than the evidence in *Morrison*. Supposing the dissenters are correct on this point, does this inconsistency between the decisions increase or decrease the continuing significance of *Morrison*? Would a challenge to Title VII, as it prohibits forms of discrimination by the states that are not covered by the Constitution (such as disparate impact), be more or less likely to succeed after *Hibbs*?

See also Robert C. Post & Reva B. Siegel, Legislative Constitutionalism and Section Five Power: Policentric Interpretation of the Family and Medical Leave Act, 112 Yale L.J. 1943 (2003), and Robert J. Kaczorowski, The Supreme Court and Congress's Power to Enforce Constitutional Rights: An Overlooked Moral Anomaly, 73 Fordham L. Rev. 153 (2004). For further discussion of *Hibbs* and earlier decisions on congressional power to abrogate state immunity under the 11th Amendment, see the Note added to Page 25 of the Casebook in this Supplement, supra.

Page 735, add at the end of the Introductory Note on Title IX and Athletics:

For criticism of the continuing exclusion of women from contact sports, see B. Glenn George, Fifty/Fifty: Ending Sex Segregation in School Sports, 63 Ohio St. L.J. 1107 (2002); Suzanne Sangree, Title IX and the Contact Sports Exemption: Gender Stereotypes in a Civil Rights Statute, 32 Conn. L. Rev. 381 (2000). See also B. Glenn George, Title IX and the Scholarship Dilemma, 9 Marq. Sports L.J. 273 (1999).

For articles generally defending the allocation of athletic opportunities in proportion to enrollments, see Kimberly A. Yuracko, One for You and One for Me: Is Title IX's Sex-Based Proportionality Requirement for College Varsity Athletic Positions Defensible?, 97 Nw. U. L. Rev. 731 (2003); Diane Heckman, The Glass Sneaker: Thirty Years of Victories and Defeats Involving Title IX and Sex Discrimination in Athletics, 13 Fordham Intell. Prop. Media & Ent. L.J. 551 (2003); Patrick N. Findlay, The Case for

Requiring a Proportionality Test to Assess Compliance with Title IX in High School Athletics, 23 N. Ill. U. L. Rev. 29 (2002); Deborah Brake, The Struggle for Sex Equality in Sport and the Theory Behind Title IX, 34 U. Mich. J. L. Reform 12 (2000–01); Joseph Z. Fleming, Title IX from The Red Rose Crew to Grutter: The Law and Literature of Sports, 14 Fordham Intell. Prop. Media & Ent. L.J. 793 (2004). See also Neena K. Chaudhry & Marcia D. Greenberger, Seasons of Change: *Communities for Equity v. Michigan High School Athletic Association*, 13 UCLA Women's L.J. 1 (2003) (arguing for increased opportunities for female high school students).

For criticism of interpretations of Title IX that rely solely upon proportionality of athletic opportunities with overall enrollment figures for male and female students, see Jessica Gavora, Tilting the Playing Field: Schools, Sports, Sex and Title IX (2002); Walter E. Block, Roy Whitehead, and Lu Hardin, Gender Equity in Athletics: Should We Adopt a Non-Discriminatory Model?, 30 U. Tol. L. Rev. 223 (1999); J. Brad Reich, All the [Athletes] Are Equal, But Some Are More Equal Than Others: An Objective Evaluation of Title IX's Past, Present, and Recommendations for Its Future, 108 Penn St. L. Rev. 525 (2003); Gary R. Roberts, Evaluating Gender Equity Within the Framework of Intercollegiate Athletics' Conflicting Value Systems, 77 Tul. L. Rev. 997 (2003).

CHAPTER VI

STRUCTURAL REFORM LITIGATION

Page 768, add a new Note:

4a. Unitariness Litigation. In the past several years, an increasing number of school districts have been declared unitary. In some cases, as in *Dowell*, the school district itself has sought dissolution of the decree. In others, federal courts have declared districts unitary in the course of other litigation, usually suits by parents who demanded race-neutral access to some particularly attractive educational opportunity.

For an interesting example of such litigation, consider the history of the school district involved in Swann v. Charlotte–Mecklenburg Board of Education, 402 U.S. 1 (1971). The Charlotte–Mecklenburg schools remained under court order well into the 1990s. In addition to race-based pupil assignment, the district also implemented a magnet school program. In September 1997, a white parent, William Capacchione, filed suit alleging that his daughter had unconstitutionally been denied admission to a magnet school program on account of her race. Other parents intervened and sought a determination that the school district had attained unitary status. At the same time, counsel for the original *Swann* plaintiffs moved to reactivate that litigation.

The District Court consolidated all these cases, conducted a lengthy trial, and determined that Charlotte–Mecklenburg had achieved unitary status. On that premise, the race-based admissions policy for magnet schools was found to violate equal protection of the laws. The District Court prohibited use of race-based preferences in student assignment and ordered that race-blind assignment policies go into effect in time for the 2000–2001 school year. Capacchione v. Charlotte–Mecklenburg Schools, 57 F.Supp.2d 228 (W.D.N.C.1999). The school board appealed, and sought a stay of the order pending the appeal. The Court of Appeals granted that stay. Belk v. Charlotte–Mecklenburg Bd. of Educ., 211 F.3d 853 (4th Cir.2000). It found that the balance of hardships tilted in favor of the school board, since immediate compliance with the District Court's order would require "redraw[ing] attendance boundaries for virtually every non-magnet school" within the district and perhaps reassigning 50,000 students.

In Charlotte–Mecklenburg, as in some other districts, the school authorities apparently wish to continue using race as a basis for pupil assignment and restrictive admissions in order to achieve integration.

Whether such programs can continue after a finding of voluntariness is not clear. In the 1970s, the Supreme Court approved race-based pupil assignments as part of voluntary desegregation plans, see McDaniel v. Barresi, 402 U.S. 39 (1971). *Barresi* has not been overruled, but its continued vitality may be open to question. In any event, *Barresi* only dealt with race-based assignments among presumably comparable schools. The more hotly contested issue is race-based admissions to magnet schools or other specialty programs. In this context, several recent decisions have disapproved race as a criterion for selective admission, outside the remedial context of eliminating de jure segregation. See, e.g., Tuttle v. Arlington County School Board, 195 F.3d 698 (4th Cir.1999) (striking down a system of admitting students to a special school pursuant to a weighted lottery that increased the chances of African–American applicants); Ho v. San Francisco Unified School District, 147 F.3d 854 (9th Cir.1998) (suggesting that it might be unconstitutional to continue a consent decree provision capping the number of students of a particular racial or ethnic group who could be assigned to a particularly desirable school). The question whether achieving or maintaining racial balance within a public school system, outside the context of required desegregation, is a sufficiently compelling state interest to justify race-based assignments or admissions has not yet reached the Supreme Court.

For articles discussing the decreased judicial involvement in school desegregation, see Sean F. Reardon, Integrating Neighborhoods, Segregating Schools: The Retreat from School Desegregation in the South, 81 N.C.L. Rev. 1563 (2003); Wendy Parker, The Decline of Judicial Decisionmaking: School Desegregation and District Court Judges, 81 N.C.L. Rev. 1623 (2003).

Page 792, add a new Note:

4. Subsequent Developments in *Jenkins*. In 1997, the District Court approved a settlement between KCMSD and the state, providing that the state would pay the district $320 million over three years, and in return, would be dismissed from the litigation. Jenkins v. Missouri, 959 F.Supp. 1151 (W.D.Mo.), aff'd, 122 F.3d 588 (8th Cir.1997). Pursuant to that settlement, the state was dismissed as a party in 1999, and the District Court set a hearing date to determine whether KCMSD had attained unitary status.

A few months later, the State Board of Education voted to withdraw accreditation of KCMSD as of May 1, 2000 because of poor student test scores. In response, KCMSD filed a motion seeking to bar the state's action on the ground that it would interfere with the remedial decree in *Jenkins*. At the end of a hearing devoted to that motion, the district court sua sponte declared the KCMSD unitary. In an en banc opinion, the Court of Appeals reversed and remanded the case for a fuller evidentiary hearing. Jenkins v. State of Missouri, 205 F.3d 361 (8th Cir.2000). The Court of

Appeals noted that "once there has been a finding that a defendant established an unlawful dual school system in the past, there is a presumption that current disparities of the sort listed in Green v. County School Board, 391 U.S. 430, 435 (1968), are the result of the defendant's unconstitutional conduct. Therefore, the burden of proving unitariness rests on the constitutional violator." It then held that the Due Process Clause meant that "[t]he parties are entitled to notice and an opportunity to prepare for a unitary status hearing.... The sua sponte ruling of the District Court, in spite of its several earlier orders setting the unitary status hearing some two months later, deprived the Jenkins Class of this constitutional guarantee." It thus remanded the case for such a hearing.

Page 852, delete Note 7 on the Prison Litigation Reform Act, which is now treated in an insert after page 856.

Page 856, add at the end of Note 8:

For an influential recent account of prison reform litigation, see Malcolm M. Feeley and Edward L. Rubin, Judicial Policy Making and the Modern State: How the Courts Reformed America's Prisons (1998, paperback ed. 2000). Finally, for an extensive empirical study of inmate litigation in the federal courts, both before and after the Prison Litigation Reform Act of 1996, see Margo Schlanger, Inmate Litigation, 116 Harv. L. Rev. 1555 (2003).

Page 856, add at the end of the current materials in Section 3:

INTRODUCTORY NOTE ON THE PRISON LITIGATION REFORM ACT

In 1996, Congress passed the Prison Litigation Reform Act (PLRA), Pub. L. No. 104–134, 110 Stat. 1321. The Act made a number of changes with respect to prisoner litigation in federal courts, including significant limitations on the ability of prisoners to proceed in forma pauperis (that is, without paying court fees) and on the award of attorney's fees. In addition, the PLRA barred prisoners from bringing § 1983 damages lawsuits for mental or emotional injuries "without a prior showing of physical injury." PLRA § 803(d) (amending 42 U.S.C. § 1997e).

Of particular salience to structural reform litigation was § 802 of the PLRA. It amended 18 U.S.C. § 3626 to provide:

(a) REQUIREMENTS FOR RELIEF.—

(1) PROSPECTIVE RELIEF.—(A) Prospective relief in any civil action with respect to prison conditions shall extend no further than necessary to correct the violation of the Federal right of a particular plaintiff or plaintiffs. The court shall not grant or approve any prospective relief unless the court finds that such relief is narrowly drawn, extends no further than necessary to correct the violation of the Federal

right, and is the least intrusive means necessary to correct the violation of the Federal right. The court shall give substantial weight to any adverse impact on public safety or the operation of a criminal justice system caused by the relief.

(B) The court shall not order any prospective relief that requires or permits a government official to exceed his or her authority under State or local law or otherwise violates State or local law, unless—

> (i) Federal law permits such relief to be ordered in violation of State or local law;
>
> (ii) the relief is necessary to correct the violation of a Federal right; and
>
> (iii) no other relief will correct the violation of the Federal right.

(C) Nothing in this section shall be construed to authorize the courts, in exercising their remedial powers, to order the construction of prisons or the raising of taxes, or to repeal or detract from otherwise applicable limitations on the remedial powers of the courts.

To what extent does this provision of the PLRA merely codify existing law after *Rhodes*? Does subsection (C) set out a different legal standard for prison cases than for school cases? Is this a permissible exercise of congressional power?

Section 802(a) also substantially restricted the ability of federal courts to enter consent judgments, providing that "[i]n any civil action with respect to prison conditions, the court shall not enter or approve a consent decree unless it complies with the limitations on relief set forth in subsection (a)," that is, the need-narrowness-intrusiveness criteria.

Consider the substantial effects of § 802(a)'s restriction of consent judgments. A large number of structural injunctions were the result of settlements, rather than fully litigated cases. As one recent commentator observes:

> The ordinary litigation incentives favoring settlement operate strongly for parties and judges in structural reform cases. Settlement saves the enormous expense and uncertainty of trial and appeal, and it gives the parties augmented control over the specifics of a remedy. More speculatively, defendants who agree to a decree may transform themselves in the eyes of the public, and even in their own eyes, from lawbreakers to law implementers. And there are also more situation-specific incentives. Plaintiffs or their counsel, and judges, may push especially hard for settlement if they believe that necessary institutional change requires the cooperation of the defendants, which is more easily obtained by

consent than by judicial fiat. Another frequently remarked dynamic favoring settlement in institutional reform cases ... is the high level of cooperation by defendants. The explanation seems clear: defendants, who are government officials operating under fiscal and political constraints, frequently win by losing. The result of a consent decree can be more resources and freedom from entrenched restrictions on changes in policy and practice. "The court is making me do it" trumps many ordinary political considerations. In the particular context of prison litigation, defendants were often themselves interested in the professionalization, and concurrent bureaucratization, of the prisons under their supervision. Finally, with a consent decree, defendant officials can even gain a power, unavailable through the ordinary political process, to bind their successors. For all these reasons, settlements of various kinds do indeed seem to be the primary source of judgments in prison and jail cases; the litigation has frequently been, to use Marc Galanter's coinage, "litigotiation"—"the strategic pursuit of a settlement through mobilizing the court process."

Schlanger, supra, at 2012–13. If defendants are forced to concede liability, are they more likely to litigate to the hilt? Will admissions of liability for purposes of a consent judgment open defendants up to § 1983 damages liability as well?

Section 802(a) also explicitly limited the authority of federal courts to order prisoners to be released—a common order in cases involving prison overcrowding—unless the court had previously entered an order for less intrusive relief that failed to remedy the deprivation of the federal right sought to be remedied through the prisoner release order and the defendant is given a reasonable amount of time to comply. It required that three-judge district courts be used to issue such orders and that the court find by "clear and convincing" evidence—rather than merely by a preponderance—that "crowding is the primary cause of the violation of a Federal right; and no other relief will remedy the violation of the Federal right."

Finally, in a provision that has prompted substantial litigation, § 802 of the PLRA codified a standard for terminating injunctive relief:

(1) TERMINATION OF PROSPECTIVE RELIEF.—(A) In any civil action with respect to prison conditions in which prospective relief is ordered, such relief shall be terminable upon the motion of any party or intervener—

(i) 2 years after the date the court granted or approved the prospective relief;

(ii) 1 year after the date the court has entered an order denying termination of prospective relief under this paragraph; or

> (iii) in the case of an order issued on or before the date of enactment of the Prison Litigation Reform Act, 2 years after such date of enactment....
>
> (2) IMMEDIATE TERMINATION OF PROSPECTIVE RELIEF.—In any civil action with respect to prison conditions, a defendant or intervener shall be entitled to the immediate termination of any prospective relief if the relief was approved or granted in the absence of a finding by the court that the relief is narrowly drawn, extends no further than necessary to correct the violation of the Federal right, and is the least intrusive means necessary to correct the violation of the Federal right.
>
> (3) LIMITATION.—Prospective relief shall not terminate if the court makes written findings based on the record that prospective relief remains necessary to correct a current or ongoing violation of the Federal right, extends no further than necessary to correct the violation of the Federal right, and that the prospective relief is narrowly drawn and the least intrusive means to correct the violation....

The PLRA also set out a set of specific procedures for termination motions, including a provision automatically "staying," that is, terminating, any prospective relief subject to a pending motion, within a relatively short time after the motion is filed. The meaning and constitutionality of the automatic stay provision were at issue *Miller v. French*.

For an extended examination of the PLRA's effects on individual claims by prisoners, see Margo Schlanger, Prison Litigation, 116 Harv. L. Rev. 1555 (2003). Professor Schlanger finds that while the PLRA reduced new federal filings by prisoners by over 40%, it also made constitutionally meritorious cases harder to bring and harder to win. She concludes that, as an effort to cope with the high volume of prisoner claims, most with a low probability of success, the PLRA has introduced as many problems as it has solved. In particular, its provisions for inmate payment of filing fees, reduced attorney's fees to prevailing plaintiffs, and exhaustion of administrative remedies have reduced the volume of meritorious and nonmeritorious claims alike, decreasing the effect of prisoner litigation as a deterrent to abusive prison conditions.

Miller v. French

Supreme Court of the United States, 2000.
530 U.S. 327.

■ JUSTICE O'CONNOR delivered the opinion of the Court.

The Prison Litigation Reform Act of 1995 (PLRA) establishes standards for the entry and termination of prospective relief in civil actions challenging prison conditions. If prospective relief under an existing injunction does not satisfy these standards, a defendant or intervenor is entitled to "immediate termination" of that relief. And under the PLRA's "automatic stay" provision, a motion to terminate prospective relief "shall operate as a stay" of that relief during the period beginning 30 days after the filing of the motion (extendable to up to 90 days for "good cause") and ending when the court rules on the motion. The superintendent of the Pendleton Correctional Facility, which is currently operating under an ongoing injunction to remedy violations of the Eighth Amendment regarding conditions of confinement, filed a motion to terminate prospective relief under the PLRA. Respondent prisoners moved to enjoin the operation of the automatic stay provision of § 3626(e)(2), arguing that it is unconstitutional. The District Court enjoined the stay, and the Court of Appeals for the Seventh Circuit affirmed....

I

A

This litigation began in 1975, when four inmates at what is now the Pendleton Correctional Facility brought a class action under § 1983.... After a trial, the District Court found that living conditions at the prison violated both state and federal law, including the Eighth Amendment's prohibition against cruel and unusual punishment, and the court issued an injunction to correct those violations.... This ongoing injunctive relief has remained in effect ever since, with the last modification occurring in October 1988, when the parties resolved by joint stipulation the remaining issues related to fire and occupational safety standards.

B

In 1996, Congress enacted the PLRA. As relevant here, the PLRA establishes standards for the entry and termination of prospective relief in civil actions challenging conditions at prison facilities. Specifically, a court "shall not grant or approve any prospective relief unless the court finds that such relief is narrowly drawn, extends no further than necessary to correct the violation of a Federal right, and is the least intrusive means necessary to correct the violation of the Federal right." 18 U.S.C. § 3626(a)(1)(A) (1994 ed., Supp. IV). The same criteria apply to existing injunctions, and a defendant or intervenor may move to terminate prospective relief that does not meet this standard. See § 3626(b)(2). In particular, § 3626(b)(2) provides:

> In any civil action with respect to prison conditions, a defendant or intervener shall be entitled to the immediate termination of any prospective relief if the relief was approved or granted in the absence of a finding by the court that the relief is narrowly drawn, extends no further than necessary to correct the violation of the Federal right, and is the least intrusive means necessary to correct the violation of the Federal right.

A court may not terminate prospective relief, however, if it "makes written findings based on the record that prospective relief remains necessary to correct a current and ongoing violation of the Federal right, extends no further than necessary to correct the violation of the Federal right, and that the prospective relief is narrowly drawn and the least intrusive means necessary to correct the violation." § 3626(b)(3)....

Finally, the provision at issue here, § 3626(e)(2), dictates that, in certain circumstances, prospective relief shall be stayed pending resolution of a motion to terminate. Specifically, subsection (e)(2), entitled "Automatic Stay," states:

> Any motion to modify or terminate prospective relief made under subsection (b) shall operate as a stay during the period—
>
> (A)(i) beginning on the 30th day after such motion is filed, in the case of a motion made under paragraph (1) or (2) of subsection (b); ... and
>
> (B) ending on the date the court enters a final order ruling on the motion.

As one of several 1997 amendments to the PLRA, Congress permitted courts to postpone the entry of the automatic stay for not more than 60 days for "good cause," which cannot include general congestion of the court's docket.

C

On June 5, 1997, the State filed a motion under § 3626(b) to terminate the prospective relief governing the conditions of confinement at the Pendleton Correctional Facility. In response, the prisoner class moved for a temporary restraining order or preliminary injunction to enjoin the operation of the automatic stay, arguing that § 3626(e)(2) is unconstitutional as both a violation of the Due Process Clause of the Fifth Amendment and separation of powers principles....

II

We address the statutory question first. Both the State and the prisoner class agree, as did the majority and dissenting judges below, that § 3626(e)(2) precludes a district court from exercising its equitable powers to enjoin the automatic stay. The Government argues, however, that § 3626(e)(2) should be construed to leave intact the federal courts' traditional equitable discretion to "stay the stay," invoking two canons of statutory construction. First, the Government contends that we should not interpret a statute as displacing courts' traditional equitable authority to preserve the status quo pending resolution on the merits "absent the clearest command to the contrary." Second, the Government asserts that reading § 3626(e)(2) to remove that equitable power would raise serious separation of powers questions, and therefore should be avoided under the canon of constitutional doubt....

The text of § 3626(e)(2) provides that "any motion to ... terminate prospective relief under subsection (b) *shall* operate as a stay" during a fixed period of time, i.e., from 30 (or 90) days after the motion is filed until the court enters a final order ruling on the motion. (Emphasis added.) The stay is "automatic" once a state defendant has filed a § 3626(b) motion, and the statutory command that such a motion "shall operate as a stay during the [specified time] period" indicates that the stay is mandatory throughout that period of time....

[The Government's interpretation] would subvert the plain meaning of the statute, making its mandatory language merely permissive. [N]ot only does the statute employ the mandatory term "shall," but it also specifies the points at which the operation of the stay is to begin and end. In other words, contrary to Justice Breyer's suggestion that the language of § 3626(e)(2) "says nothing ... about the district court's power to modify or suspend the operation of the 'stay,' " § 3626(e)(2) unequivocally mandates that the stay "shall operate during" this specific interval. To allow courts to exercise their equitable discretion to prevent the stay from "operating" during this statutorily prescribed period would be to contradict § 3626(e)(2)'s plain terms....

Viewing the automatic stay provision in the context of § 3626 as a whole further confirms that Congress intended to prohibit federal courts from exercising their equitable authority to suspend operation of the automatic stay. The specific appeal provision contained in § 3626(e) states that "any order staying, suspending, delaying, or barring the operation of the automatic stay" of § 3626(e)(2) "shall be appealable" pursuant to 28 U.S.C. § 1292(a)(1). § 3626(e)(4). At first blush, this provision might be read as supporting the view that Congress expressly recognized the possibility that a district court could exercise its equitable discretion to enjoin the stay. The two Courts of Appeals that have construed § 3626(e)(2) as preserving the federal courts' equitable powers have reached that conclusion based on this reading of § 3626(e)(4). They reasoned that Congress would not have provided for expedited review of such orders had it not intended that district courts would retain the power to enter the orders in the first place. In other words, "Congress understood that there would be some cases in which a conscientious district court acting in good faith would perceive that equity required that it suspend" the § 3626(e)(2) stay, and "Congress therefore permitted the district court to do so, subject to appellate review."

The critical flaw in this construction, however, is that § 3626(e)(4) only provides for an appeal from an order preventing the operation of the automatic stay.... If the rationale for the provision were that in some situations equity demands that the automatic stay be suspended, then presumably the denial of a motion to enjoin the stay should also be appealable. The one-way nature of the appeal provision only makes sense if the automatic stay is required to operate during a specific time period, such that any attempt by a district court to circumvent the mandatory stay is immediately reviewable.

... Given that curbing the equitable discretion of district courts was one of the PLRA's principal objectives, it would have been odd for Congress to have left enforcement of § 3626(e)(2) to that very same discretion. Instead, Congress sensibly chose to make available an immediate appeal to resolve situations in which courts mistakenly believe—under the novel scheme created by the PLRA—that they have the authority to enjoin the automatic stay....

Thus, although we should not construe a statute to displace courts, traditional equitable authority absent the "clearest command," Califano v. Yamasaki, 442 U.S. 682, 705 (1979), or an "inescapable inference" to the contrary, Porter v. Warner Holding Co., 328 U.S. 395, 398 (1946), we are convinced that Congress' intent to remove such discretion is unmistakable in § 3626(e)(2). And while this construction raises constitutional questions, the canon of constitutional doubt permits us to avoid such questions only where the saving construction is not "plainly contrary to the intent of Congress." Edward J. DeBartolo Corp. v. Florida Gulf Coast Building & Constr. Trades Council, 485 U.S. 568, 575 (1988).

III

The Constitution enumerates and separates the powers of the three branches of Government in Articles I, II, and III. ... While the boundaries between the three branches are not "hermetically sealed," the Constitution prohibits one branch from encroaching on the central prerogatives of another. The powers of the Judicial Branch are set forth in Article III, § 1, which states that the "judicial Power of the United States shall be vested in one supreme Court and in such inferior Courts as Congress may from time to time ordain and establish," and provides that these federal courts shall be staffed by judges who hold office during good behavior, and whose compensation shall not be diminished during tenure in office. As we explained in Plaut v. Spendthrift Farm, Inc., 514 U.S. 211, 218–19 (1995), Article III "gives the Federal Judiciary the power, not merely to rule on cases, but to decide them, subject to review only by superior courts in the Article III hierarchy."

Respondent prisoners contend that § 3626(e)(2) encroaches on the central prerogatives of the Judiciary and thereby violates the separation of powers doctrine. It does this, the prisoners assert, by legislatively suspending a final judgment of an Article III court in violation of *Plaut* and Hayburn's Case, 2 U.S. (2 Dall. 408) 408 (1792). According to the prisoners, the remedial order governing living conditions at the Pendleton Correctional Facility is a final judgment of an Article III court, and § 3626(e)(2) constitutes an impermissible usurpation of judicial power because it commands the district court to suspend prospective relief under that order, albeit temporarily. An analysis of the principles underlying *Hayburn's Case* and *Plaut*, as well as an examination of § 3626(e)(2)'s interaction with the other provisions of § 3626, makes clear that § 3626(e)(2) does not offend these separation of powers principles....

[*Hayburn's Case*] "stands for the principle that Congress cannot vest review of the decisions of Article III courts in officials of the Executive Branch." *Plaut*, 514 U.S. at 218. As we recognized in *Plaut*, such an effort by a coequal branch to "annul a final judgment" is "an assumption of Judicial power and therefore forbidden."

Unlike the situation in *Hayburn's Case*, § 3626(e)(2) does not involve the direct review of a judicial decision by officials of the Legislative or Executive Branches. Nonetheless, the prisoners suggest that § 3626(e)(2) falls within *Hayburn's* prohibition against an indirect legislative "suspension" or reopening of a final judgment, such as that addressed in *Plaut*. In *Plaut*, we held that a federal statute that required federal courts to reopen final judgments that had been entered before the statute's enactment was unconstitutional on separation of powers grounds. The plaintiffs had brought a civil securities fraud action seeking money damages. While that action was pending, we ruled in [an unrelated case] that such suits must be commenced within one year after the discovery of the facts constituting the violation and within three years after such violation. In light of this intervening decision, the *Plaut* plaintiffs' suit was untimely, and the District Court accordingly dismissed the action as time barred. After the judgment dismissing the case had become final, Congress enacted a statute providing for the reinstatement of those actions, including the *Plaut* plaintiffs', that had been dismissed under [our decision] but that would have been timely under the previously applicable statute of limitations.

We concluded that this retroactive command that federal courts reopen final judgments exceeded Congress' authority. [O]nce a judicial decision achieves finality, it "becomes the last word of the judicial department." And because Article III "gives the Federal Judiciary the power, not merely to rule on cases, but to decide them, subject to review only by superior courts in the Article III hierarchy," the "judicial Power is one to render dispositive judgments," and Congress cannot retroactively command Article III courts to reopen final judgments.

Plaut however, was careful to distinguish the situation before the Court in that case—legislation that attempted to reopen the dismissal of a suit seeking money damages—from legislation that "altered the prospective effect of injunctions entered by Article III courts." ... Prospective relief under a continuing, executory decree remains subject to alteration due to changes in the underlying law....

[T]he automatic stay of § 3626(e)(2) does not unconstitutionally "suspend" or reopen a judgment of an Article III court. Section 3626(e)(2) does not by itself "tell judges when, how, or what to do." Instead, § 3626(e)(2) merely reflects the change implemented by § 3626(b), which does the "heavy lifting" in the statutory scheme by establishing new standards for prospective relief. Section 3626 prohibits the continuation of prospective relief that was "approved or granted in the absence of a finding by the court that the relief is narrowly drawn, extends no further than necessary to correct the violation of the Federal right, and is the least intrusive means to correct the violation," § 3626(b)(2), or in the absence of "findings based on the record that prospective relief remains necessary to correct a current and ongoing violation of a Federal right, extends no further than necessary to correct the violation of the Federal right, and that the prospective relief is narrowly drawn and the least intrusive means necessary to correct the violation," § 3626(b)(3). Accordingly, if prospective relief under an existing decree had been granted or approved absent such findings, then that prospective relief must cease, see § 3626(b)(2), unless and until the court makes findings on the record that such relief remains necessary to correct an ongoing violation and is narrowly tailored, see § 3626(b)(3). The PLRA's automatic stay provision assists in the enforcement of §§ 3626(b)(2) and (3) by requiring the court to stay any prospective relief that, due to the change in the underlying standard, is no longer enforceable, i.e., prospective relief that is not supported by the findings specified in §§ 3626(b)(2) and (3).

By establishing new standards for the enforcement of prospective relief in § 3626(b), Congress has altered the relevant underlying law. The PLRA has restricted courts' authority to issue and enforce prospective relief concerning prison conditions, requiring that such relief be supported by findings and precisely tailored to what is needed to remedy the violation of a federal right. We note that the constitutionality of § 3626(b) is not challenged here; we assume, without deciding, that the new standards it pronounces are effective. [W]hen Congress changes the law underlying a judgment awarding prospective relief, that relief is no longer enforceable to the extent it is inconsistent with the new law. Although the remedial injunction here is a "final judgment" for purposes of appeal, it is not the "last word of the judicial department." The provision of prospective relief is subject to the continuing supervisory jurisdiction of the court, and therefore may be altered according to subsequent changes in the law. See Rufo v. Inmates of Suffolk County Jail, 502 U.S. 367, 388 (1992). Prospective relief must be "modified if, as it later turns out, one or more of the obligations placed upon the parties has become impermissible under federal law."

The entry of the automatic stay under § 3626(e)(2) helps to implement the change in the law caused by §§ 3626(b)(2) and (3). If the prospective relief under the existing decree is not supported by the findings required under § 3626(b)(2), and the court has not made the findings required by § 3626(b)(3), then prospective relief is no longer enforceable and must be stayed. . . .

For the same reasons, § 3626(e)(2) does not violate the separation of powers principle articulated in United States v. Klein, 80 U.S. (13 Wall.) 128 (1872). In that case, Klein, the executor of the estate of a Confederate sympathizer, sought to recover the value of property seized by the United States during the Civil War, which by statute was recoverable if Klein could demonstrate that the decedent had not given aid or comfort to the rebellion. In United States v. Padelford, 76 U.S. (9 Wall.) 531, 542–43 (1870), we held that a Presidential pardon satisfied the burden of proving that no such aid or comfort had been given. While Klein's case was pending, Congress enacted a statute providing that a pardon would instead be taken as proof that the pardoned individual had in fact aided the enemy, and if the claimant offered proof of a pardon the court must dismiss the case for lack of jurisdiction. *Klein*, 80 U.S., at 133–34. We concluded that the statute was unconstitutional because it purported to "prescribe rules of decision to the Judicial Department of the government in cases pending before it."

Here, the prisoners argue that Congress has similarly prescribed a rule of decision because, for the period of time until the district court makes a final decision on the merits of the motion to terminate prospective relief, § 3626(e)(2) mandates a particular outcome: the termination of prospective relief. As we noted in *Plaut*, however, "whatever the precise scope of *Klein*, ... later decisions have made clear that its prohibition does not take hold when Congress 'amends applicable law.'" The prisoners concede this point but contend that, because § 3626(e)(2) does not itself amend the legal standard, *Klein* is still applicable. As we have explained, however, § 3626(e)(2) must be read not in isolation, but in the context of § 3626 as a whole. Section 3626(e)(2) operates in conjunction with the new standards for the continuation of prospective relief; if the new standards of § 3626(b)(2) are not met, then the stay "shall operate" unless and until the court makes the findings required by § 3626(b)(3). Rather than prescribing a rule of decision, § 3626(e)(2) simply imposes the consequences of the court's application of the new legal standard.

Finally, the prisoners assert that, even if § 3626(e)(2) does not fall within the recognized prohibitions of *Hayburn's Case*, *Plaut*, or *Klein*, it still offends the principles of separation of powers because it places a deadline on judicial decisionmaking, thereby interfering with core judicial functions. Congress' imposition of a time limit in § 3626(e)(2), however, does not in itself offend the structural concerns underlying the Constitution's separation of powers. ... Respondents' concern with the time limit ... must be its relative brevity. But whether the time is so short that it deprives litigants of a meaningful opportunity to be heard is a due process question, an issue that is not before us. We leave open, therefore, the question whether this time limit, particularly in a complex case, may implicate due process concerns.

In contrast to due process, which principally serves to protect the personal rights of litigants to a full and fair hearing, separation of powers principles are primarily addressed to the structural concerns of protecting the role of the independent Judiciary within the constitutional design. In this action, we have no occasion to decide whether there could be a time constraint on judicial action that was so severe that it implicated these structural separation of powers concerns. The PLRA does not deprive courts of their adjudicatory role, but merely provides a new legal standard for relief and encourages courts to apply that standard promptly....

■ JUSTICE BREYER, with whom JUSTICE STEVENS joins, dissenting.

[The provision of the PLRA at issue in this case] means approximately the following: Suppose that a district court, in 1980, had entered an injunction governing present and future prison conditions. Suppose further that in 1996 a party filed a motion under the PLRA asking the court to terminate (or to modify) the 1980 injunction. That district court would have no more than 90 days to decide whether to grant the motion. After those 90 days, the 1980 injunction would terminate automatically—regaining life only if, when, and to the extent that the judge eventually decided to deny the PLRA motion.

The majority interprets the words "shall operate as a stay" to mean, in terms of my example, that the 1980 injunction must become ineffective after the 90th day, no matter what. The Solicitor General, however, believes that the view adopted by the majority interpretation is too rigid and calls into doubt the constitutionality of the provision. He argues that the statute is silent as to whether the district court can modify or suspend the operation of the automatic stay. He would find in that silence sufficient authority for the court to create an exception to the 90-day time limit where circumstances make it necessary to do so. As so read, the statute would neither displace the courts' traditional equitable authority nor raise significant constitutional difficulties.

I agree with the Solicitor General and believe we should adopt that "reasonable construction" of the statute.

I

At the outset, one must understand why a more flexible interpretation of the statute might be needed. To do so, one must keep in mind the extreme circumstances that at least some prison litigation originally sought to correct, the complexity of the resulting judicial decrees, and the potential difficulties arising out of the subsequent need to review those decrees in order to make certain they follow Congress' PLRA directives. A hypothetical example based on actual circumstances may help.

In January 1979, a Federal District Court made 81 factual findings describing extremely poor—indeed "barbaric and shocking"—prison conditions in the Commonwealth of Puerto Rico. Morales Feliciano v. Romero Barcelo, 497 F.Supp. 14, 32 (D.P.R.1979). These conditions included prisons typically operating with twice the number of prisoners they were designed to hold; inmates living in 16 square feet of space (i.e., only 4 feet by 4 feet); inmates without medical care, without psychiatric care, without beds, without mattresses, without hot water, without soap or towels or toothbrushes or underwear; food prepared on a budget of $1.50 per day and "tons of food ... destroyed because of ... rats, vermin, worms, and spoilage"; "no working toilets or showers," "urinals [that] flush into the sinks," "plumbing systems ... in a state of collapse," and a "stench" that was "omnipresent"; "exposed wiring ... no fire extinguisher, ... [and] poor ventilation"; "calabozos," or dungeons, "like cages with bars on the top" or with two slits in a steel door opening onto a central corridor, the floors of which were "covered with raw sewage" and which contained prisoners with severe mental illnesses, "caged like wild animals," sometimes for months; areas of a prison where mentally ill inmates were "kept in cells naked, without beds, without mattresses, without any private possessions, and most of them without toilets that work and without drinking water." These conditions had led to epidemics of communicable diseases, untreated mental illness, suicides, and murders.

The District Court held that these conditions amounted to constitutionally forbidden "cruel and unusual punishment." It entered 30 specific orders designed to produce constitutionally mandated improvement by requiring the prison system to, for example, screen food handlers for communicable diseases, close the "calabozos," move mentally ill patients to hospitals, fix broken plumbing, and provide at least 35 square feet (i.e., 5 feet by 7 feet) of living space to each prisoner.

The very pervasiveness and seriousness of the conditions described in the court's opinion made those conditions difficult to cure quickly. Over the next decade, the District Court entered further orders embodied in 15 published opinions, affecting 21 prison institutions. These orders concerned, inter alia, overcrowding, security, disciplinary proceedings, prisoner classification, rehabilitation, parole, and drug addiction treatment. Not surprisingly, the related proceedings involved extensive evidence and argument consuming thousands of pages of transcript. Their implementation involved the services of two monitors, two assistants, and a Special Master. Along the way, the court documented a degree of "administrative chaos" in the prison system, and entered findings of contempt of court against the Commonwealth, followed by the assessment and collection of more than $74 million in fines.

Prison conditions subsequently have improved in some respects. Morales Feliciano v. Rossello Gonzalez, 13 F.Supp.2d 151, 179 (D.P.R.1998). I express no opinion as to whether, or which of, the earlier orders are still needed. But my brief summary of the litigation should illustrate the potential difficulties involved in making the determination of continuing necessity required by the PLRA. Where prison litigation is as complex as the litigation I have just described, it may prove difficult for a district court to reach a fair and accurate decision about which orders remain necessary, and are the "least intrusive means" available, to prevent or correct a continuing violation of federal law. The orders, which were needed to resolve serious constitutional problems and may still be needed where compliance has not yet been assured, are complex, interrelated, and applicable to many different institutions. Ninety days might not provide sufficient time to ascertain the views of several different parties, including monitors, to allow them to present evidence, and to permit each to respond to the arguments and evidence of the others.

It is at least possible, then, that the statute, as the majority reads it, would sometimes terminate a complex system of orders entered over a period of years by a court familiar with the local problem—perhaps only to reinstate those orders later, when the termination motion can be decided. Such an automatic termination could leave constitutionally prohibited conditions unremedied, at least temporarily. Alternatively, the threat of termination could lead a district court to abbreviate proceedings that fairness would otherwise demand. At a minimum, the mandatory automatic stay would provide a recipe for uncertainty, as complex judicial orders that have long governed the administration of particular prison systems suddenly turn off, then (perhaps selectively) back on. So read, the statute directly interferes with a court's exercise of its traditional equitable authority, rendering temporarily ineffective pre-existing remedies aimed at correcting past, and perhaps ongoing, violations of the Constitution. That interpretation, as the majority itself concedes, might give rise to serious constitutional problems.

II

The Solicitor General's more flexible reading of the statute avoids all these problems. . . . The language [of the stay provision] says nothing . . . about the district court's power to modify or suspend the operation of the "stay." In the Solicitor General's view, the "stay" would determine the legal status quo; but the district court would retain its traditional equitable power to change that status quo once the party seeking the modification or suspension of the operation of the stay demonstrates that the stay would cause irreparable injury, that the termination motion is likely to be defeated, and that the merits of the motion cannot be resolved before the automatic stay takes effect. . . .

Is this interpretation a "reasonable construction" of the statute? I note first that the statutory language is open to the Solicitor General's interpretation. A district court ordinarily can stay the operation of a judicial order (such as a stay or injunction), when a party demonstrates the need to do so in accordance with traditional equitable criteria (irreparable injury, likelihood of success on the merits, and a balancing of possible harms to the parties and the public.) There is no logical inconsistency in saying both (1) a motion (to terminate) "shall operate as a stay," and (2) the court retains the power to modify or delay the operation of the stay in appropriate circumstances. The statutory language says nothing about this last-mentioned power. It is silent. It does not direct the district court to leave the stay in place come what may.

Nor does this more flexible interpretation deprive the procedural provision of meaning. The filing of the motion to terminate prospective relief will still, after a certain period, operate as a stay without further action by the court. Thus, the motion automatically changes the status quo and imposes upon the party wishing to suspend the automatic stay the burden of demonstrating strong, special reasons for doing so....

In addition, the surrounding procedural provisions are most naturally read as favoring the flexible interpretation. The immediately preceding provision requires the court to rule "promptly" upon the motion to terminate and says that "mandamus shall lie to remedy any failure to issue a prompt ruling." 18 U.S.C. § 3626(e)(1). If a motion to terminate takes effect automatically through the "stay" after 30 or 90 days, it is difficult to understand what purpose would be served by providing for mandamus—a procedure that itself (in so complicated a matter) could take several weeks. But if the automatic stay might be modified or lifted in an unusual case, providing for mandamus makes considerable sense....

Finally, the more flexible interpretation is consistent with Congress' purposes as revealed in the statute. Those purposes include the avoidance of new judicial relief that is overly broad or no longer necessary and the reassessment of pre-existing relief to bring it into conformity with these standards. But Congress has simultaneously expressed its intent to maintain relief that is narrowly drawn and necessary to end unconstitutional practices. The statute, as flexibly interpreted, risks interfering with the first set of objectives only to the extent that the speedy appellate review provided in the statute fails to control district court error. The same interpretation avoids the improper provisional termination of relief that is constitutionally necessary. The risk of an occasional small additional delay seems a comparatively small price to pay (in terms of the statute's entire set of purposes) to avoid the serious constitutional problems that accompany the majority's more rigid interpretation....

■ JUSTICE SOUTER, with whom JUSTICE GINSBURG joins, concurring in part and dissenting in part.

I agree that 18 U.S.C. § 3626(e)(2) is unambiguous and join Parts I and II of the majority opinion. I also agree that applying the automatic stay may raise the due process issue, of whether a plaintiff has a fair chance to preserve an existing judgment that was valid when entered. But I believe that applying the statute may also raise a serious separation-of-powers issue if the time it allows turns out to be inadequate for a court to determine whether the new prerequisite to relief is satisfied in a particular case. I thus do not join Part III of the Court's opinion and on remand would require proceedings consistent with this one. I respectfully dissent from the terms of the Court's disposition.

A prospective remedial order may rest on at least three different legal premises: the underlying right meant to be secured; the rules of procedure for obtaining relief, defining requisites of pleading, notice, and so on; and, in some cases, rules lying between the other two, such as those defining a required level of certainty before some remedy may be ordered, or the permissible scope of relief. At issue here are rules of the last variety.

Congress has the authority to change rules of this sort by imposing new conditions precedent for the continuing enforcement of existing, prospective remedial orders and requiring courts to apply the new rules to those orders. If its legislation gives courts adequate time to determine the applicability of a new rule to an old order and to take the action necessary to apply it or to vacate the order, there seems little basis for claiming that Congress has crossed the constitutional line to interfere with the performance of any judicial function. But if determining whether a new rule applies requires time (say, for new factfinding) and if the statute provides insufficient time for a court to make that determination before the statute invalidates an extant remedial order, the application of the statute raises a serious question whether Congress has in practical terms assumed the judicial function. In such a case, the prospective order suddenly turns unenforceable not because a court has made a judgment to terminate it due to changed law or fact, but because no one can tell in the time allowed whether the new rule requires modification of the old order. One way to view this result is to see the Congress as mandating modification of an order that may turn out to be perfectly enforceable under the new rule, depending on judicial factfinding. If the facts are taken this way, the new statute might well be treated as usurping the judicial function of determining the applicability of a general rule in particular factual circumstances.

Whether this constitutional issue arises on the facts of this action, however, is something we cannot yet tell, for the District Court did not address the sufficiency of the time provided by the statute to make the findings required by § 3626(b)(3) in this particular action. Absent that determination, I would not decide the separation-of-powers question, but simply remand for further proceedings. If the District Court determined both that it lacked adequate time to make the requisite findings in the period before the automatic stay would become effective, and that applying the stay would violate the separation of powers, the question would then be properly presented.

NOTE ON THE RETROACTIVE APPLICATION OF THE PLRA

As both the majority and the dissenting opinions note, the PLRA changes the substantive standard for granting injunctive relief in prison condition cases. As Schlanger suggests in the excerpt quoted in the Introductory Note preceding *Miller v. French,* for a variety of reasons many existing decrees do not comply with the specificity and judicial findings requirements of the PLRA and are thus vulnerable to attack.

For another example of the retroactive application of the PLRA, see Martin v. Hadix, 527 U.S. 343 (1999). The respondents were prisoners who had filed two federal class actions in 1977 and 1980 against prison officials challenging the conditions of confinement in the Michigan prison system under § 1983. The plaintiffs prevailed in both suits, and the district court held that they were entitled to attorney's fees under § 1988 for postjudgment monitoring of the defendants' compliance. The district court's order specified the hourly rate at $150 per hour.

Section 803(d)(3) of the PLRA, however, limits the size of fees that may be awarded to attorneys who litigate prisoner lawsuits. In the Eastern District of Michigan, the cap is $112.50 per hour. After the effective date of the PLRA, the respondents' attorneys made fee requests for work performed both before and after the Act's effective date. They sought to be paid at their prior rate for all the work.

In an opinion by Justice O'Connor, the Supreme Court held that § 803(d)(3) did not limit fees for monitoring performed before the effective date of the PLRA, but that it did limit attorney's fees for postjudgment monitoring services performed after the PLRA's effective date, despite the prior order setting the fees at a higher rate. For monitoring performed before the PLRA's effective date, the attorneys had a reasonable expectation that work they performed would be compensated at the pre-PLRA rates set by the District Court. If applied to work performed before its effective date, the PLRA would alter the fee arrangement post hoc by reducing the compensation rate. With respect to monitoring performed after the PLRA's effective date, by contrast, the Court saw no retroactive effect. It held that the PLRA provided the attorneys with notice that their hourly rate had been adjusted. Once the PLRA took effect, any expectation of compensation at the pre-PLRA rates was therefore unreasonable.

The Court also rejected the contention that the PLRA had an impermissible retroactive effect because it attached a new legal consequence (namely, a lower pay rate) to conduct completed before the PLRA went into effect—the attorneys' initial decision to file suit on behalf of prisoners. The Court found that argument based on an erroneous assumption that the attorneys' initial decision to file a case was irrevocable. Since they were free to withdraw from the case if they were dissatisfied with the fee set by the PLRA, there was no retroactive effect.

†